The New Resource Wars

The New Resource Wars

Native and Environmental Struggles Against Multinational Corporations

Al Gedicks

Foreword by Winona LaDuke

South End Press
Boston MA

Cover design by Karyl Klopp
Text design and production by the South End Press collective
Printed in the U.S.A.

Library of Congress Cataloguing-in-Publication Data
Gedicks, Al.
  The new resource wars : native and environmental struggles against multinational corporations / by Al Gedicks.
        p. cm.
Includes bibliographihcal references and index.
ISBN 0-89608-463-9 (cloth) : $35.00. – ISBN 0-89608-462-0 (pbk.) : $ 15.00
        1. Ojibwa Indians–Mines and mining–Law and legislation. 2. Ojibwa Indians–Land tenure. 3. Ojibwa Indians–Politics and government. 4. Strip mining–Environmental aspects–Wisconsin. 5. International business enterprises–Wisconsin–Case studies. 6. Sustainable development–Law and legislation–Wisconsin. 7. Indians–Land tenure. 8. Indians–Politics and government. I. Title.
E99.C5G44 1993
333.8'514'09775–dc20   93-22108
                                            CIP

South End Press, 116 Saint Botolph Street, Boston, MA 02115
        99 98 97 96 95 94 93   1 2 3 4 5 6 7 8 9

Table of Contents

Acknowledgements

I would like to thank the University of Wisconsin System Faculty Development Fund and the UW La Crosse for their support while I wrote the first draft of this manuscript in the fall of 1991. I am also grateful for the support I received from the Department of Sociology/Archeology, especially the word-processing assistance of Mary Clements.

Joyce Melville, my friend and fellow activist, patiently read and provided insightful comments on successive drafts of this book. Many others have read and commented on parts of the manuscript, including Roscoe and Evelyn Churchill, Marian Havlik, Dick Brooks, Sandy Lyon, Jeff Peterson, Jim Wise, Karl Fate, Bob Gough, Daniel Poler, Jr., Walt Bresette, Rick Whaley, and Gaiashkibos. Special thanks to Steve Chase at South End Press for his encouragement and expert advice in revising this manuscript for publication.

Portions of this manuscript have appeared in several publications, including *Dollars & Sense, Race and Class, Raw Materials Report, Political Power and Social Theory,* and *The Wisconsin Sociologist.* My thanks to them for their permission to include this work here.

Finally, I would like to express my appreciation for all those who have inspired this book by their actions in defense of the earth and the peoples of the earth.

—Al Gedicks

A Society Based On Conquest Cannot Be Sustained

Winona LaDuke

We have come to the edge of the woods,
out of brown grass where we slept, unseen,
out of knotted twigs, out of leaves creaked shut,
out of hiding.

At first the light wavered, glancing over us.
Then it clenched to a fist of light that pointed,
searched out, divided us.
Each took the beams like direct blows the heart answers.
Each of us moved forward alone.

We have come to the edge of the woods,
drawn out of ourselves by this night sun,
this battery of polarized acids,
that outshines the moon...

From *Jacklight,* by Louise Erdrich

Native people are at the center of a crossroads. Native communities possess the experience of sustainability, learned from years of observation, careful behavior, and strong community—evidenced in thousands of years of living in the same place, whispering the same prayers, and walking the same paths. Native people also find themselves to be a target of industrialism's struggle to dominate the natural world; they are possessed of resources, lands, and waters, now demanded by urban areas and industrial machinery often thousands of miles distant.

Al Gedicks' book is a strong testimony to this conflict, through careful and compassionate documentation of the oral and written histories of communities facing huge multinational corporations and governments wedded to international debt and the pursuit of industrial-based development plans. While each story told occurs in an "isolated" part of this world, together they form the patchwork of peoples and struggles in which we find ourselves today: a conflict central to who we are now, and who we, collectively, will come to be. That is the power of this book, and that is our lesson.

Let me place it in my own context, one which is specific, yet indicative of the larger context. Indigenous societies, the estimated 5,000 of them on a worldwide scale, hold much in common, yet diversity, along with adaptation to specific circumstances and ecosystems, are also commonalities. Overall, however, I believe that one truth predominates: Natural Law is pre-eminent and, as such, should provide the guiding principles upon which societies and peoples function.

Laws made by nations, states, and municipalities are inferior to this supreme law, and should be treated as such; that is the experience of sustainability. Within this context, Anishinabé (Chippewa) people, those about whom much of this book is written, have developed a code of ethics and a value system which guides our behavior in accordance with Natural Law: *mino bimaatisiiwin*—alternately translated as "the good life" or "continuous rebirth." This *mino bimaatisiiwin* guides behavior toward others, toward animals, toward plants and the ecosystem, and it is based on tenets of reciprocity and cyclical thinking.

Reciprocity or reciprocal relations define the responsibilities and ways of relating between humans and the ecosystem. Simply stated, "the resources" of the ecosystem, whether corn, rocks, or deer, are viewed as "animate" and, as such, gifts from the Creator. Thus, one could not take life without reciprocal offering, usually tobacco or *saymah,* as it is called in our language. Within this act of reciprocity is also an understanding that "you take only what you need and leave the rest." Implicit in the understanding of Natural Law is also the understanding that most of what is natural is cyclical: whether our bodies, the moon, the tides, seasons, or life itself. Within this natural cycling is also a clear sense of birth and rebirth, a knowledge that what one does today will affect us in the future, on the return.

These tenets, and the overall practice of *mino bimaatisiiwin,* imply a continuous inhabiting of place, an intimate understanding of the relationship between humans and the ecosystem, and the need to maintain the balance. For the most part, social and economic systems based on these values are decentralized, communal, self-reliant, and very closely based on the land of that ecosystem. This way of living has enabled indigenous communities to live for thousands of years upon their land as, quite frankly, the only examples of continuous sustainability which exist on Turtle Island (North America). We hope there will be more.

This is in stark contrast to another way of living—that of industrial society, or as some call it, "settler society." In industrial society, "man's dominion over nature" has preempted the perception of Natural Law as central. Linear concepts of "progress" dominate this worldview. From this perception of "progress" as an essential component of societal development (defined as economic growth and technological advancement) comes the perception of the natural world as a wilderness in need of "cultivation" or "taming," and of some peoples as being "primitive" while others are "civilized." This, of course, is the philosophical underpinning of colonialism and "conquest."

This way of thinking is also present in scientific systems of thought like "Darwinism," as well as in social interpretations of human behavior such as "Manifest Destiny," with its belief in some god-ordained right of some humans to dominate the earth. These concepts are central to the legacy of the Columbus quincentennary and the present state of relations between native and settler in North America and elsewhere. This conflict, in its present state, is also indicative of the scope of the problem—and the reality that a society based on conquest cannot survive.

During the last 100 years, this society has caused the extinction of more species than have disappeared in the period between the Ice Age and the nineteenth century; and in the past 400 years, an estimated 2,000 indigenous peoples have been made extinct. The present rate of extinction of indigenous peoples in the Amazon rainforest alone is one indigenous nation per year. As one reporter noted:

> The Yesinbetheri is a 13 member Yanomami group struc-
> tured around three brothers and a sister. They live in the
> state of Roraima, in Amazonia, and just a few days ago
> they were 14 in number. The middle brother, known as
> Fraquinho ("Weakie"), died, probably from malaria. He
> was the only member of the group whose wife was at
> childbearing age. The elder brother, Chiquinho, is rais-
> ing an orphan to become his wife. The younger brother,
> Kobaxi, works with the family of another group in order
> to have permission to marry one of its daughters.
> Chiquinho's and Kobaxi's wives died. Kobaxi was left
> alone with a ten-day-old infant, who is being taken care of
> by officials of the National Indian Foundation...Hundreds
> of Yanomami Indians have died mainly because of the
> presence of gold prospectors in their traditional terri-
> tory...[1]

Extinction is about peoples, as well as species. Extinction is the price of colonialism and conquest. It is the price indigenous peoples resist paying, and people of conscience should work to stop. World-wide, and certainly in North America, native peoples are at the center of the present environmental and economic crisis. This is no coinci-dence. Five hundred years after the European invasion, native peo-ples still maintain a significant presence on the North American continent, and in the western hemisphere overall. Over 700 native communities remain on the continent—200 in Alaska alone, 80 in California, and hundreds more scattered as islands in a sea of what is called the United States and Canada, retaining lands reserved by treaty or other agreement.

While native peoples represent a demographic minority population in North America, we still maintain land occupancy over substantial areas of the continent. In many regions in the United States, we are the majority population—in parts of New Mexico, Arizona, northern Minnesota, the Dakotas, and Montana, for example. But even more striking are the statistics for the Arctic and subarctic. The native population is the majority population in the upper two-thirds of Canada, or about one-third of the North American continent. The Northwest Territories, for instance, are under legislative mandate to divide the land into two native territories—one Dene and one Inuit. But elsewhere across the north—northern Quebec, Newfoundland, Labrador, Ontario, all the way to British Columbia—the northern population is also decidedly native.

Within this context, native thinking, the survival of native communities, and the issues of sovereignty and control over natural resources become central to North American resource politics and the challenge for North Americans of conscience. Consider these facts:

- Over 50 million indigenous people inhabit the world's remaining rainforests.
- Over one million indigenous people are slated to be relocated for hydroelectric dam projects in the next decade.
- All nuclear weapons that have been "tested" by the United States have been detonated in the lands of indigenous peoples, over 600 tests within the Shoshone nation alone.
- Two-thirds of all uranium resources within the "borders of the United States" lie under native reservations, with Indians producing 100 percent of all federally-controlled uranium in 1975.
- Fifteen of the present 18 so-called monitored retrievable nuclear storage sites are in Indian communities.

- The single largest hydroelectric project on the continent—
  James Bay hydroelectric project—is on Cree and Inuit lands
  in northern Canada.

These are just some of the issues at the center of Al Gedicks'
skillfully written book, a series of testimonies to the struggle between
industrial society and indigenous society, a struggle which ultimately
encompasses us all. These stories, whether of the Chippewa in
Wisconisn facing Exxon or Rio Tinto Zinc, the people of Sarawak
fighting for their survival, or tales still untold—the Lone Fighters
Society opposing a huge dam project in Alberta, or the Inuit opposing
NATO base siting and new dams in Newfoundland, Labrador, and
Quebec—all of these stories are about our own future.

Gedicks' writing helps us to understand how these struggles
have taken place, why and what we can do in the future. He tells these
stories not as a journalist, or even as an interested observer, but
rather as an integral part of many battles over mining and energy
development in North America. Al Gedicks, for the two decades that
I've known him, has always provided a reassurance in the knowledge
that he is there, vigilantly defending land and people, and never
wavering in his principles or his honesty. I invite you to learn from
his work, and hope that this reading will expand not only your
intellectual understanding, but also your courage, for that is the
substance of this resistance. Courage, I sincerely believe, is our path
back to *mino bimaatisiiwin.*

We smell them behind it
but they are faceless, invisible.
We smell the raw steel of their gun barrels,
mink oil on leather, their tongues of sour barley.
We smell their mothers buried chin-deep in wet dirt.
We smell their fathers with scoured knuckles,
teeth cracked from hot marrow.
We smell their sisters of crushed dogwood, bruised apples,
of fractured cups and concussions of burnt hooks.

We smell their breath steaming lightly behind the jacklight.
We smell the itch underneath the caked guts on their clothes.
We smell their minds like silver hammers
cocked back, held in readiness
for the first of us to step into the open.

We have come to the edge of the woods,
out of brown grass where we slept, unseen,
out of leaves creaked shut, out of our hiding.
We have come here too long.

It is their turn now,
their turn to follow us. Listen,
they put down their equipment.
It is useless in the tall brush.
And now they take the first steps, not knowing
how deep the woods are and lightless.
How deep the woods are.

From *Jacklight,* by Louise Erdrich

Inside the Native-Environmental Alliance

Contrary to the common, culturally-ingrained misreading of history, the disappearance of native peoples and the degradation of the natural world is not the result of some abstract and inevitable "development" process. Both these evils can be traced to a particular and identifiable source—the resource-acquisition and profit-maximizing activities of some of the most powerful institutions in the industrial global economy. More satisfying, more sustainable ways of living on this planet are possible, of course. Many alternatives to multinational capitalist industrialism already exist; others are being envisioned and developed by communities all over the world. Social "progress" does not have to be defined by genocide, social hierarchy, an out-of-control technology, a nonrenewable resource addiction, life-threatening pollution, massive habitat destruction, and endless material growth. We do not have to submit or acquiesce to the multinational corporations' ongoing war of aggression against native peoples and the natural world. We can, in fact, fight back and help give birth to more democratic and humane societies that are better able to protect and restore the earth.

My own involvement in these struggles as an environmental/native solidarity activist originally grew out of my interest, as a young sociologist, in exposing the critical role of U.S. copper corporations in the 1973 overthrow of the democratically-elected, socialist government of President Salvador Allende in Chile. At the time when the U.S. Central Intelligence Agency (CIA) and the Kennecott Copper Corporation were waging a covert war against the Allende government in response to its nationalization of Chile's copper mines, I was the research coordinator for a Madison, Wisconsin anti-imperialist collective called Community Action on Latin America. Many of us in the collective had actively opposed the Vietnam War and were determined to prevent future Vietnams in Latin America and the rest of the Third World.

My research, however, tended increasingly to focus on the plight of North America's native nations and non-native rural communities, particularly in northern Wisconsin. As economic nationalists in Chile and all over the Third World began to assert their right to control their own natural resources, I noticed that Kennecott had begun an active mineral exploration program near Ladysmith, Wisconsin. Exxon Minerals was also exploring next to the Sokaogon Chippewa reservation, near Crandon, Wisconsin, and Phelps Dodge, a major copper producer, was exploring next to the Lac du Flambeau Chippewa reservation, near Woodruff-Minocqua, Wisconsin.[1]

This did not bode well for either the native or non-native peoples of Wisconsin. Historically, mining has been an ecological, cultural, and economic disaster for the region. In the early 1800s, the U.S. government forced Native American populations off the known mineral-rich lands of Wisconsin, Michigan, and Minnesota, causing untold suffering. The profits from the early iron ore mines sited on this land then laid the foundations for J.P. Morgan's U.S. Steel Corporation. Beginning in the 1890s, and continuing for the next half-century, the iron mines of the Lake Superior region shipped over four billion tons of iron ore to U.S. steel mills, accounting for more than three-quarters of the nation's iron ore. Yet, the enormous wealth of the region did not bring economic prosperity to the vast majority of the region's inhabitants. At the end of World War II, U.S. Steel and Hanna Mining shut down their midwest iron mining operations and invested in potentially competitive sources of iron ore in Brazil, Venezuela, Canada, and Australia. This sudden withdrawal of capital ended the Great Lakes iron boom and threw an entire regional economy based on mining into a severe economic depression. To this day, the region suffers from widespread poverty and some of the highest unemployment rates in the nation. In 1974, I interviewed many of the retired miners in these communities for a documentary film called *The Shape of an Era*. The film addressed two major questions: where had all the wealth of the region gone to; and what were the underlying power relationships which facilitated this transfer of wealth to absentee-owned steel corporations like U.S. Steel and Hanna Mining?

It was during this period in the mid-1970s that I began to work with citizen action groups and Indian tribes that were resisting corporate and governmental pressures to transform northern Wisconsin into a new mineral resource colony. In 1975, I was invited to a tribal council meeting on the Lac du Flambeau Chippewa reservation, where the Phelps Dodge Corporation wanted to acquire the mineral rights to potential copper deposits on the reservation. Company representatives laid a minerals contract on the table and expected the tribal council to approve the contract that evening.

Fortunately, the tribe had hired Charles Lipton, an international minerals lawyer, to examine Phelps Dodge's offer. "No company that I have seen in recent times," said Lipton, "would dare to suggest such terms now to a developing nation overseas."[2] The agreement specified that, if the tribe desired to be a partner, it would have to put up $250,000 to participate in the exploration stage of the project. Lipton advised the tribe not to pay anything for Phelps Dodge to explore on their land. Later, the tribe responded with a counterproposal: after the exploration stage was completed and the tribe had access to the corporation's economic feasibility report, the tribe would consider further negotiations with the company. Phelps Dodge abruptly ended its negotiations with the tribe. This episode helped me to see how a non-Indian consultant could provide valuable information and analysis that would enable tribes to make more informed choices about different kinds of resource development.

More importantly, however, the resistance of the Lac du Flambeau Chippewa to a colonial-style contract was indicative of the changes that were occurring in the self-images of American Indians during the late 1960s and early 1970s. Through the analysis and activities of the American Indian Movement (AIM) and the more mainstream Americans for Indian Opportunity (AIO), Indian tribes began to see themselves in analogous positions to those of Third World resource colonies dominated by multinational mining and energy corporations. In 1977, the American Indian Policy Review

Commission reflected a widespread perception that "Indian people can regain their historic economic self-sufficiency only if they regain control over their natural resources and begin to develop those resources themselves."[3] For some of the energy-rich tribes in the western United States, this resulted in demands for more equitable mineral leasing agreements and higher mineral royalties for the tribes. In other cases, especially in water-rich areas like the upper midwest, this meant a renewed effort to save tribal lands from ecologically destructive mining and energy projects. This situation seemed to hold out the possibility for a potentially powerful alliance of native peoples and environmentalists.

In 1976, I was invited to speak to Wisconsin tribal representatives attending an AIO conference on mining held in Racine, Wisconsin. Exxon Minerals had just announced its discovery of one of the world's largest and richest zinc-copper deposits immediately adjacent to the Sokaogon Chippewa reservation at Mole Lake, Wisconsin. Two members of the Sokaogon Chippewa tribal council asked me to provide assistance to the tribe in its dealings with Exxon. The tribe needed technical assistance, legal help, and fundraising support to develop an effective counterstrategy to Exxon's mining plans. Most of the media and even many mainstream state environmental groups had already written off Exxon's proposed mine near Crandon as a lost cause. By any objective measure, the tribe's chances of success against the world's largest corporation were not good. The Sokaogon Chippewa band was the smallest tribe in Wisconsin, with just over 200 members and a tiny land base of approximately 1,900 acres. The tribe's annual budget was $1,200; the value of Exxon's energy reserves alone exceeded $1.3 trillion![4]

Before the company even began the mine permitting process, they were predicting the start of mining by 1981. Even some of my friends in the Madison chapter of the Union of Radical Political Economists (URPE) told me not to waste my time on a hopeless cause. To these nay-sayers, native struggles to defend their lands and resources appeared to be throwbacks to struggles already waged and lost during the 19th century. I took great exception to this view on both ethical and political grounds. I felt there was a moral imperative to support native struggles because it was not just a matter of preserving this piece of land or that particular resource; it was a matter of preserving an entire way of life. Their right to self-determination demands recognition. Those cultures are unique and deserve to be protected because they are part of the diversity of human life. Their loss affects all of us.

Beyond the morality of the situation, I also found compelling political reasons to support native struggles. I challenged my fellow radical colleagues to consider the possibility that Native American struggles over land and resources might prove to be the "Achilles heel" of U.S. imperialism. The successful assertion of Native American sovereignty would not only deprive U.S. imperialism of a much needed source of cheap raw materials for expansion but would also provide concrete examples of how economic development could take place on a basis other than the self-expansion of multinational corporate capital.[5] Whether raw material supply was the "Achilles heel" of U.S. imperialism or whether the struggle for native self-determination could aid the cause of environmentalism were not questions that could be answered in the abstract; one had to develop a political strategy and put it to the test.

It was at this point I decided that if I was going to work with the Sokaogon Chippewa it would take a major organizational commitment of time, resources, and energy. Through my work with Community Action on Latin America, I had become aware of the work of Shelton Davis and the Anthropology Resource Center in Cambridge, Massachusetts, as well as the work of Roger Moody and Colonialism and Indigenous Minorities Research/Action in London.[6] With these organizational models in mind I developed the idea for a Center for Alternative Mining Development Policy to provide technical assistance and organizational support for Indian and non-Indian rural communities targeted for mining projects. Several church funding agencies, including the Campaign for Human Development (U.S. Catholic Conference) and the Committee for the Self-Development of People (United Presbyterian Church), provided the initial funding for the Center. Dan Bomberry of the Seventh Generation Fund in Forestville, California also provided technical support and contacts with private foundations for the Sokaogon Chippewa tribal mining committee.

As I was finishing my doctoral degree in sociology during this period, I also offered to use my university connections in Madison to try to assemble an interdisciplinary research team that could provide the tribe with a social, economic, and environmental assessment of Exxon's proposed mine. The result of that effort was the formation of COACT Research, Inc. This group of radical academics helped document the hypocrisy of Exxon, which sought to project the public image of a socially and environmentally responsible corporation, by detailing Exxon's negative track record with other mining projects. This information provided the Sokaogon Chippewa with a way of gauging the reliability of Exxon's promises, based on the company's past performance record.

Ultimately, the tribe decided to resist Exxon's efforts to establish a mine near or on their land. The key, of course, to developing an effective counterstrategy to corporate resource colonialism is to identify the weakest, most vulnerable aspect of the project (for example, financing, dangerous or unproven technologies, violation of native land rights, failure to comply with applicable environmental laws, etc.) and organize a campaign around these issues. With the assistance of Wisconsin Indian Legal Services, the Sokaogon Chippewa identified mining impacts upon their wild rice lake as one of the critical legal issues in the mine permiting process. Any withdrawal of groundwater, or dewatering, of the proposed underground mine could harm the rice lake and provide the tribe with legal grounds to request a state denial of a mine permit.

This approach seemed increasingly realistic. By the time that Exxon filed its mine application with the Wisconsin Department of Natural Resources in December 1982, grassroots environmental organizations like the Rusk County Citizens Action Group in Ladysmith were traveling to the Rhinelander-Crandon area and meeting with the Sokaogon Chippewa. To counteract Exxon's propaganda, the Sokaogon Chippewa and their environmentalist allies decided to form a statewide environmental organization to focus attention on the negative effects of Exxon's proposed mine and the whole issue of resource colonialism in northern Wisconsin. The result was the Wisconsin Resources Protection Council (WRPC). As WRPC executive secretary, it was my job to initiate a dialogue between the tribes who would be affected by the Exxon mine—the Sokaogon Chippewa, the Forest County Potawatomi, and the Menominee—and their non-Indian neighbors. All around me, I could see a growing native-environmentalist alliance taking up its position in the new resource wars.

This new alliance, while one of the most promising developments of the last two decades, is still very fragile. It is often plagued by distrust, covert anti-Indian racism, and potentially competing agendas. I know of very few non-Indians, for example, who have worked with native peoples for any length of time who have not experienced some level of suspicion by Indians about their motives for doing this work. I have been accused of "using" Indians to advance my own political agenda on several occasions. In some sense, this is true. While I have a very strong political/ethical commitment to native sovereignty, I am also an environmentalist with my own serious objections to mining in ecologically sensitive areas. This puts me at odds with the aspirations of some Indians. From an ecological perspective, whether the industrial resource extraction process is controlled by the multinational mining companies or the tribes themselves makes relatively little difference.

When I describe the emerging "native-environmentalist" alliance in opposition to corporate resource extraction projects, I do not mean to suggest that all natives are environmentalists (or that all environmentalists are white). There are significant differences among native nations as well as within native nations on the question of resource development. One cannot speak about *the* native response to corporate-initiated resource development any more than one can speak about *the* white response to such development. Both in the past and in the present, these issues have divided one tribal group against another.[7] Multinational mining corporations and the Bureau of Indian Affairs have frequently exploited these divisions to neutralize resistance to resource extraction projects on Indian lands. Nonetheless, I find the term "native-environmentalist" useful in describing a growing political tendency within native communities and within the mainstream and grassroots environmental movement, a tendency that sees the integral connection between native struggles for cultural survival and struggles to protect the natural world.

For white environmentalists, this holistic perspective stands in sharp contrast to the distorted white supremacist and industrial notions they have grown up with.[8] For native traditionalists, this perspective has deep historical and cultural roots. It reflects the wisdom of their ancestors and elders that sees the fate of the world as intimately bound up with how human beings treat each other and "Mother Earth." As the editors of *Akwesasne Notes,* a Mohawk publication, argue, "Participation in a process which is certain to destroy the local ecology, deplete the water table, and make human occupation of the land a tenuous if not impossible prospect, has to be seen in terms which go beyond a simple moral breakdown. That participation has to be seen as a form of self-destructive madness."[9] Theirs is a potent warning for all native peoples:

> The development of profitable mining and refining processes requires exorbitant amounts of capital (money), and requires supportive structures that most Indian people never think much about. But the real reason for objection to that line of thought and course of action is that it requires the same kind of technology and will produce the same kinds of long-term results. Putting stripmining machinery in the hands of Indians won't make it any less polluting and environmentally destructive than it is in the hands of Exxon or Tenneco. The objection to that kind of development is not that such development is only an exploitation of native people and their lands. The real objection is that the technology will make human occupation of Indian country impossible. It does happen to be true, however, that the economic exploitation continues even when Indian people try to purchase the equipment and to extract the resources themselves. The real question is much more important

than the economic questions. What do the Indian people do, three or four decades hence, when the water is all gone or polluted for generations to come, when the land is all stripmined, or sold off, or occupied by summer beach houses, or made into golf courses, or paved by highways, or turned to desert (where there isn't supposed to be a desert)?[10]

What indeed do any of us do? We need to join and build the native-environmentalist alliance today and struggle for a more just, more sustainable, more desirable world. This movement, as this book attests, has already taken root throughout the world. Chapter One examines three international native-environmental resistance campaigns to hydroelectric, logging, and oil drilling megaprojects. Chapter Two turns to the question of mining, perhaps the most destructive extractive industry in the world. Chapters Three through Six explore case studies of resource wars over mining in northern Wisconsin and the Indian-environmental coalition that has arisen to challenge resource colonialism there. Chapter Seven looks at how white racism has been fanned and used to spearhead the assault on native lands in northern Wisconsin. Chapter Eight explores further how the defense of treaties and native sovereignty can be used to protect both Indian and non-Indian communities from being pillaged by resource extractive industries. Hopefully this book will inspire organizing, coalition-building, and personal action. The future, after all, is in our hands.

Part I
Up Against the Multinationals

Chapter 1

Resource Colonialism and International Native Resistance

Native peoples are under assault on every continent because their lands contain a wide variety of valuable resources needed for industrial development. From the Amazon Basin to the frozen stretches of northern Saskatchewan, to the tropical rainforests of Southeast Asia and Central Africa, energy, mining, logging, hydro-electric, and other megaprojects have uprooted, dislocated, and even destroyed native communities. In the early 1960s, Darcy Ribeiro, a Brazilian anthropologist, summarized the effects of resource coloni-zation on the Indians of the Amazon Basin: "The discovery of any-thing which can be exploited is tantamount to the crack of doom for the Indians who are pressured to abandon their lands or be slaugh-tered on them. And economic discoveries do not have to be excep-tional for the Indians to be plundered."[1] The Yanomami Indians, the largest unacculturated tribe in Brazil, now face extinction because valuable deposits of tungsten, titanium, gold, uranium, bauxite, and tin have been discovered on their lands.[2] The mercury effluent from the mining has poisoned the rivers, killing the fish and destroying the Indians' water supply. The Yanomami are dying from diseases brought in by the miners, such as malaria, TB, flu, and respiratory infections to which they have no immunity. The American Anthropo-logical Association has estimated that at least 15 percent of the Yanomami have died from malaria.[3]

A basic aspect of the resource colonization process is, as John Bodley has emphasized in his classic work, *Victims of Progress,* "that the prior ownership rights and interests of the aboriginal inhabitants are totally ignored as irrelevant by both the state and the invading individuals."[4] Exxon's investment in the El Cerrejón project in Co-lombia, South America is a case in point. El Cerrejón is one of the richest undeveloped coal-fields in the world and the largest project of any kind ever undertaken in Colombia. It is a joint venture of Intercor, a subsidiary of Exxon, and Carbocol, a Colombian government corporation. The project is located on the lands of the Guajiros, Colombia's largest group of native people. Although a four-volume environmental impact statement was prepared on the project, the presence of the Guajiros was practically omitted from the report. The land the Guajiros have occupied for centuries is called *vacante* (vacant). "The overall impression," according to one critic of the study, "is of a wasteland inhabited by a few unorganized and insignificant indigenous groups, in which the construction of a road, port, and workers' camps can proceed without problem. Not a word is said about Guajiro history, culture, social organization, or economy."[5]

Despite such cases, well-documented by groups like Survival International, Cultural Survival, the International Work Group for Indigenous Affairs, and the Anthropology Resource Center, there is an extraordinary reluctance in mainstream media to assign responsibility to the practices of specific corporations, banks, and government agencies. For example, *Time* magazine recently ran a cover story on "Lost Tribes, Lost Knowledge," which lamented that "the world's tribes are dying out or being absorbed into modern civilization. As they vanish, so does their irreplaceable knowledge."[6] Never once in that long article does the author mention that the ecologically destructive megaprojects which threaten native peoples around the world are being promoted by multinational corporations and international financial organizations like the World Bank. Nowhere is there mention of how multinational corporations and development-oriented governments have long waged relentless resource wars against native peoples.[7] Instead, we are treated to a photo gallery of native faces that will be preserved for the viewer while the resource wars continue unabated. This exercise in romantic nostalgia is reminiscent of Edward S. Curtis, the turn-of-the-century photographer who wanted to preserve the images of American Indian life even as the U.S. government was trying to eradicate native cultures.[8] Curtis' large-scale photographic project was financed, appropriately enough, by J. P. Morgan, one of the original "robber barons," whose fortune was built, in part, on the iron ore wealth stolen from the Chippewa of the Lake Superior region.[9]

Also missing from the article is any mention of the fact that corporate and governmental attempts to gain access to cheap energy or cheap timber on native lands have often been met with fierce resistance from native peoples. Blending traditional forms of defending their cultures with the most sophisticated forms of political protest, coalition-building, and international networking with environmental and human rights organizations, these groups have demonstrated that such ecologically-destructive megaprojects can be slowed down, modified, and even stopped.[10] In this chapter, we will examine three cases of the new resource wars that are on the cutting edge of international native resistance to resource colonization.

Growing Native Resistance to Dams: James Bay II, Quebec, Canada

Certainly one of the most serious threats to native peoples comes from the damming of rivers to generate hydroelectric power. From the Amazonian rainforests to the Canadian subarctic region, the insatiable demand for cheap energy has threatened to literally submerge the lands of tribal hunters and gatherers. One of the largest projects, and one which has generated fierce resistance among the Cree and Inuit Indians, is located in northern Quebec, on the shores of James Bay.

Here the Cree and Inuit are fighting Hydro-Quebec, a $50-billion utility that is wholly-owned by the Quebec government. It would be hard to conceive of two opponents that are more unevenly matched. In monetary terms, Hydro-Quebec is the largest nonfinancial institution in Canada, accounting for 5 percent of Quebec's gross domestic product and employing 22,000 people.[11] Totally unregulated, its finances shielded from public scrutiny, it has become "a state within the state."[12] Robert Bourassa, the Quebec prime minister and original mastermind of the James Bay project, sees hydropower as the key to the province's economic and political independence from Canada. Northern Quebec, he wrote in a 1985 book, *Power from the North,* is a "vast hydroelectric project-in-the-bud, and every day millions of potential kilowatt hours flow downhill and out to the sea. What a waste!"[13] Several critics have noted the symbolism of Bourassa's office being located in the Montreal headquarters of Hydro-Quebec.[14]

Hydro-Quebec wants to spend $12.6 billion Canadian dollars to tap hydropower on the Great Whale River, which flows into Hudson Bay. The 3,100-megawatt project, known as James Bay, Phase II, would feed the energy demands of cities like Montreal, Boston, and New York. Phase III of the project, known as the Nottaway-Broadback-Rupert project, would divert the Nottaway and Rupert rivers into the Broadback River and flood 5,000 square miles of wildlife habitat. The lower parts of the diverted rivers would be transformed into dry bedrock. If the project is completed, "it will have reduced to servitude every major river flowing from Quebec into James Bay and southern Hudson Bay save one."[15] The entire James Bay project will generate, at peak output, some 27,000 megawatts of power, equivalent to about 13 Niagara Falls. It is one of the largest construction projects ever undertaken. Stephen Hazell, executive director of the Canadian Arctic Resources Committee in Ottawa, refers to the utility as a "bureaucracy run wild...with no checks or counterchecks. Hydro-Quebec is in the business of building dams at all costs."[16]

Those costs would fall heavily on both the region's native people and the delicate ecosystems that the natives depend upon for their economy and culture. The series of dams, water diversions, and hydroelectric projects planned for James Bay, Phase II, would flood an area roughly 2,700 square miles in a subarctic region where 10,000 Cree and 5,000 Inuit have hunted and trapped for thousands of years. Even now, over 40 percent of the Cree make their living off the land.[17] Many of the place names in the Great Whale area reflect the importance of mammals, birds, and fish for Cree survival. For example, the proposed site of the Great Whale-2 generating station is called *Masmakwisich* (Place of the Speckled Rainbow Trout).[18] Of all the animals, fish remains the most important part of the Cree diet, accounting for about one-quarter of the total community wild food harvest.[19]

One of the unforeseen results of the first phase of the James Bay project on the La Grande River was the contamination of the fish with mercury in the impounded areas. The massive flooding caused the death of plant material which produced bacteria that transformed naturally-occurring mercury in the soil and vegetation into toxic methylmercury. The mercury moved up the food chain to the fish and ultimately to the Cree, who depended on the fish for their diet. "In some species of fish," says Hazell, "particularly the predatorial species like large pike and lake trout in the reservoirs of the La Grande project, mercury levels have reached as high as four to five parts per million, which is roughly ten times the legal limit for the sale of fish in Canada. Hydro-Quebec admits that there is no feasible solution to the problem."[20] The contamination of the fish with mercury also poisons the other animals that the Cree depend on because they also eat fish. Despite this assault on native health and traditional economy, Hydro-Quebec plans to go ahead with the Phase II project and the Nottaway-Broadback-Rupert Project and exacerbate what is already the most significant mercury contamination in North America. In 1984, notes Hazell, "two-thirds of the people in Chisasibi, at the mouth of the La Grande River, had levels of mercury in their bodies that exceeded the World Health Organization limits. Some of the older people in Chisasibi had levels so high that they were exhibiting symptoms of methylmercury poisoning, Minamata disease."[21] Among these symptoms are irreversible neurological damage such as numbness of limbs and loss of peripheral vision. In classic blaming-the-victim style, the Cree have been told to restrict their consumption of several species of fish throughout the La Grande River drainage.

But for the Cree, the issue goes far beyond a change in their diet. "Telling us that we'll be OK if we don't eat fish is like telling us that we will be OK if we just cut our own legs off," says Andrew Natachequan, a Cree elder in the village of Whapmagoostui.[22] The contamination of natural resources with methylmercury strikes at the very core of native culture and "promotes a feeling of loss of control over their environment and their very lives. Mercury contamination thus can become a serious mental health issue."[23] Whenever core cultural values are undermined, community cohesion is threatened. Among the hidden social costs of hydroelectric development may be higher rates of suicide and homicide.[24]

The assault against the economy and culture of native peoples cannot be separated from the assault on the complex and delicate ecosystems of James Bay and Hudson Bay. Migratory birds are critically dependent upon the James Bay coast as a staging area where they store up on food resources to make their annual migrations. Chris Rimmer, director of research at the Vermont Institute of Natural Science, notes that "the coastlines of James and Hudson bays constitute an immense, natural migratory funnel along which millions of subarctic and arctic breeding waterfowl, shorebirds, raptors, and passerine birds pass during spring and autumn migrations."[25] The massive flooding and water diversions of the James Bay project would, according to the National Audubon Society, "make James Bay and some of Hudson's [sic] Bay uninhabitable for much of the wildlife dependent on it."[26] Other hydroelectric projects, in the provinces of Ontario and Manitoba, will also have significant environmental impacts on the James Bay and Hudson Bay ecosystems.[27] To date, there has been no attempt to provide a comprehensive assessment of the cumulative impacts of these projects upon the ecosystem.

How is it possible that such a large project with such enormous destructive potential has never been subjected to a comprehensive environmental review process? Matthew Coon-Come, Grand Chief of the Grand Council of the Cree of Quebec and chair of the Cree Regional Authority, puts it bluntly: "Projects on this scale are only possible in areas which are uniquely inhabited by indigenous peoples...We think of these projects as a form of racism. Our way of life, our lands, our communities, and our people would all be sacrificed if these projects are allowed to go ahead. Projects built on indigenous lands inevitably are built without the benefit of a full environmental and social impact assessment. We call this environmental racism because of the vast environmental impacts of these projects and because review processes are not properly implemented when development occurs on indigenous lands. What is especially disturbing about these projects is that they will degrade the environment in northern Quebec for thousands of more years."[28] Were it not for the determined resistance of the Cree and the Inuit, none of these issues would have arisen and become the focal point for international discussion and action. How did this happen?

The Cree and the Inuit living in northern Quebec were never consulted about the James Bay project. They learned about the project from newsreports on the radio or in the newspapers. By that time, planning was already well underway. The Cree had to act quickly if they were going to resist the damming of rivers that would flood the land where they hunted, fished, and trapped. When Cree from the scattered villages of northern Quebec came together to discuss the project, it was the first time they had all come together. It was the beginning of "the process by which the Cree of Quebec have come to see themselves as belonging not just to family and village, but to a regional ethnic and political unit, to a nation."[29] The Indians of Quebec Association assisted the Cree in their early organizing efforts, as did a number of non-Native advisers and experts, including anthropologist Harvey Feit and attorney James O'Reilly.

While the Cree, the Quebec Association, and their consultants were preparing the legal case against the project, others, like Helene Lajambe, an economics student at McGill University, was organizing a grassroots opposition movement. In February 1972, Lajambe and others founded the James Bay Committee, which brought together hunting and fishing groups, various Indian organizations, and a host of environmental and conservation groups.[30]

In April 1972, the Cree asked the Superior Court of Quebec to order a halt to further construction of the James Bay project because it would damage their lands and destroy their way of life. Government lawyers argued that since the Cree and Inuit people had no rights in James Bay, there was no need for a hearing on the request for an injunction.[31] As far as the Quebec government was concerned, the Cree were squatters on public land. James O'Reilly countered with a bold assertion of native land rights: "Petitioners are invoking not only their collective territorial rights, also known at times as aboriginal rights, in the land; they are also invoking rights presently recognized by the province of Quebec to hunt and trap exclusively in all of the territory which will be affected, to use the navigable waters, the highways of the north in summer as in winter."[32]

Judge Albert Malouf agreed with O'Reilly and granted the Cree the opportunity to present their case against the James Bay project to the court. For the next six months the Cree and their expert witnesses presented detailed testimony about the cultural and environmental impacts of the project. Some of the most damming testimony came from Daniel J. Khazzoom, an econometrics professor at McGill University who had previously served as the chief econometrist for the U.S. Federal Power Commission. He testified that Hydro-Quebec's projections of energy needs were not based upon the energy needs of the province but upon the corporate growth needs of Hydro-Quebec. This resulted in greatly exaggerated estimates of energy needs. Furthermore, by simply negotiating contracts for interruptable power with industrial consumers, "the entire La Grande project would be made unnecessary."[33]

On November 15, 1973, Judge Malouf issued a strongly worded verdict in favor of the Cree and Inuit and ordered an immediate halt to all construction on the La Grande project. In his 170-page opinion the judge declared: "In view of the dependence of the indigenous population on the animals, fish, and vegetation in the territory, the works will have devastating and far-reaching effects on the Cree Indians and the Inuit living in the territory and the lands adjacent thereto."[34]

The immediate response of the developers (the James Bay Development Corporation, the James Bay Energy Corporation, and Hydro-Quebec) to the judge's order was to "seize the territory, seal it off from outside observers and continue the work."[35] Meanwhile, the Quebec government and the corporations launched a media campaign to emphasize how much the work stoppage was costing the people of Quebec. Within a week, the Quebec Appeals Court suspended Malouf's ban, arguing that construction was too far along to stop and that the needs of millions of the province's energy consumers outweighed the concerns of a few thousand natives.

The Cree went directly to the Supreme Court of Canada in Ottawa to appeal the suspension of Malouf's injunction. The Supreme Court refused to hear the case before the Quebec Appeals Court heard the case against Malouf's judgment. The earliest that the Appeals Court could hear the case would be eight months; in the meantime, construction work proceeded.

Even though Malouf's injunction was suspended, the Cree had won important legal recognition of their land rights. Prime Minister Bourassa realized that the land claims of the Cree could throw a legal monkey wrench into the James Bay project as they made their way through the courts. An out-of-court settlement with the Cree would remove a potential legal obstacle to the completion of the project and reassure nervous investors. The Cree could expect little sympathy from the Quebec Appeals Court and they knew that as construction proceeded, the chances of stopping the project were remote. After a long, tough negotiating process, the James Bay and Northern Quebec Agreement was signed in November 1975.

The Cree reluctantly ceded their rights to lands affected by the project in return for local self-government, some cash compensation, and exclusive hunting, fishing, and trapping rights in some areas of the territory. In addition, the Cree and Inuit secured a regional environmental and social protection regime which guarantees their right to have a say in future projects. The agreement is the first modern land claims agreement negotiated in Canada and the first test of a "technique for giving local land-based indigenous communities more effective participation in the regulation of development activities in their regions."[36] A Cree Regional Authority was established to administer the provisions of the social and environmental protection regime. While the Cree and Inuit lost the battle to stop Phase I of the James Bay project, they acquired invaluable political experience, organizational skills, and a network of non-Native American experts and advisers to help them wage the battle against Phase II.

Since the 1975 treaty was signed, the Quebec government has gone ahead with Phase II of the James Bay project without consulting the Cree. In 1989, the Cree began new litigation, based upon their right to be consulted about future projects. In November 1990, in order to get around the detailed environmental impact assessment requirements of the agreement, Hydro-Quebec decided to split the Great Whale project into two parts—first, the roads, airports, and other access infrastructure, then the dam construction. This is the classic foot-in-the-door strategy and the Cree were not about to participate in this sham review process. If Hydro-Quebec were allowed to get away with this segmented review process, the principal parts of the project could be built and assessed in isolation from each other, and from their cumulative impacts. Once the access infrastructure was built, there would be a powerful momentum to approve the rest of the project, regardless of the environmental consequences.[37] In September 1991, a federal judge in Ottawa ruled that the 1975 treaty requires the consent of the Cree before the project is constructed. The court ordered the federal government to carry out a new assessment of the project that will give federal authorities the right to stop it. "It's no secret that the Cree's ultimate objective is to stop this project," said Bill Namagoose, executive director of the Grand Council of the Cree of Quebec. "One of the ways to stop it is to have full public...environmental assessments."[38]

Namagoose listed a number of conditions that would have to be met before the Cree agreed to participate in the environmental review. The conditions include: a moratorium on the Great Whale project; no time limit on the review; full funding for any group or citizen to intervene and state their views; and a complete discussion of the justification for the project. This latter point has proven to be a most embarrassing public relations issue for Hydro-Quebec and has drawn public attention to the secrecy surrounding the project's finances.

The Cree have raised significant doubts about the need for the project in Quebec, suggesting that the real beneficiaries of the Great Whale project will not be the public but the energy-intensive industries along the St. Lawrence River. In January 1991, Hydro-Quebec's contract with Norsk Hydro, a Norwegian company that operates a magnesium smelter on the St. Lawrence River, was leaked to a

Canadian Broadcasting reporter. Hydro-Quebec went to court to suppress the publication of the contract's details. Some of the details leaked out anyway, thanks to the Sierra Club and the Solidarity Foundation in the United States. They disclosed that "power that cost Hydro-Quebec 2.4 cents per kilowatt-hour to produce was being sold to Norsk Hydro for 1.5 cents—in effect, forcing Quebec ratepayers, who were then being charged 4.2 cents per kilowatt-hour, to subsidize the company."[39] Although only the Norsk Hydro contract has been made public, it is widely believed that the utility had offered cut-rate deals to all 13 companies on the St. Lawrence River. Laval University economist Jean-Thomas Bernard estimates that Hydro-Quebec loses $300 million a year on these contracts.[40]

The disclosure of the Norsk Hydro contract also created other problems for Hydro-Quebec. Under the terms of the U.S.-Canada Free Trade Agreement, the United States can slap duty on imports of subsidized products. The Utah-based Magnesium Corporation of America has already brought a case before the U.S. International Trade Commission, charging unfair competition and seeking import duties on refined magnesium from the Norsk Hydro smelter in Quebec.[41]

How did Hydro-Quebec get itself into such a financial mess? The Cree had already presented evidence before Judge Malouf that the utility had overestimated the demand for electricity. When James Bay, Phase I started to come on line in the late 1970s, there was an energy surplus in Quebec. Hydro-Quebec had to spill water over the dams because there was no market for all this power.[42] To create markets for this electricity, Prime Minister Bourassa encouraged energy-intensive industries, like aluminum smelters, to locate in Quebec. The strategy was successful. Southern Quebec is now known as "Aluminum Valley," where, according to Daniel Green of the Montreal-based *Societe pour Vaincre la Pollution* (Society to Overcome Pollution), "the largest concentration of aluminum smelters in any hydrographic basin in the world" releases pollutants into the St. Lawrence River.[43] The Cree and their economic advisers have suggested that the only justification for building the Great Whale

project was to meet the demand created by these sales and anticipated export sales to the United States.[44]

To counter this part of Hydro-Quebec's marketing strategy to
export electricity to the United States, the Cree and Inuit developed
an extensive and sophisticated international network of support
groups that targeted the electrical export contracts in Maine, Vermont, and New York. As with so many of the current resource wars
against native peoples, the Cree and Inuit are raising issues that go
far beyond cultural survival and regional environmental impacts. Increasingly, they are also addressing issues of economics and energy
conservation/energy efficiency from an international perspective.

In their attempt to stop James Bay II, the Cree and Inuit have
enlisted the help of several national and international environmental
action organizations including the Sierra Club, the National Audubon
Society, the Natural Resources Defense Council, Greenpeace, and
Earth First!. They have also established contact with the Kayapo
Indians of Brazil, who have also been fighting large hydroprojects in
their territory.[45] In the spring of 1990, a delegation of the Cree and
Inuit paddled down the Hudson River to New York City on their
specially-made *odeyak*—half canoe, half kayak. They stopped at numerous points along the way to bring their urgent message to a U.S.
audience. Hydro-Quebec has sold this project to U.S. utilities as
"cheap and clean." But, according to Whapmagoostui Chief Robbie
Dick, "it's not cheap for us. When you turn on your switch, you're
killing us."[46] Through videos and other media events, like the Fall
1991 "Ban the Dam Jam" rock concerts in New York City, the Cree
and Inuit have brought international attention to their battle. Far from
framing it as a "Canadian" issue, the Cree and Inuit have emphasized
the crucial role that international energy contracts play in the destruction of their cultures and ecosystems. Seven U.S. utilities in New
York and New England have entered into long-term contracts to
purchase power from Hydro-Quebec. "Our aim," says Matthew
Mukash, a Whapmagoostui council liaison officer who holds a degree in political science, "is to kill contracts in the United States."[47]

The initial efforts of U.S.-based groups to oppose James Bay II
were focused on the construction of huge transmission lines through

New York and Maine. No Thank Q Hydro-Quebec, a grassroots environmental group in Maine, campaigned against the power line and the contract. In January 1989, Maine backed out of a $15 billion contract "because the Maine utility had not proven that importing electricity from Quebec would be cheaper than options such as investing in improvements in energy efficiency."[48] Grassroots opposition also led to the cancellation of several small contracts in Vermont. In New York City, Jeffrey Wollock of the Solidarity Foundation helped found the James Bay Defense Coalition, comprising some 24 environmental and native rights organizations. The coalition's objective is to get the state to cancel the $19 billion New York Power Authority (NYPA) contracts. The NYPA is Hydro-Quebec's largest export customer. This may also be the Achilles' heel of the entire project because Hydro-Quebec has borrowed heavily to finance construction. At the end of 1990, the corporation's long-term debt was $25.6 billion, including $7.5 billion in U.S. dollars, making it one of the largest debts held by a North American corporation. If these contracts are canceled, says Robert Blohm, a U.S. investment banker in Montreal, the company could be "dangerously exposed to risk on the American portion of its debt."[49]

In August 1991, after a meeting with Matthew Coon-Come, New York Governor Mario Cuomo announced that the NYPA would postpone finalizing its contracts with Hydro-Quebec until November 1992. He also announced that he had requested an economic and environmental study of the impacts of the contract. Meanwhile, activists in the James Bay Defense Coalition continued to hold debates, protests, concerts, and other events designed to keep the issue in the political spotlight. Several religious orders holding Con Edison stock, working through the New York-based Interfaith Center on Corporate Responsibility, filed a shareholder resolution on the James Bay issue. As the state's largest utility, Con Edison was scheduled to receive nearly half of the NYPA's purchases from Hydro-Quebec. The resolution asked management to report on the reasons why it needs power from the James Bay project, to provide an evaluation of the proposed energy cost versus conservation investment, and to summarize the environmental and social impacts on the native people in Quebec.[50]

On the legislative front, Representative William B. Hoyt of Buffalo introduced a bill in the New York State Assembly which required all foreign energy purchases to meet the state's environmental guidelines. The bill passed the State Assembly in mid-March 1992 by an overwhelming majority. Before the bill could be introduced in the State Senate, Governor Cuomo announced that New York State was canceling a 20-year contract to buy power from Hydro-Quebec. He said the decision was made "primarily on economic grounds." His energy advisers "calculated that signing the Quebec contracts would actually be slightly more expensive for New York consumers than relying on conservation and other energy sources."[51]

Equally significant is the fact that Con Edison canceled its contract with the NYPA. Prior to canceling its contract the utility admitted that it had overestimated its energy needs. It is now convinced that it can meet all demand growth in coming years by a combination of conservation and demand management through pricing adjustments.[52] This turnaround is a confirmation of many of the economic arguments the Cree and their allies had been making for years. In challenging Hydro-Quebec's export contracts, the James Bay Defense Coalition exposed the erroneous economic assumptions of the project to public scrutiny. "It's a case where environmentalists used the power of the marketplace to halt a destructive project," says David R. Wooley, a law professor at Pace University's Center for Environmental Legal Studies. "Conservation competes very well when you give it a chance."[53]

While Governor Cuomo's March 27, 1992 announcement is a major victory for the native rights and environmental coalition opposed to James Bay II, this is not the end of the battle. Hydro-Quebec is determined that Phase II will proceed regardless of the financial uncertainties. The collapse of the NYPA contract will at least delay the construction for several years, however. In the meantime, the Interfaith Center on Corporate Responsibility has focused its attention on Merrill Lynch and Shearson Lehman, the Wall Street invest-ment firms that are still involved as underwriters of the project.[54]

The Cree will continue to argue their case in the courts, in environmental hearings, and in the mass media. They will also use direct action if necessary. In the spring of 1991, 600 Cree blockaded a construction site on the La Grande River, stopping work for hours. Whether the provincial government is prepared to deal with mass nonviolent civil disobedience remains to be seen. The province is reported to be training a special SWAT team to occupy Cree villages in the event of civil disorder.[55] However, in light of the international prominence of this struggle, Prime Minister Bourassa would risk inter-national condemnation for any military response to the ongoing conflict. In the meantime, the Cree and the Inuit have demonstrated that native peoples are capable of blending their assertion of treaty rights with the most innovative and militant forms of environmental activism to chal-lenge the most powerful institutions of a large nation-state.

Blockading the Loggers: Native Resistance to Deforestation in Malaysia

There are about 250 million native people worldwide, many of whom live within or on the margins of tropical rainforests in South-east Asia, Central and South America, and Central Africa.[56] They depend upon the forests for their food, medicines, clothes, and building materials. However, the extensive and accelerating exploi-tation of the rainforests for timber, minerals, oil, hydroelectric en-ergy, cattle ranching, and plantation agriculture makes them "the most seriously threatened habitat of indigenous peoples."[57]

At present, Malaysia is the country where deforestation is most rapid. The highest rate of commercial deforestation in the world, encompassing some 2,100 acres per day, occurs in the Malaysian state of Sarawak, in the northwest part of the island of Borneo.[58] The rainforests of Sarawak are also home to 220,000 tribal peoples collec-tively known as Dayaks or Orang Ulu ("peoples of the interior"). They include the Iban, Kayan, Kelabit, Kenyah, Kejaman, Punan Bah, Tanjong, Sekapan, Lahanan, and Penan peoples. Over the past quarter century, some 30 percent of Sarawak's unique tropical forests have been logged.[59] If present trends continue, warned the European Parliament in a 1989 resolution, "by 1995 more than 60 percent of the forests of Sarawak are likely to disappear with disastrous consequences for the environment and the continued existence of the aboriginal population."[60] The fiercest resistance to logging on native lands has come from the Penan, one of the few remaining nomadic hunting and gathering rainforest tribes in the world.

In 1983, Malaysia accounted for 58 percent of the total world export of tropical logs. Eighty percent of the timber is sold to Japan, and the remaining 20 percent goes to Europe, the United States, Singapore, and Korea.[61] By 1985, Sarawak accounted for 40 percent of Malaysia's total log production. The government of Sarawak routinely grants logging licenses to timber companies without any notice to the native peoples who have lived on these lands for at least 50,000 years. Under *adat,* or customary law, anyone who occupies or cultivates the land is entitled to its use. This customary right to land, as practiced by the natives, is recognized in the Sarawak Land Code.[62] Nonetheless, the timber companies have concessions to 60 percent of the forest area of Sarawak. Between 1968 and 1984 the area under Communal Forest shrunk from 303 square kilometers to only 56 square kilometers.[63] Forest concessions are routinely given in areas within traditional village boundaries. It is not unusual for the native people to wake up in the morning and see bulldozers and chainsaws leveling their farms, desecrating sacred ancestral burial grounds, and opening roads through their property. When these communities apply to the government for Communal Forest Reserves to protect the land around their settlements, they are routinely denied while the same forest is opened up to the timber companies. Top government officials hand out logging concessions to friends, relatives, and political allies. James Wong, Sarawak's minister for the environment and tourism, is also the owner of one of Malaysia's most prosperous logging companies, Limbang Trading, which controls over 300,000 hectares of timber concessions in Sarawak. Robin Hanbury-Tenison, the president of Survival International, once asked Wong whether he was concerned about the likely climatic effects of deforestation. Wong replied, "We get too much rain in Sarawak. It stops me from playing golf."[64]

To extract the great mahogany trees and the other valuable woods, bulldozers tear up entire forests, washing vast amounts of earth and topsoil into the river system. The most pervasive effects of logging in hilly terrain is "the reduced water-holding capacity of the land and increased erosion from rain. Many plant and animal species, at all levels of the food web are affected or destroyed as a result."[65] Thousands of native people are being forced off the land and into the towns where they face slum housing, malnutrition, unemployment, alcoholism, and prostitution.

In February 1987, the Penan, whose way of life is entirely dependent on the forest, appealed to the State Government:

> Stop destroying the forest or we will be forced to protect it. The forest is our livelihood. We lived here before any of you outsiders came. We made our sago meat and ate fruit of the trees. Our life was not easy, but we lived it in contentment. Now the logging companies turn rivers into muddy streams and the jungle into devastation. The fish cannot survive in dirty rivers and wild animals will not live in devastated forests.[66]

When the authorities ignored their appeals, the Penan decided to erect barricades across logging roads. The barricades consist of logs and the bodies of hundreds of men, women, and children standing across the logging roads, blocking the timber lorries from getting through. Liman Awun, a Penan from Long Beluk, says "I want to block so the *kompeni* [loggers] won't behave like thieves. We'll tell the police this is not wrong. It's our land but they've destroyed it. We will *matep* [blockade] till it's given back to us." Sarina Oho, a Penan from Long Terawan, adds another important dimension to the assault on Penan culture:

> The *kompeni's* men not only kill the forest, they go after our women too. One night when my husband was away,

the men from the timber camp climbed up to our hut and asked for girls. They have disturbed many women, married or single. When we complained, the men just laughed and made dirty gestures." The Penan were enraged when some politicians referred to them as "animals." A Penan blockader told a reporter that "We are human beings like the leaders. But they look down on us. That's why they don't recognize our land rights but give licenses to timber companies."[67]

The Penan were soon joined by other Dayak tribes and members of environmental groups. At least nine timber companies were affected, including Limbang Trading, Wong Tong Kwong, Samling Timber, Merlin Timber, Sarsin, Keruntum, Marabong, and Baya Lumber.[68] The blockades began in March 1987 and involved several thousand native people from over 30 communities in the Baram and Limbang districts where the logging was heaviest. The timber industry was paralyzed for several months because the timber lorries couldn't move.

As long as the blockades were in effect the government was losing potential timber revenues. The Dayaks were soon faced with whole platoons of heavily-armed, paramilitary police who forced them at gunpoint to dismantle their blockades. In November 1987, 42 Penan and Kayan blockaders were arrested. The Malaysian government also invoked its emergency "Internal Security Act" to close down three national newspapers, ban public rallies, and arrest 103 citizens, including prominent environmentalists, lawyers, and tribal rights activists.[69] Among those detained was Harrison Ngau, a Kayan who works with Sahabat Alam Malaysia (SAM, or Friends of the Earth, Malaysia). SAM had been in the forefront of organizations appealing to the federal and state governments of Malaysia and Sarawak to protect the lands, forests, and resources of the Dayaks. The arrests provoked worldwide protests with the International Commission of Jurists in Geneva, Switzerland. In January 1988, the government released all but 33 of the 145 citizens jailed in the November sweep. Shortly thereafter, the chief minister, Datuk Patinggi Hj Abd

Taib Mahmud, announced that he had frozen 25 timber concessions worth more than $22.5 billion, covering some 3 million acres of land. In making this announcement, he noted that the concessions were "concentrated in the hands of a few," most notably the relatives and friends of former Chief Minister Tun Rahman.[70]

After the arrest of the blockaders, however, the government passed a law which prohibits the setting up of blockades on logging roads. Violation of the law carries a two-year jail term and a fine of $6,000. In February 1988, 71 of the arrested Penan met and decided that the new law was unjust because it denied their legally recognized customary land rights. "We are the owners preventing outsiders from coming onto our property," they said. "We are not doing something wrong on other people's property."[71] In the meantime, the logging companies were working 24 hours a day with the help of floodlights. This renewed assault resulted in a series of blockades and new arrests, bringing the total arrested since 1987 to 300. Using a network of environmental and human rights groups, SAM organized an international campaign to draw world attention to the April 1989 trial of the 42 Penan and Kayan blockaders. In North America, the Rainforest Action Network organized extensive showings of the video "Into Darkest Borneo." News updates on the Penan struggle were also made available on the EcoNet computer network.

Survival International and the International Union for the Conservation of Nature and Natural Resources intervened with the Sarawak government to recognize and uphold the Dayak people's rights to their lands and to withdraw the licenses of the logging companies working on native lands. Because most of Sarawak's timber exports go to Japan, demonstrations were organized at Japanese embassies around the world during World Rainforest Week in October 1988.[72] In April 1989, SAM hosted the World Rainforest Movement Meeting in Penang, Malaysia. More than a dozen organizations were in attendance, from Indonesia, the Philippines, Thailand, India, Japan, Australia, Canada, Great Britain, and the United States. Participants drafted an emergency call to action for the forests, their people, and life on earth. Included in this declaration was a call to ban all imports of tropical timber from natural forests and tropical wood products.[73]

With all the international publicity focused on the Sarawak government's treatment of the Dayak blockaders, the prosecution decided to withdraw all the charges against the 42 Penans and Kayans arrested in October 1987. They were discharged on April 24, 1989. Shortly thereafter they filed a lawsuit against the government, charging it with human rights abuses, including incarceration in overcrowded and filthy jails, being subjected to severe and unwarranted interrogation, and wrongful imprisonment.[74]

Green parties staged protests in European cities in September 1989 as part of their Anti-Tropical Hardwoods Campaign. In November 1989, the European Parliament passed a resolution which "sympathizes with the steps taken by the Penan, Kelabit, and Kayan, with a view to combatting the further destruction of their surroundings," and "calls on the Sarawak Government to release immediately those arrested and to initiate genuine negotiations with representatives of the indigenous people."[75] Shortly thereafter, Deputy Prime Minister Abdul Ghafar Baba announced the possibility of a ban on log exports from Sarawak and Sabah. However, the ban was never implemented and Sarawak has continued to arrest native blockaders. To date, 500 Dayaks have been arrested for blockading the logging roads into their forest. The situation of the Dayaks remains of paramount concern to international human rights and environmental organizations.

The most recent effort to present a united front against the assault on the rainforests took place in February 1992 when tribal peoples from tropical forests around the world came together to form the International Alliance of the Indigenous Tribal Peoples of the Tropical Forests at a conference held in Penang. Marcus Colchester of the World Rainforest Movement describes this "historic new alliance" of forest-dwelling peoples as the necessary prerequisite "to confront those who are responsible for destroying their forests and undermining their livelihoods and who are already united and organized."[76] The conference also adopted a "Charter of the Indigenous Tribal Peoples of the Tropical Forests," which places the rights of the forests' original inhabitants at the center of any rational or sustainable development of the forests. This is an important principle because logging is not the only threat to rainforest communities.

Big Oil Invades the Ecuadorian Amazon Rainforest

The Amazon region of northeast Ecuador, known as the Oriente, is home to eight different native groups, comprising about 75,000 individuals.[77] They include the Shuar, Achuara, Quichua, Cofan, Siona, Huaorani, and Secoya Indians. Since the late 1960s, they have had to defend their lands and communities against oil drilling, road construction, and the invasion of colonists who pour into the jungle along oil company roads. In 1967, *The New York Times* reported that "a vast helicopter operation, believed to be second only to that in Vietnam, is rushing oil-drilling rigs and supplies into the rugged northern region of Ecuador."[78] This massive invasion was led by the Texaco-Gulf consortium, with the help of a 1.4 million hectare concession from Ecuador's military junta (1963-66). In 1972, Ecuador enacted legislation which created a state oil corporation, now called Petroecuador, and replaced the concession system with "association contracts" between its state company and foreign oil companies. The government then became a profit-sharing partner in oil production rather than being paid in royalties.[79] Oil production now accounts for 70 percent of Ecuador's exports, and oil revenues finance the nation's massive $12.4 billion foreign debt obligations.[80] Neither the Ecuadorian government nor the oil companies recognize the rights of native peoples who have always lived in the rainforest. "In some cases," reports Survival International, "oil wells have been placed actually within lands which have been already properly titled to Indian communities—making conflict inevitable."[81]

Texaco-Gulf first struck oil at Lago Agrio, just north of the territory of the Huaorani—one of the last hunting and gathering native groups in the Oriente. During the 1960s, Texaco-Gulf worked closely with the North American missionaries of the Summer Institute of Linguistics (SIL) to secure the territory of the Huaorani and other native groups for the consortium.[82] Bill Eddy, a pilot for the SIL-affiliated Jungle Aviation and Radio Service, described the relationship between SIL's missionary work among the Huaorani (sometimes pejoratively referred to as *Auca,* meaning "savage") and the advance of the oil companies into native territory:

> Twenty-five years ago the Shell Oil Company lost many workers to Auca spears. For several reasons Shell decided to leave Ecuador. Suddenly with the discovery of a vast reserve of oil under the Eastern Jungle, 21 companies are working 1,500 men there. As they advance, we fly ahead of them and explain to Aucas living in their path that they are coming. We persuade them that they should move out of the way. This is done by Auca Christians through a loud speaker mounted on the plane. As the Indians move we notify the oil companies. As a result of this close coordination by radio and telephone through our Quito office there has been not one life lost to date. PRAISE GOD!!![83]

Other oil discoveries quickly followed. By 1971, Texaco-Gulf reported the extraordinary record of finding oil in 74 out of 78 wells drilled.[84] By 1972, the 310 miles of the Trans-Ecuadorian pipeline connected Lago Agrio across the Andes to the Pacific port of Esmeraldas. In that same year, Ecuador had become the second largest oil producer in South America. Twenty-eight international oil companies joined the oil rush and obtained concessions on 15 petroleum blocks in the jungle. Ten major oil companies invaded Huaorani lands and sank exploratory wells without consulting the Huaorani. These companies include Petro-Canada, Arco, Braspetro, Texaco, Conoco, BP, Elf-Aquitane, Esso, Unocal, and Petroecuador.

SIL missionaries were not always successful in "pacifying" the natives. Violent confrontations between oil companies and native groups were not uncommon. In November 1977, for example, Texaco-Gulf tried to penetrate the territory of Tihueno. The Huaorani killed three members of an exploration team, while defending their lands. Shortly afterward, the Ecuadorian government sent the army to wipe out the native resistance.[85] As the oil companies continue to build roads into the jungle, they are accompanied by army escorts. Both Arco and Unocal have been using armed Ecuadorian military to defend their sites from native peoples protesting the invasion of their homelands.[86]

Over the past 20 years, the international oil industry has placed some 330 wells and pumping stations in the jungle, and extracted 1.5 billion barrels of crude. Almost half of the Amazon crude ends up in the United States.[87] More than 12 million acres of forest have been consumed in this process, including some of the most biologically diverse zones on earth. The environmental cost has been staggering: "16.8 million gallons of oil spilled, 19 million gallons of toxic chemicals, heavy metals, and hydrocarbons dumped, 2.35 million cubic feet of gas burned without any emission control whatsoever and tens of thousands of hectares of forest cleared."[88] The results of this contamination are increased illnesses and poverty for the native peoples. "Children are severely affected by skin diseases and the polluted water is directly responsible for chronic diarrhea and intestinal ailments, and, indirectly, for malnutrition."[89] The game the Huaorani depend on for food has been driven out, and the fish in many lakes and rivers has been killed. Moreover, as soon as the access roads are built, the Huaorani face a rush of non-Indian colonists who further encroach on Indian lands and make it difficult to subsist from the forest.

And the oil rush is only the beginning. The Ecuadorian government is also encouraging exploration and possible mining of gold, uranium, vanadium, lead, zinc, and copper in the rainforest. Since 1982, more than 90 percent of Ecuador's Podocarpus National Park has been opened to gold miners. The mercury used in the gold extraction process has already found its way into the Nangaritza, Loyola, San Luis, Sabanilla, and Bombuscaro rivers.[90] And 35,000 Quichua people are now threatened by palm oil plantations, which have moved into the jungle in recent years. The pesticides used by one plantation company have already killed the fish in the Huashito River.[91]

In 1983, the government gave the Huaorani title to a 67,000-hectare reserve and the right to hunt in another 250,000-hectare forest reserve known as Yasuni National Park. The park is one of the most valuable natural reserves in the world and was declared a "world biospheric reserve" by the United Nations Educational, Scientific, and Cultural Organization. Despite repeated promises to protect Huaorani land rights, the government has failed to demarcate Huaorani lands or to prevent oil exploration in the park. Indeed, Survival International, which has been campaigning for Huaorani land rights since 1982, has suggested that "some so-called conservation zones were created deliberately to keep areas clear of settlers so that oil extraction can take place unhindered."[92]

In the fall of 1990, the Ecuadorian government opened up the last refuge of the Huaorani to oil development. Conoco Ecuador, a subsidiary of the U.S.-based Dupont Corporation, is most interested in Blocks 16 and 22, which cover 900,000 acres of rainforest. Much of this falls within the boundaries of Yasuni National Park. Conoco was the corporation that financed the government's preliminary management plan for the park. Not surprisingly, the plan allows more than half of the area to be available for industrial use. There are no provisions for recognition of Huaorani land rights.

The controversy over the Yasuni National Park has become the focal point for an international battle involving Conoco, the Ecuadorian government, the Confederation of Indian Nations of the Ecuadorian Amazon (CONFENIAE), and North American environmental and native rights groups. The controversy took an unexpected turn in the spring of 1991 when an Ecuadorian environmental law firm known as the Corporation for the Defense of Life obtained copies of the minutes of meetings between Conoco and the Natural Resources Defense Council (NRDC). A year earlier the NRDC and the Boston-based Cultural Survival began talks with Conoco exploring a negotiated compromise that would permit drilling in part of the Yasuni National Park in return for a multi-million-dollar corporate-funded grant to Amazon Indian federations. Robert Kennedy, Jr. was the NRDC staff attorney in these negotiations and had written the preface to the NRDC's expose of Ecuador's oil industry, *Amazon Crude*. Nevertheless, Kennedy was convinced that drilling was "inevitable." From NRDC's perspective, the best that could be done was "to make a deal that would at least have it proceed in a clean, well-monitored fashion, with local Indians the beneficiaries of Conoco's financial largess."[93]

When those private talks were exposed, Ecuadorian environmental groups were furious. The Corporation for the Defense of Life, after unsuccessfully filing suit to block Conoco's drilling in protected parks, accused Kennedy of selling-out the native peoples of the Oriente. The major objection of Ecuadorian environmentalists and Indians seemed to center on the secrecy of the negotiations and the near-colonial presumption that the NRDC was capable of representing the voice of all native groups in the Oriente.

The NRDC negotiations were also condemned by U.S.-based groups like the Rainforest Action Network, Friends of the Earth, and the Sierra Club Legal Defense Fund. The latter group had filed a complaint on behalf of the Ecuadorian Indian federation to the Inter-American Commission on Human Rights, arguing that drilling on native lands constitutes a human rights violation.[94] Sierra Club lawyer Karen Parker had been working with CONFENIAE for two years but had no idea that NRDC was talking with Conoco. "Maybe [NRDC's motivation] was altruistic, but its [behavior was] also very American, very paternalistic."[95]

On October 11, 1991, Conoco announced it was pulling out of oil development in the Yasuni National Park. That same day the Maxus Energy Corporation, an independent oil company from Dallas, Texas, announced it was taking over the Conoco project. While the threat to the Huaorani has not disappeared, the withdrawal of Conoco is eloquent testimony to the effectiveness of international campaigns that focus public attention on specific corporations that are engaged in gross abuse of human rights and the environment.

The Rainforest Action Network, in conjunction with an international coalition of native, environmental, and human rights organizations, has targeted Maxus, ARCO, Occidental, and other U.S.-based oil companies operating in the Oriente. At the same time, one of the most well-organized Indian movements in the hemisphere has put increasing pressure on the Ecuadorian government to recognize native land rights. In April 1992, 1,500 natives from Ecuador's Amazon rainforest walked 140 miles to Quito, the country's capital. There they negotiated with the government for titles to about 13,000 square miles of ancestral lands. "The urgency we have is that the Amazon Indian peoples [in Ecuador] have already lost almost the majority of our traditional territory," said Leonardo Viteri, coordinator of the Organization of Indigenous Peoples of Pastaza.[96] The Indians received title to their lands but the government retained mineral rights to the lands and shows no sign of slowing down the oil rush. "The Indians must understand that Ecuador lives off oil," said Diego Bonifaz, who was President Rodrigo Borja's chief negotiator with the Indians.[97]

The powerful interests working against the Huaorani should not be underestimated. In recent years, U.S.-based oil companies have drastically cut back on domestic exploration and production and have greatly increased their foreign investments because these properties are seen as the cheapest to drill.[98] Governments that are heavily dependent on oil revenues have been reluctant to criticize oil operations in their country. The long-term strategy of those opposed to the oil industry's assault on the native peoples of the Ecuadorian Amazon rainforest is to make the real costs of the U.S. energy addiction a political issue in the United States, in Ecuador, and in the international community.

The outcomes of all the resource wars described in this chapter remain unclear. Yet, they provide an excellent window into the workings of the modern resource colonialism of multinational corporations, international finance, and development-hungry governments. They also suggest that successful resistance is possible. Dams, logging, and oil drilling are not the only dangers native peoples face, however. After surveying the major threats confronting native peoples worldwide, Julian Burger, the director of research at the Anti-Slavery Society in London, concluded that "Mining is the greatest single threat to indigenous people. It pollutes vital water supplies, it imposes a debilitating economy and alien social values, it destroys sacred sites, disfigures familiar landscapes, and separates people from their homes, their past, and each other. It causes deep pain, cultural disintegration, and sometimes death."[99] It is to the environmental and cultural costs of the international mining industry that we now turn.

Chapter 2

The Special Case of Mining

The *Global 2000 Report* projects that the total land area that will be disturbed by the mining industry during the last quarter of this century will be approximately 60 million acres, 94,000 square miles—an area roughly equal to that of West Germany.[1] This projected figure is misleadingly small, however, because it does not take into account the fact that mining operations are responsible for air and water pollution, for destruction of fish and wildlife habitats, for erosion, and for toxic and radioactive contamination many miles from the mine sites. Nor does it take into account that the infrastructure (roads, railways, airstrips, power lines, hydroelectric plants, dams) and processing (smelters) associated with mining can be as damaging as the mining itself. Smelter pollution, according to a recent Worldwatch Institute paper, "has created biological wastelands as large as 10,000 hectares, and accounts for a significant portion of the world's acid rain."[2]

For example, the smelters for Brazil's Carajás iron ore project in eastern Amazonia will require an area of rainforest the size of Wisconsin.[3] The energy to run the smelters will come from the Tucuruí hydroelectric dam and reservoir, the fourth largest in the world. The infrastructure and processing facilities associated with the Carajás project have the potential to displace 100,000 people, including 13,000 Indians. The official mythology of Amazonia is that it is "a land without people, for a people without land."[4]

Internal Colonialism

The current mining wars originated in the revolts that swept the Third World in the 1960s. The resulting shaky investment climates—with threats of expropriation, nationalization, and higher

taxes—scared many mining firms considering the billion-dollar capital outlay and the decade-long lead time needed to reap profits. To
lessen the risks, multinationals intensified the search for raw materials in the United States, Canada, South Africa, and Australia. Since
the early 1970s, nearly 80 percent of the world's spending on mineral
exploration has occurred in these nations.[5] The lead time between
discovery of a mineable deposit and actual mine construction can be
anywhere between five and ten years. It is only in the last few years,
as environmental regulations have been strengthened in the advanced capitalist countries, that multinational mining companies
have begun to look seriously again at major investments in the Third
World. In the meantime, the scramble for the world's remaining
energy and mineral resources continues to fall heavily upon native
lands in the advanced capitalist countries.

Uranium is the raw material used to fuel nuclear power plants
and to make nuclear weapons. Uranium mining is thus the first step
in the nuclear fuel chain. The correspondence between some of the
world's richest uranium deposits and these internal colonies is particularly striking.[6] In Australia, three of the four largest uranium
deposits, with over 80 percent of the country's reserves, are on
aboriginal lands.[7] Rio Tinto Zinc (RTZ) operates the Rossing uranium
mine, the largest open pit uranium producer on aboriginal land in
Namibia, a former colony of South Africa. The highest grade of
uranium in the world is found on native lands in northern Saskatchewan, Canada.[8] And in the United States, Indian uranium holdings
range from 16 to 37 percent of the nation's total.[9]

A substantial share of the nation's other energy and mineral
resources happens to lie on the remaining land base of American
Indian reservations.[10] *Forbes* magazine (the self-proclaimed "Capitalist Tool") has summarized the strategic importance of American
Indian resources as follows: "Now, at a time when the United States
seems to be running out of practically everything, the 272 federally-
recognized Indian reservations constitute one of the largest and least
known mineral repositories on the continent—nearly 5 percent of the
U.S. oil and gas, one-third of its strippable low-sulfur coal, one-half of
its privately owned uranium...'From a national standpoint,' says

David Baldwin, an Osage who heads the technical division of the BIA's Office of Energy and Minerals, 'you are talking in the neighborhood of 25 percent of the U.S.' mineral wealth located on Indian lands.'"[11]

Since the mid-1970s, multinational mining and energy corporations have intensified their efforts to exploit these low-cost resources as a hedge against Third World economic nationalists and because of growing fears of scarcity.[12] During Ronald Reagan's first presidential campaign, a new twist was added to the fear of resource scarcity: the possibility of a "resource war" with the Soviet Union that could block U.S. access to "strategic" (military-related) metals like chromium, cobalt, manganese, and the platinum group metals.[13] During his campaign, Reagan emphasized the importance of decreasing U.S. dependence on foreign mineral sources. After the election, he established a Strategic Minerals Task Force to make policy recommendations. Among those named to the task force were top executives from major mining companies like Asarco, Kennecott, Amax, Phelps Dodge, Newmont, as well as a representative from the Council on Economics and National Security, a project of the right-wing National Strategy Information Center.[14] In 1980, the American Mining Congress published a 12-page color brochure on "The Resources War." It depicted the United States' vulnerability to supply disruptions of minerals essential to national defense. Many of these minerals could be provided by domestic production, according to the American Mining Congress, if only the federal government would open wilderness areas to mining and relax environmental restrictions. Charles F. Barber, chair of the Asarco Mining Company and a member of President Reagan's Strategic Minerals Task Force, blamed "professional environmentalists" for restricting mining on public lands.[15]

The Reagan administration's response to the carefully orchestrated hysteria over strategic minerals was twofold: to relax environmental, health, and safety laws that were seen as obstacles to mining and minerals processing; and to propose a "New Indian Policy," reflecting the recommendations of the conservative Heritage Foundation, that would incorporate Indian resources into a program of U.S. "energy independence."[16] From the very beginning, the corporate assault on the environment and the assault on Indian tribal sovereignty were inseparable. Even with the end of the Cold War, the Pentagon proclaims that one of the main reasons for the continuing buildup of U.S. military power is to "ensure access to...mineral resources..."[17] This colonial mindset leads to a vicious circle where "raw materials are needed to prepare for war, and war is needed to gain control over the sources of those materials."[18] Those "sources" of raw materials are increasingly concentrated on the lands of native peoples. Anishinabé activist Winona LaDuke and Creek/Cherokee Metis activist Ward Churchill have suggested that those opposed to North American imperialism have frequently overlooked the strategic significance of native peoples because of their small numbers. But any anti-imperialist movement that wants to strike at the heart of the problem cannot afford to ignore the "absolutely crucial nature of the existence of these colonies, by virtue of their resource distribution and production, to the maintenance and expansion of North American imperialism."[19]

The penetration of Indian lands by multinational mining corporations seeking to extract valuable mineral and energy resources has resulted in what one Native American sociologist has described as the transformation of Indian tribes "from captive nations into internal colonies."[20] Although Indian tribes theoretically "own" all reservation resources, the lands are held "in trust" by the U.S. government through the U.S. Bureau of Indian Affairs (BIA). As recently as 1970, practically all Indian mineral and energy resources were effectively controlled by large multinational corporations through lease agreements worked out between the BIA and the corporations.[21] Through such leases, multinational corporations paid Indian nations as little as 2 percent of the value of the minerals extracted.[22] "Measured by international standards," said the American Indian Policy Review Commission in 1977, "the leases negotiated on behalf of Indians are among the poorest agreements ever made."[23] Charles Lipton, the international minerals lawyer who advised the Lac du Flambeau Chippewa in their mineral negotiations, has referred to these leases as "colonial style mineral leases in that minerals are obtained cheaply and the profits made and taxes paid elsewhere."[24] The result is that resource extraction from Indian lands is "hastening the process of internal colonialism and this process is revolutionizing the status of American Indian tribes on a scale equal to the restriction of their political powers in the 19th century."[25]

The Environmental Assault

In addition to the economic and political dimensions of internal colonialism, there is also an important, but frequently overlooked, environmental dimension. Jerry Mander has observed that most Indian struggles take place far away from mass media, "in the central Arizona desert, in the rugged Black Hills, the mountains of the Northwest, or else on tiny Pacific islands, or in the icy vastness of the far north of Alaska. *The New York Times* has no bureau in those places; neither does CBS...As a result, some of the most terrible assaults upon native peoples today never get reported."[26]

The Church Rock Tailings Dam accident on the Navajo reservation is a good example of a major environmental catastrophe that received very little media attention. In July 1979, 100 million gallons of radioactive sludge spilled into the Rio Puerco River from United Nuclear Corporation's uranium tailings pond when its dam broke. Those hardest hit by the spill were the approximately 1,700 residents of the Rio Puerco Valley, mostly Navajo Indians. The Navajos used the river water for their livestock, grazed their cattle and sheep in the river bed, and drank from nearby wells. While the spill remains the largest one-time release of radioactive wastes ever in the United States, it received hardly any media attention at the time. *The New York Times* mentioned the spill in a short news story 12 days after it happened. *The Los Angeles Times* gave slightly more coverage, largely because California officials were concerned that the contamination could reach the southern California water supply coming from Lake Mead, Arizona.

An engineering report on the cause of the dam break attributed it to the shifting and settling of the soil underneath the dam and United Nuclear's failure to perform routine maintenance of the dam.

The company had known about serious problems with the site two years before the accident.[27] The ultimate costs of the spill to the Navajo may never be calculated. The final report of the federal Centers for Disease Control argued that epidemiological studies of mortality and morbidity rates in Church Rock should not be undertaken due to the difficulty in detecting risks associated with radiation exposure in a small population. In other words, the Navajo were expendable.

Indians and Environmentalists Join Forces

The process whereby multinational corporate capital extracts resources without regard to its effects upon the land and people of resource-rich areas has met significant resistance from both the native rights and environmental movements. At the 1977 International Non-Governmental Organizations Conference on Discrimination against Indigenous Populations in the Americas, the delegates recommended that the United Nations Committee on Trans-National Corporations "conduct an investigation into the role of multinational corporations in the plunder and exploitation of native lands, resources, and peoples in the Americas."[28] With considerable information about these costly and destructive mining and energy projects at hand, native peoples and their allies began planning counterstrategies. Organizations like People Against Rio Tinto Zinc and its Subsidiaries (PARTIZANS) in England, the Aboriginal Mining Information Centre in Australia, and the Center for Alternative Mining Development Policy in Wisconsin have been in the forefront of an international network providing information and analysis of multinational mining corporations to those directly affected by those operations. In this way, native communities, who are otherwise isolated from the centers of political and economic power, can forge effective links with environmental, labor, religious, and human rights organizations in the home territory of the multinational mining corporations.

The results of this international networking have been most dramatically illustrated by the appearance of native delegations from Australia, New Zealand, and Wisconsin at the annual general meetings of the London-based RTZ corporation, the largest mining company in the world. These appearances make it impossible for stockholders and the general public to ignore the devastating consequences of corporate mining activity on native communities. Native peoples from every continent also testified before the 1992 World Uranium Hearings in Salzburg, Austria, about "the destruction being inflicted upon their cultures, lives and lands by a civilization addicted to nuclear weaponry and energy."[29]

There is every reason to expect a growing alliance between native rights and environmental movements that will exacerbate the political and ecological contradictions of the resource extraction technology of the multinational mining corporations. This is due to several factors. First, the exhaustion of the most accessible mineral deposits, that is, those which cost the least to exploit, constitutes a physical limitation to the ability of industrial capital to return a profit.[30] The industry's response to the depletion of high-grade mineral deposits is to "dig deeper." However, newly discovered mineral deposits cannot be exploited except at a higher cost of investment than in the past. As higher-grade ore reserves are exhausted, the direct energy requirements of mining and milling rise rapidly as more ore must be mined and milled for each ton of metal recovered.[31]

Copper, for example, is mined at a grade of about .6 percent. That means that 420 units of material must be handled for every one unit of marketable material that is produced. The high ratio of "material handled" to "marketable product" is due primarily to the low percentage of metal in the ore and to the mining methods and processes that must be used. The case of uranium is even more dramatic. Over 6,900 units of material must be handled to obtain one marketable unit of uranium.[32] To produce a ton of copper also requires a great deal of energy—about 112 million BTUs, or the equivalent of the energy in about four metric tons of Wyoming coal or nearly 18 barrels of oil.[33]

Mining is now the most capital-intensive of all industries. Single projects can cost as much as $1 billion dollars or more. A 100,000-ton-per-year copper project (mine to refinery) can cost $700-800 million. A 500,000-ton-per-year aluminum project, from mine to smelter, can cost about $2 billion.[34] The capital requirements for the worldwide metallic minerals industry, in 1991, were $55 billion.[35] The size of these investments makes it increasingly difficult for mining companies to finance new projects without seeking capital from the international oil corporations.[36] I will return to this point when I discuss Exxon's interest in developing a zinc-copper mine next to the Sokaogon Chippewa reservation in Wisconsin.

The extraction of ore from lower-grade deposits produces larger volumes of waste which scar the landscape and pose serious environmental and health problems. A recent cover story in *U.S. News and World Report* underscored the sheer magnitude of the problem:

> The U.S. Bureau of Mines estimates that 10,000 miles of rivers have been contaminated by mine wastes. Some 3.6 billion tons pile up each year, largely immune from federal hazardous-waste regulations. Acid drainage and metallic poisons seep continually from old diggings...An estimated 500,000 acres of worked-out claims now lie barren and abandoned, and 48 of the Environmental Protection Agency's Superfund sites are mine-cleanup projects.[37]

Of even greater concern, as the EPA noted in its report to Congress, is the potential danger to human health from mining wastes. The report notes, "Mining wastes may contain constituents, such as heavy metals, other toxic elements, radionuclides, cyanide compounds, and asbestos, that may be dangerous to human health and the environment."[38]

By the mid-1960s, the visibility of the damage from past mining practices in places like Appalachia had already contributed to a growing public perception of the conflict between environmental protection and corporate growth and expansion. A decade later, Hans

Landsberg of Resources for the Future, a liberal think-tank in Washington, D.C., warned that a large and growing segment of society had developed an intense hostility toward mining activities: "The emergence of this hostility and its reflection in recent laws are not, of course, fortuitous. At the rate of exploitation...over the past three decades, the scars inflicted on the environment, animate and inanimate, are correspondingly large and conspicuous...If that is the way to wrest materials from their habitat, let it occur elsewhere, seems to be the spreading attitude."[39] At a recent conference of the Institute of Mining and Metallurgy in Edinburgh, Scotland, Leonard Harris of Newmont Mining Corporation noted that mining has a public image around the world "as dirty, dangerous work that pollutes and degrades the environment."[40]

This social awareness of the effects of mining has frequently resulted in costly delays, more stringent regulations, and higher taxes for the industry. A recent report by Metals and Minerals Research Services of London notes with alarm that environmental laws are becoming "more widespread and stringent and, in many cases, being framed according to perceived (and not necessarily scientifically proved) environmental risks and public health hazards."[41]

This growing concern with protecting the environment comes into direct conflict with the physical requirements for the reproduction of large industrial capital. As early as 1972, the National Materials Advisory Board warned that the environmental costs of mining, already severe, would increase still further: "To produce, fabricate, and dispose of wastes from ever larger quantities of metals obtained from ever leaner deposits demands ever larger investments of energy and creates a growing potential for damage to all aspects of our environment on, above, and below the land surface, including living organisms."[42] The note of alarm in the Metals and Minerals report previously mentioned had to do with the observation that lawmakers seem not to be concerned whether mining companies can actually meet the new environmental standards being proposed.

For the first time since the beginning of the U.S. environmental movement, there is a national consensus among the largest environmental organizations that mine waste is a top priority issue. In 1990, many of these groups, including the Sierra Club, National Audubon Society, Natural Resources Defense Council, Trout Unlimited, Environmental Defense Fund, and over a dozen grassroots organizations formed the Environmental Mining Network to participate in the EPA's development of regulations for mine waste. The U.S. Congress is now considering revisions to the 1976 Resource Conservation and Recovery Act that would provide a framework for the regulation of mine wastes as hazardous wastes. Depending on the assumptions employed, the additional annual cost of such regulation for the metal mining industry could be as low as $7 million or as high as $854 million. Under the highest-cost scenario, the incremental compliance costs would average 20 percent of current operating costs for the lead mining sector on the low end, to 120 percent of the current operating costs for the copper mining sector on the high end. The higher costs for copper mining reflect the larger quantities of waste and their higher potential for environmental damage.[43]

Much of the conflict between environmental protection and corporate growth and expansion comes down to a political struggle over who pays the costs of mine pollution. This increased potential for environmental conflict occurs at the precise moment when the risks of mining are already exacerbated by the large capital outlays required for new mining projects and the long lead time before production begins to return a profit on investment. Thus the growth of both environmental and native rights activism has become a central concern of the mining industry in the large mining countries—Australia, Canada, and the United States. In September 1991, the world's largest mining companies established the International Council on Metals and the Environment so that the industry could "respond internationally to the growing pressures it faces on health, safety and environmental matters."[44] Among the Council's North American members are Noranda, Cominco, Falconbridge, Asarco, the Doe Run Company, Minorco, and Phelps Dodge.

Jeffrey Zelms, president of the Doe Run Company, a U.S.-based lead mining operation, recently sounded the alarm about environmental activism in the *Engineering and Mining Journal:* "If we're to be in business in the year 2000, we need to take action today." He warned that "today's environmental activism is as much a battle of public perception as it is of facts. Substance does not always prevail over style. And mischievous entities should not be underestimated in their ability to misrepresent mining."[45] All of a sudden, it seems, environmental activists like those represented in the Environmental Mining Network have replaced communists as the major threat to U.S. business and western civilization. Perry Pendley, of the conservative Mountain States Legal Foundation, told the Wyoming Mining Association that environmentalists are the same people who used to be communists before the fall of the Soviet Union. He said environmentalists are like "watermelons" because "they're green on the outside and red on the inside."[46]

At the root of this industry's insecurity and hostility toward environmental activism is the realization that the time has long passed when mining companies could assume an automatic public acceptance of extractive resource technologies in potential mining areas. The case studies from Wisconsin that form the heart of this book are important because they provide critical insights into how the world's largest and most powerful energy (Exxon) and mining (RTZ) corporations are trying to gain control of new mineral supplies in the face of significant resistance from both Indian and non-Indian communities.

From Old to New Resource Wars in Wisconsin

Such efforts are best seen in historical context. The current mining wars in Wisconsin are not new in the sense of being the first struggles between native peoples and mining-oriented industrialists in the region. Long before Columbus set sail for the New World, the Chippewa who inhabited the Lake Superior region knew of the existence of rich copper deposits in Lake Superior's Ontonagan country, Keeweenaw Peninsula, and Isle Royale. Some of these deposits had been worked by pre-Columbian miners. Reports of the rich copper came through French explorers and missionaries, and, in 1771, an Englishman tried unsuccessfully to mine the deposits.[47] Despite the British mining failure, farsighted businessmen alerted Benjamin Franklin to the rich copper deposits of Lake Superior, especially those of the ancient mines of Isle Royale. As a result of this concern, Isle Royale was the only island of the Great Lakes specifically mentioned in the Treaty of Paris in 1783.[48]

By the time of one of the first treaties between the United States and the Chippewa, made at Fond du Lac in 1826, Henry Schoolcraft, the famous geologist-explorer, had confirmed the existence of rich copper deposits along the shores of Lake Superior: "No part of the union presents a more attractive field for geological investigation or mineral discoveries. Its copper, iron, and lead promise to become important items in the future commerce of the country. The beds of iron and sand along the shore exceed everything of the kind found in the United States."[49]

As superintendent of the Office of Indian Affairs, Schoolcraft dealt with the Chippewa "as a geologist committed to American Manifest Destiny and who actively promoted mineral development."[50] Over the next 28 years, the United States negotiated a series of four treaties with the Chippewa which removed them from the mineral districts and opened the land to white miners. The 1826 Treaty at Fond du Lac gave the United States the mining rights to all of Chippewa country. The 1828 Treaty of Green Bay dispossessed the Winnebago, Potawatomi, and Chippewa of their lead mines. The 1842 "Miners Treaty" of La Pointe dispossessed the Chippewa of the Keeweenaw copper districts. The western boundary of this treaty was first drawn at the Montreal River, Michigan's border with Wisconsin. But when Michigan's Indian superintendent, Robert Stuart, learned that the copper veins extended even further west, he urged the government to include all unalienated Chippewa lands along Lake Superior. The "main importance" of the Wisconsin territory, according to Stuart, "is owing to its supposed great mineral productiveness."[51]

Finally, the Chippewa were dispossessed of the iron wealth of northern Minnesota in the Treaty of 1854.[52] In all of these transactions, "The federal government, state governments, and Indian tribes all understood the stakes in the four treaties. In each instance, the tribes resisted and the white man triumphed..."[53] The amount of wealth the United States acquired as a result of the treaties with the Chippewa has been calculated by historian David Wrone as follows:

- 100 billion board feet of timber;
- 150 billion tons of iron ore;
- 13.5 billion pounds of copper;
- 19 million acres of land;
- water, ports, power sites, and quarries; and
- fish, fowl, and game numbering into the billions.[54]

This wholesale dispossession impoverished the Lake Superior Chippewa and enriched several generations of East Coast copper- and iron-mining families, including the Aggasizs and the Rockefellers.[55] It also set in motion the great mining and lumber booms that went bust and left large portions of the Lake Superior region in a severe economic depression that continues today.

Now, more than a century after the first mining treaty with the Chippewa, the competition for Indian land and resources continues. The Lake Superior region of northern Wisconsin, northern Minnesota, and the Upper Peninsula of Michigan is considered a prime place for mineral deposits because it lies in the southern tip of the Canadian Shield (formerly known as the Chippewa Lobe). Its Precambrian glacial rock is believed to be some two billion years old. Up until the late 1960s, little was known about the distribution of metallic ores because the region was overlain by a concealing layer of glacial debris. After a decade of geophysical exploration, however, it is clear that the Chippewa, Potawatomi, Menominee, Stockbridge-Munsee, Oneida, and Winnebago were resettled in the mineral-rich area of the Canadian Shield.

In 1975, the U.S. Bureau of Mines, under contract with the Bureau of Indian Affairs, began a systematic mineral resource evaluation of Indian reservations in the United States. In 1976, the BIA reported that there were possible copper and zinc deposits on the reservation lands of the Sokaogon Chippewa, the Lac du Flambeau Chippewa, the Lac Courte Oreilles Chippewa, and the Potawatomi of

Wisconsin. Geological formations which have yielded copper in Michigan extend to the reservations of the Bad River Chippewa and the St. Croix Chippewa; gold and uranium might also occur in the Precambrian conglomerates on the Potawatomi and Lac Courte Oreilles lands.[56] Finally, the granite bedrock of northern Wisconsin is an attractive target for uranium exploration. A U.S. Department of Energy report noted that "this vast expanse is bound to become one of the principal exploration areas of the future."[57]

While Exxon was proceeding with its mine plans next to the Sokaogon Chippewa reservation, Kerr-McGee, Getty Oil, Minatome (France), and Uranerz (West Germany) were exploring for uranium. The Center for Alternative Mining Development Policy was tracking these companies through their mineral lease contracts, which had to be filed with the county clerk's office, and from their drilling permits with the Wisconsin Department of Natural Resources.[58] Kerr-McGee approached Potawatomi tribal leaders several times for permission to explore on reservation lands. Each time, the tribe turned down the request. This did not stop Kerr-McGee, however. In May 1980, the Center for Alternative Mining Development Policy informed the Forest County Potawatomi that Kerr-McGee had acquired lease options to 22 percent of the reservation.[59] Tribal chair James Thunder's response to this news was unequivocal: "The Potawatomi are not about to become the guinea pigs for the nuclear industry in the 1990s as the Navajo and Pueblo Indians were in the 1950s."[60] After the tribe hired an attorney to challenge the leases, Kerr-McGee offered to withdraw them.

Faced with tribal bans on uranium exploration and mining, U.S. Department of Energy subcontractors have intruded on Indian lands without the knowledge or permission of the tribes and collected water samples as part of the Department's National Uranium Resource Evaluation program. Employees of private mining companies like Exxon and Uranerz have also been caught taking unauthorized water and rock samples from the Lac Courte Oreilles Chippewa reservation.[61]

For Exxon Minerals, the Crandon, Wisconsin zinc-copper deposit, on land claimed by the Sokaogon Chippewa, represented the company's diversification from energy production into base metal mining. If Exxon succeeded at Crandon, it would be well on its way to becoming one of the largest and most diversified natural resource corporations in the world. In a similar fashion, Kennecott/RTZ's interest in the Flambeau copper deposit at Ladysmith, Wisconsin, on treaty-ceded lands of the Lake Superior Chippewa, was linked to its interest in opening up a new mining district in northern Wisconsin. Neither Exxon nor Kennecott/RTZ anticipated the strength and determination of the resistance that emerged from both the Indian and non-Indian communities, however. The lessons that are learned from these struggles in the heart of the beast will enable other resource-rich communities to anticipate and respond to the new corporate strategies for waging resource wars in the future.

Part II
Mining Wars in Wisconsin

Chapter 3

The Sokaogon Chippewa Take On Exxon

Where the trout rose to the fly
Where the loon gave forth his cry
Where the mushrooms hugged the ground
Only mining can be found.

No more pine trees to the sky
No more whip-or-wills to cry
Where it opened up the door
God's country is no more.

"Copper Mining Aftermath"
Elizabeth and George Ballard, Ripon, Wisconsin

Since the late 1960s, environmental movements have arisen in all advanced industrialized societies. Over the past 15 years, these movements have grown in size, broadened their mass appeal, and developed strategies and tactics which have made them a significant force in domestic politics. At the same time, there has been a dramatic shift in the focus of public concern over environmental issues. After surveying over 360 environmental battles in the United States during the 1970s, business economist Thomas Gladwin concluded that the focus of environmental conflict has shifted "from old to new targets, from existing pollution problems to potential environmental impacts, and from 'band aid' remedies to preventive or risk reduction measures."[1]

The following case study of opposition to a proposed underground zinc-copper mine in northeastern Wisconsin is an example of this dramatic shift. The Ballards' poem above is not referring to an existing mine but a proposed mine. The poem was set to music by a local bluegrass band and became a rallying cry for grassroots opposition to the proposed mine. The battle began in 1975 as a highly unequal contest between Exxon Minerals, a subsidiary of Exxon, and the Sokaogon Chippewa—the smallest, poorest Indian tribe in the state of Wisconsin. It ended in December 1986 with Exxon's withdrawal from the project after a decade of intense controversy which brought together Indian tribes and environmentalists in an unprecedented and highly effective coalition.

While there are severe limitations on how much one can generalize from specific environmental conflicts, I have attempted to situate the specific issues, opponents, and tactics of this case study in the context of Gladwin's large-scale statistical study of environmental conflict over industrial facilities. The overall picture that emerges is of a growing environmental movement in the United States that threatens investment in new mines, nuclear power plants, oil refineries, petrochemical plants, and electric utilities. Several resource economists have concluded that this new environmental opposition might reduce the ability of the world to meet its anticipated increase in demand for mineral and energy materials.[2]

The implications of this trend have profound consequences for the future of industrialized societies but are rarely discussed by social scientists. During this decade-long conflict, non-Indian groups and Indian tribes have shaped public discussion and debate on a number of political ecological issues including tribal sovereignty over Indian resources, the wisdom of resource extraction in ecologically fragile environments, the distribution of costs and benefits between mining corporations and the local community, and the adoption of less-polluting technologies. As these kinds of issues become incorporated into the political rhetoric of environmental conflict, opposition to new facilities tends to challenge the system's own reproducibility and sharply poses the question of alternative modes of development. In this sense, as authors Paul Piccone and Victor Zaslevsky have noted, the ecological movement is even more radical than it claims.[3] The starting point for this analysis is the recent entry of the largest oil companies into the mineral industry.

Big Oil in the Mineral Industry

Exxon's projected $900 million investment in developing the Crandon, Wisconsin zinc-copper discovery was part of the oil giant's diversification into the minerals industry. "By the mid-1980s," stated the *Engineering and Mining Journal* in 1978, "Exxon may become a significant producer of copper and zinc at facilities based on the massive sulphide deposit discovered by the company at Crandon, Wisconsin."[4] Exxon described the deposit as one of the ten largest known metallic sulphide deposits in North America.

Exxon's diversification into base metal mining (copper, zinc, and lead) was part of a long-term oil industry strategy. Faced with the prospects of nationalization of their supply sources in the Third World and the eventual depletion of their remaining crude oil reserves, the oil companies began searching out profitable areas for investment. In the mid-1960s, they began buying into the mineral industry by acquiring coal and uranium reserves. This trend accelerated after the 1973 jump in oil prices and profits. During this same period, when copper prices were depressed and their stocks undervalued, oil companies bought up copper companies at bargain basement prices.[5] By 1981, Big Oil had major interests in seven of the top ten U.S. copper producers and controlled more than 55 percent of domestic primary copper production capacity (see Table 1). Seven of the ten largest oil companies had investments in minerals, either through acquisition of existing mining companies or through building up their own mineral reserves through exploration and development.

Big Oil viewed mining as a logical extension of its expertise in natural resource extractive industry and as a convenient outlet for its rapidly accumulating cash reserves. All of the oil companies underestimated the problems inherent in the mineral industry, however. While both industries involve extraction, depend on exploration, and are highly capital intensive, there are some fundamental differences. First, the development of mineral resources takes more time, and discovery of new supplies is more difficult. Second, the demand for minerals is more cyclical than the demand for oil. Third, the payback period for mineral investments is three to four times as long as that

Table 1
Oil Firms in the Copper Business

Copper Producer	Acquiring Oil Company	Date of Acquisition	Current Annual Copper Mine Capacity (short tons)
Tennessee and Miami Copper	Cities Service	1963	95,000
Duval Corporation	Penzoil	1968	135,000
Anaconda	Atlantic Richfield	1977	200,000
Copper Range	Louisiana Land	1977	80,000
Cyprus Mines	Standard Oil of Indiana	1979	125,000
Amax	Standard Oil of California	1981	60,000
Kennecott	Standard Oil of Ohio1963	1981	450,000

Source: Simon D.Strauss, "Oil and Copper Don't Mix," *The New York Times*, April 12, 1981.

for oil. Whereas an oil well starts contributing revenues almost immediately, a mine may not start contributing revenues until five or ten years after construction begins.

Moreover, oil company managements tend to stress higher and faster rates of return on investment than traditional mining company managements. Thus, when Exxon's president was asked if his company's nonenergy businesses could ever prove as profitable as oil and gas, he replied: "We're not interested in being in businesses long-term that don't meet the kinds of return criteria we see in oil and gas...if you can't see the results in a two-to-four year period, then you'd better start reexamining your whole card."[6] A mining company's operations are also much more visible, in a sociopolitical sense, than those of an oil company. According to one consultant to multinational corporations, "The development of a mine assaults the physical, the cultural, and the economic environments, all by its very nature. Therefore, mining companies have a very different socio-political vulnerability pattern than oil companies, even though both are extracting nonrenewable resources."[7] This is especially the case as the higher-grade resources are exhausted and new mining ventures exploit lower-grade deposits in less accessible and more fragile environments. This is precisely the situation Exxon confronted at Crandon, Wisconsin.

In May 1976, Exxon first announced its discovery of a major zinc-copper deposit near the town of Crandon in northeastern Wisconsin, just a mile from the Chippewa's wild rice lake. The rice is an essential part of the Chippewa diet, an important cash crop, and a sacred part of the band's religious rituals.[8] Should Exxon build the mine, acid runoff and seepage could destroy the lake. The Chippewa were not reassured when Exxon's biologist mistook their wild rice for "a bunch of weeds." Exxon's own environmental impact report blandly mentioned that "the means of subsistence on the reservation" may be "rendered less than effective."[9]

From Exxon's perspective, there was never any question of whether there was going to be a mine, only when. The attitude goes to the core of the colonization process and the expendability of native peoples: "Simply stated, the difference between the economics of the 'old colonialism' with its reliance on territorial conquest and manpower, and the 'new colonialism,' with its reliance on technologically-oriented resource extraction and transportation to the metropolitan centers, is the expendable relationship of the subject peoples to multinational corporations," observe Robert Davis and Mark Zannis in their 1973 book, *The Genocide Machine in Canada.*[10]

Situated at the headwaters of the Wolf River in Forest County, the proposed mine would have generated enormous quantities of toxic waste that could threaten both surface water and groundwaters with contamination. Over the 20-year life of the mine, an estimated 58 million tons of acidic waste would be generated. Approximately half of this tonnage would consist of fine tailings, with the consistency of talcum powder, and would contain high levels of acid-generating sulfides and other heavy metals (arsenic, lead, cadmium, zinc, copper, mercury, etc.). These would be stored in tailings ponds covering approximately 400 acres. Each pond would be 90 feet deep.[11] The remaining coarse tailings would be redeposited in the mine as backfill. An Exxon engineer once pointed to the terrain map of the mine and said that, from the standpoint of the wetlands, the groundwater, and the overall topography, "You couldn't find a more difficult place [in the world] to mine."[12]

The environmental consequences of the proposed mine would have extended far beyond the boundaries of the Sokaogon Chippewa reservation. According to a report done for the Menominee, whose reservation lies 30 miles downstream on the Wolf River, "The development of the [Exxon] orebody poses a potential threat to the Wolf River basin…Groundwater contamination will be especially hard to detect and contain. The residual effects may not, in some cases, express themselves until years after the development has occurred." If Exxon's plan to contain the tailings fails, pollutants "could ruin life in the Wolf River."[13] Despite the fact that the Menominee were in the direct path of pollutants from the mine, Exxon deliberately omitted any mention of the tribe from their maps showing Native American lands and the local study area.

For the Forest County Potawatomi, whose reservation is near the proposed mine, the potential socio-economic impacts of the mine overshadowed the purely physical impacts on the environment. The Potawatomi have always occupied a marginal position in the local economy and have had a long-standing conflict with the Crandon public school system over the treatment of Indian children in the schools. Potawatomi tribal leaders feared that the already marginal status of tribal members would be further marginalized by social interaction with white mineworkers who migrated to the area in search of jobs. The social dislocation resulting from intense competition with white mineworkers for jobs, housing, recreation, fishing, hunting, and gathering, etc. could spell the end of Potawatomi tribal cohesion and solidarity.[14]

From the perspective of the area's Indian tribes—the Sokaogon Chippewa, the Potawatomi, the Menominee, and the Stockbridge Munsee—the environmental and social impacts of the proposed mine were inseparable. Any contamination of the area's surface or groundwaters was a threat to survival. And Exxon's own geologist admitted that "contamination is bound to occur no matter how wisely a mine is designed or how diligent are the operators."[15]

All of this raised the issue of Chippewa treaty rights, an issue that would come back to haunt Exxon in the form of stockholder resolutions and a federal lawsuit. Sokaogon Chippewa tribal leaders claimed that the orebody, which extends under their reservation, lies in the middle of a 92,000-acre tract of land that the U.S. government promised them following an 1854 treaty. In September 1975, Exxon gave a $20,000 check to the Sokaogon Chippewa tribal chairperson for the right to explore on their tiny 1,900-acre reservation. If Exxon liked what it found it could go ahead and mine it. At the same time, Exxon began making offers, including one of $200,000 for just 40 acres of corporate-owned timberland a mile away. A week later, the tribal council found out about Exxon's check, tore it to pieces, and reasserted the Sokaogon Chippewa's treaty claim to the lands encompassing the Exxon discovery site.[16] Tribal member Myra Tuckwab summed up the feelings of many reservation residents: "We like where we're living. They put us here years and years ago on federal land and now that we're here—they discover something—and they either want to take it from us or move us away from it. We don't want to do this. This is where I belong. This is my home. This is where my roots are and this is where I'm gonna stay."

If Exxon could have limited the conflict over the mine to a contest between itself and the Sokaogon, there would not have been a decade-long protracted environmental conflict. Multinational mining companies have a long record of overwhelming native peoples whose resources they have sought to control. In each case, the strategy has been the same: reduce corporate political and financial risks as much as possible. They have done this by limiting the arena of conflict so that the victims are completely exposed to the reach of the corporation but only one tentacle of the corporation's worldwide organization is exposed to the opposition.[17] "There are a lot of businesses where you have the sense of betting the company every once in a while," says one Exxon executive. "But perhaps you don't ever bet Exxon—not even when you bet $3 or $5 billion on a project."[18]

The nature of the proposed mine, however, posed a number of environmental threats that were of major concern to local residents, environmental groups, sportspersons, other Indian tribes, and the public intervenor's office in the Wisconsin Department of Justice. As one EPA official put it, "Tailings ponds are the last major industrial facility of that size to be regulated so loosely."[19] Furthermore, Exxon's proposed mine would not only affect the entire Wolf River watershed but it would also set a precedent for at least a dozen other mining companies who were eagerly awaiting the outcome of Exxon's mine permit application. Since the mid-1970s, multinational mining corporations have quietly leased the mineral rights to over 300,000 acres of land in northern Wisconsin.[20] The list of top corporate leaseholders reads like a *Who's Who* of the international mining industry: Kerr-McGee, Universal Oil Products, Amoco Minerals, Noranda (Canada), Kennecott, Phelps Dodge, BHP-Utah, and Urangesellschaft (Germany). These corporations envision northern Wisconsin as one of the last resource frontiers—a colony where rich deposits of base metals (copper, zinc, and lead) and radioactive minerals (uranium and thorium) could be mined at minimal cost, while leaving behind the toxic and radioactive wastes. [21]

The reaction of non-Indian communities was muted and mixed at first, however. The mine and mill complex, a taxable industrial property, would be located entirely in Lincoln Township, while the tailings ponds would be located entirely in Nashville township. Since most of the taxable revenues from the mine would benefit Lincoln Township, the Lincoln Town Board granted Exxon the necessary local permits to begin construction of the mine in 1986. While Nashville Township would experience negative impacts associated with the tailings ponds, this did not become an issue until the latter stages of Exxon's permit application process. Prior to 1982, the Nashville Town Board did not raise public objections to Exxon's proposal. One of the major reasons for this political quiescence was the domination of the town board by a large lumber family that employed many of Nashville's north-side residents in the logging industry. The history of the entire area is closely tied to the various lumber company families, who had established company towns like Laona, just east of Crandon. The people in Nashville who stood to gain the most from the mine were the owners of corporate timberland who had leased their lands to Exxon for mineral royalties that would be paid once production began.

At the southern end of the township, however, it was a different story. The area was populated with many retired people and part-time residents who had second homes on the many lakes in the area. By the time that Exxon submitted its environmental impact report to the Wisconsin Department of Natural Resources (DNR) in December 1982, several respected members of the community from the southern end had begun to raise serious concerns about the mine. First, they feared that dewatering, the constant pumping of groundwater out of the underground mine, would dry up wells and springs and lower area lakes up to several feet. Second, they feared that acid drainage from the tailings ponds would contaminate their wells and pose a potential human health hazard. Finally, they feared that the township would be financially overburdened by the costs associated with the expansion of services for large numbers of newcomers to the area—the "boomtown" syndrome.[22]

When these concerns fell on the deaf ears of the Nashville Town Board, the "south-enders" began to use the existing organizational network of the area lake associations to formulate their positions, talk to their neighbors, run political candidates for the town board, and seek out allies who were also concerned about the mine. The closest allies were the Sokaogon Chippewa. This Chippewa-citizens alliance worked to challenge the complacency of the Nashville Town Board. At their 1983 annual town meeting, Nashville residents voted 41 percent in favor of an immediate moratorium on granting mining permits. The following year an outspoken Chippewa critic of the mine ran for Nashville town chair on a write-in ballot. While the Chippewa candidate did not win, he made an impressive showing in the non-Indian community. The multiple environmental concerns of this Indian-citizens alliance became a central focus of town politics thereafter.

Further downstream from the proposed mine, the Menominee and non-Indian residents were concerned about Exxon's plan to dump 3,000 gallons of waste water per minute from the mine into a tributary of the Wolf River over the 20- to 30-year life of the mine. This raised major human health concerns as well as the prospect of adverse impacts on the tourism industry. The Wolf River, in Langlade and Menominee counties, is the state's largest whitewater trout stream, supporting brown-, brook-, and rainbow-trout fisheries. Over 50,000 tourists are attracted to the area every year to enjoy trout fishing, whitewater rafting, and canoeing. The lower half of the river is also designated a National Wild and Scenic River. Under the provisions of the Wild and Scenic Rivers Act, the Department of the Interior must review and approve any federal licenses required for proposed projects.

In February 1985, Herb Buettner, owner of the Wild Wolf Inn and secretary of the Wolf River Conservation Club, initiated a petition campaign that focused on Exxon's responsibility to use all available technology to avoid toxic discharges into the Wolf River, and to remove the acid-generating pyrites from mine waste before its placement in the tailings ponds. The separation of the pyritic content of the tailings would significantly reduce the potential for acid mine drainage from the tailings ponds, one of the most significant environmental impacts of the proposed mine. The technology for this is already available and would be economical as a pollution-control measure over the life of the tailings facility. Exxon had even commissioned a feasibility study on the technology but concluded that there was an insufficient market for the byproducts of the process and thus rejected the technology.[23]

Opponents of the mine were not persuaded by Exxon's narrow cost-benefit view of this technology. In April 1985, Buettner told the packed audience at a mining forum sponsored by the Antigo Chamber of Commerce that "Industry must assume responsibility for the waste it generates and the cost of proper disposal. If we can't mine it clean, leave it in the ground."[24] The message did not go over well with the Antigo business community who anticipated economic benefits from the mine, but it was well received by residents in communities along the river, the tourist businesses, and well-established sports groups like Trout Unlimited. By the time that the DNR held public hearings on the draft environmental impact statement in June 1986, over 10,000 signatures had been collected on petitions asking the governor, the legislature, and the DNR to oppose any dumping into the Wolf River. This early resistance is consistent with the pattern observed by Gladwin: over the last decade there has been a shift of environmental targets from pre-existing to proposed industrial facilities.[25] This potential opposition was not lost on Exxon. As a 1980 article in *American Metal Market* noted, "Exxon Corporation expects to begin serious prospecting of a rich 70 million ton zinc and copper orebody at Crandon, Wisconsin next year while it works to neutralize objections from environmentalists, residents, and Indian tribes in the area."[26]

The Opponents

At the earliest stage of this battle (1976-81), the Sokaogon Chippewa feared that the final showdown would be between them and Exxon, and they took steps to prepare for that eventuality. They formed a tribal mining committee, hired a well-known Madison law firm, and sought technical and financial assistance from a variety of organizations: Americans for Indian Opportunity, the Center for Alternative Mining Development Policy, private charitable foundations, and the Bureau of Indian Affairs.

The tribe also sought grassroots allies and established contact with the Rusk County Citizens Action Group (discussed in detail in

Chapter Four) in north-central Wisconsin. This group had success-fully mobilized public opinion against an open-pit copper mine pro-posed by the Kennecott Copper Corporation. In July 1982, the Sokaogon Chippewa mining committee and the Rusk County group were among the dozen smaller groups which established the Wis-consin Resources Protection Council (WRPC) to coordinate a re-sponse to Exxon's mine permit application. The council presented a new model for grassroots environmental organizing. In a state where Indian reservations were targeted for several new mines and a pro-posed nuclear waste dump (the Menominee reservation), there had been little contact or communication between Indians and environ-mentalists. And with the exception of the Black Hills Alliance in South Dakota, there had been very little coordination between environmen-talists and Indians anywhere in the United States.[27]

The WRPC organized several public forums on mining in the Crandon area and brought together Indians and non-Indians to discuss their common concerns. The local chapter of WRPC cam-paigned on behalf of the Chippewa candidate for the chair of the Nashville Town Board in 1984. The organization also enlisted the support of the Sinsinawa Dominican Sisters of Wisconsin to present the concerns of the tribe to Exxon stockholders at the corporation's annual meeting.

By the final stage of the permitting process, it was clear that Exxon's proposed mine had all the elements necessary to bring together a diverse opposition: it was a large-scale, precedent-setting, and highly threatening facility. In addition to the Indian tribes and local communities already mentioned, there were several statewide and nationally-affiliated environmental organizations (Wisconsin's Environmental Decade, Wisconsin Wildlife Federation, Sierra Club, Audubon Society, Citizens for a Better Environment), sports fishing organizations (Trout Unlimited, Wolf River Conservation Club), two federal agencies (the Environmental Protection Agency and the Department of the Interior), and the public intervenor's Office in the Wisconsin Department of Justice involved in the controversy.

As Wisconsin public intervenor in the Exxon permit applica-tion, Waltraud Arts was charged with representing public rights in the environment. This involved efforts to ensure that the DNR fulfilled its obligation to encourage public participation in the permit review process and in the critical evaluation of the DNR's environmental impact statements. The public intervenor also played a critical role in establishing a division of labor among the many groups interested in the multitude of issues raised by Exxon's project.

The Tactics

The pattern of opposition described above is consistent with the trend data analyzed by Gladwin: a gradually expanding role for local governmental bodies, increasingly greater involvement of local residents, more frequent grassroots mobilization, and strong representation in environmental conflicts by national environmental groups interested in precedent-setting cases.[28] As one mining industry report noted, "Another adverse factor is that time delay enables opposition to a project, frequently minimal in the early stages, to develop, many times through dissemination of misinformation or rumor."[29]

As we have seen, the Exxon battle brought together a wide range of opponents concerned about different aspects of the project. This diversity was also reflected in the tactics used against Exxon. These included: (1) governmental legal action; (2) governmental administrative action; (3) private legal action; (4) petitions and referenda; (5) lobbying; (6) press campaigns; and (7) shareholder resolutions. Gladwin would describe the first two as regulatory tactics and the rest as social mobilization tactics.[30] The Exxon opposition used both types of tactics in roughly equal proportion over the decade-long conflict. Four tactics were particularly successful and had a significant influence on the outcome of the battle: (1) the challenge to Exxon's prospecting permit in 1980; (2) the Langlade County Board's 1985 resolution opposing Exxon's pipeline to the Wolf River; (3) the town of Nashville's 1986 socioeconomic mitigation ordinance; and (4) the Exxon shareholder campaign from 1982 to 1985. All are worth exploring.

Exxon's Prospecting Permit

A large part of Exxon's early success in mobilizing local public opinion in favor of the mine was due to a public relations campaign that sought to convince people that the mine was inevitable and that environmental opposition was unthinkable against such a "clean" mine. Exxon's project timetable reinforced this sense of inevitability by calling for the construction of a "test mine" in 1981 before any public hearings on a final environmental impact statement. Under a loophole in Wisconsin law, the DNR can issue a prospecting permit without requiring a full statement on the entire project. The prospecting permit would have allowed Exxon to begin construction of a mine shaft and extract a 70,000-ton bulk sample for analysis. Once the mine shaft was in place, of course, the bureaucratic momentum in favor of issuing the final permits would be overwhelming.

Exxon's plans went awry in August 1980 when they secretly obtained a draft copy of COACT Research Inc.'s report to the Sokaogon Chippewa on the environmental impacts of the proposed mine. The report challenged Exxon's public statements about the "minimal impact" of a test mine. Exxon was also aware of the rumors circulating in Crandon that the tribe was planning to challenge any prospecting permit issued by the DNR. Because of the federal government's special trust responsibility toward the tribe, any lawsuit would automatically involve the federal government and the federal courts. This could delay the project for several years. In September 1980, Exxon made a surprise announcement that it was abandoning its plans to apply for a prospecting permit.[31] The tribe's organizational capacity, information base, legal resources, and political determination posed a sufficient threat to persuade Exxon to change its timetable. This delay bought invaluable time for the opposition and challenged the widespread public perception that the mine was inevitable.

The Langlade County Board Resolution

County board resolutions are also very effective devices for localizing environmental conflict by raising the public visibility of controversy and drawing out the opposition in open confrontation. In June 1985, the Langlade County Board passed a resolution written by the Wisconsin Resources Protection Council and the Wolf River Conservation Club. The resolution called for the board to inform the governor, the DNR, and the legislature that Langlade County was opposed to Exxon's plan to store toxic mine waste at the headwaters of the Wolf River and the corporation's plan to dump mine waste water into the Wolf River.

This resolution caught Exxon by surprise. Exxon's local affairs coordinator had not been aware that the resolution was even on the agenda. When the *Antigo Journal* asked Exxon for a comment, a spokesperson downplayed the significance of the resolution by saying it was worded similarly to county board resolutions passed in other parts of the state. Several months later, however, Exxon appeared before the board and asked them to reconsider their resolution. The Exxon local affairs coordinator was particularly upset with the reference to "contaminated discharges" in the resolution. The board refused to overturn the resolution.

Over and above the legal significance of the resolution in the final permit proceeding, the resolution demonstrated that the supposed economic benefits of the mine did not outweigh the potential contamination of the Wolf River in the minds of the county board members. Moreover, Exxon's sudden about-face on the significance of the resolution made it clear that the county had found a vulnerable point in Exxon's public relations campaign.

The Town of Nashville's Socioeconomic Mitigation Ordinance

In the early stages of the mine controversy in the town of Nashville (1982 to 1985), the principal focus of public concern was the physical impact of the mine on area lakes, streams and private wells. By 1985, however, the local WRPC chapter also began to focus public attention on the potential "boomtown" problems resulting from the large influx of workers and their families to the Crandon area. Forest County had the lowest population density of any county in the state and had geared its facilities and services to that low density. Yet the draft environmental impact statement projected a conservative estimate of a 12 percent population increase in the project area during the peak year of mine construction.[32] This sudden influx of population had the potential not only to disrupt traditional rural lifestyles but also to impose economic hardships on the township because public facilities and services would be needed before local revenues became available.

During the spring of 1986, George Rock, president of the local WRPC chapter, appeared at numerous town board meetings and presented documented case studies of energy boomtowns in the western United States where communities were burdened with excessive costs that were not offset by increased tax revenues. Of particular interest to town officials was Grand Junction, Colorado, where Exxon had invested in a $5 billion synthetic fuels project, the largest commercial-scale oil shale operation in the United States. In May 1982, after two years of unprecedented boomtown growth, Exxon announced its withdrawal from the project. More than 2,000 construction workers were immediately laid off. Randall Meyer, the president of Exxon, said the company had miscalculated the costs of the project.[33] The Colorado Department of Natural Resources estimated that western Garfield County, the heart of oil shale country, lost an annual payroll of $93 million.[34] Exxon representatives responded to these concerns by pointing to the numerous compensation programs that Wisconsin had available to take care of these costs. All of these programs, however, were dependent upon a profitable mine contributing tax revenues to the state. George Rock pointed to the depressed market for copper and zinc and suggested that these tax payments might never materialize.

In April 1986, the township adopted a socioeconomic mitigation provision to its zoning ordinance. This provision, modeled after similar legislation in the western United States, made the issuance of a mine construction permit contingent upon Exxon's agreement to reimburse the township for any project-related expenses that exceeded the tax revenues available to the community. This action effectively shifted the economic burden of socioeconomic impact mitigation from the community to Exxon.

The Exxon Shareholder Campaign

In recent years, various church groups who own stock have raised "corporate responsibility" issues, ranging from ending nuclear weapons production to divesting in South Africa, at annual stockholders meetings of the nation's largest corporations. While the resolutions rarely win large numbers of votes, they do succeed in dramatizing issues and forcing corporations to publicly state their position on them. The Sokaogon Chippewa and Forest County Potawatomi tribes have made effective use of this tactic with the help of WRPC and church stockholders. For example, as soon as Exxon filed its mining application with the Wisconsin DNR in December 1982, the Sinsinawa Dominican Sisters of Wisconsin entered a stockholder resolution with Exxon, asking that the company postpone any further investment in the project until Chippewa treaty claims had been settled.

Prior to Exxon's annual meeting, the Investor Responsibility Research Center (IRRC), a private research service in Washington, D.C., prepared a background report on the resolution which was sent out to major institutional shareholders (churches, universities, insurance companies, etc.). The report concluded that Exxon might not have adequately considered the social and environmental impacts of its mining operation on the Chippewa and that this might end up creating additional financial risks for the corporation.[35]

The resolution could not have come at a more critical moment for the Crandon project. One year earlier, William McCardell, president of Exxon Minerals, had told Exxon employees that "some of the lower priority [minerals] projects will be re-evaluated and may fall by the wayside."[36] In August 1982 the *Wall Street Journal* ran a cover story on Exxon's mining problems and speculated that the parent company would eventually pull the plug on the minerals division.[37] The fate of the Crandon project was by no means clear and this stockholder resolution brought this embarrassing issue to the attention of the shareholders.

When the Chippewa tribal chair walked up to the microphone to speak on behalf of the resolution, silence descended upon the auditorium. It is a rare occasion when native people address Exxon shareholders about the effects of their investments. The Dominican Sisters' resolution received 2.5 percent of the vote in 1983. A similar resolution received 3.5 percent of the vote in 1985. The persistence of the tribe and the Dominican Sisters in submitting resolutions served as a powerful reminder to Exxon's top management that this $900 million investment carried enormous financial and political risks. Just prior to the 1985 shareholders meeting, Exxon Minerals outlined a proposal to reduce the size of the Crandon project by mining only the zinc portion of the orebody, leaving the remaining copper portion for some unspecified future mine development. This "downsizing" of the project was an attempt to justify the investment to shareholders in the context of depressed prices for both copper and zinc. It also reduced the estimated costs from $900 to $540 million. However, the political cost to Exxon of this project revision would be a further delay in the timetable for obtaining mining permits.

The Sokaogon Chippewa also used the threat of a resolution to force Exxon's top management to negotiate with them in 1984 about investing in pyrite-removal technology for the tailings ponds. Exxon's vice-president for shareholder relations, along with the top Crandon project staff, met with a delegation from the Chippewa and the Dominican Sisters and tried to persuade them to withdraw their resolution. Since Exxon Minerals would not agree to invest in the technology, the Chippewa refused to withdraw their resolution. At that point Exxon petitioned the Securities and Exchange Commission to disqualify the resolution. Just before Exxon's shareholder proxy went to press, the Securities Exchange Commission ruled the resolution out of order because it did not affect a significant proportion of Exxon's overall operations. While the resolution was suppressed, the Chippewa had once again demonstrated that they could effectively translate widespread local discontent with the project into political action that reached into the center of the parent company's decisionmaking process. Many of the tactics used in the Exxon conflict—private legal action, petitions and referenda, and shareholder campaigns—have been widely used by environmentalists in their efforts to delay, modify, or block new industrial projects.[38]

Just when the Indian-environmentalist opposition was at its peak, however, Sokaogon Chippewa tribal chair Arlyn Ackley announced that he had been talking with officials at Ernest Lehman and Associates, a Minneapolis mining exploration company, about developing an ore deposit on the reservation. In 1982, the Bureau of Indian Affairs had estimated the value of the copper, zinc, and silver on the reservation at more than $1 billion. Ackley said the possibility of milling ore at the proposed Exxon mine would make the development of the tribal deposit more feasible and that he had considered the possibility.[39] Just prior to Ackley's announcement, the Wisconsin Justice Department issued a 28-page legal opinion which said that the Sokaogon Chippewa could mine the deposit on their reservation without paying Wisconsin mining tax or receiving a state permit. Since subsurface minerals on the reservation were under federal, rather than state jurisdiction, any mining permits would be issued from the U.S. Department of the Interior. Such a permit could be issued in a year or two. The Wisconsin attorney general's opinion was drafted in response to a request from pro-mining governor Anthony Earl, on behalf of Ackley.[40]

The timing of this announcement had all the elements of a well-coordinated political strategy to split the Chippewa-environmentalist alliance against the Exxon project. This last minute attempt to coopt the tribal opposition failed when the on-reservation mine proposal was blocked by the Sokaogon Chippewa tribal council. The depth and breadth of opposition by tribal members could not be ignored by the tribal council.

The Outcome

On December 10, 1986, after more than a decade of opposition, Exxon announced it was abandoning its plans to construct an underground mine at Crandon. Citing low metal prices, the company asked the DNR to suspend the permiting process just as it was entering its final phases. The DNR had just released a final environmental impact statement on the project in November 1986, and a master hearing had been scheduled for March 1987. Barry Hansen, Exxon's permiting manager, denied that pressure from Indians and environmentalists forced the action. "There's no question this was a marketing-driven decision," he said.[41]

But mine critics had long argued that depressed metal prices should have led Exxon to abandon the $600 million project years ago. Exxon's response had always been the same: first we'll get the mining permits, then we'll make a decision based on market conditions.[42] With mining permits in hand, Exxon would have had a number of options. It could sit on the deposit for years before it made a decision about further investment in development. It could also have sold the property, complete with permits, to another mining company. As late as May 1986, Exxon was talking to other mining companies about a joint venture. Without the permits, Exxon would have had a hard time selling the property to another buyer.

If Exxon's withdrawal from the Crandon project was not a marketing-driven decision, then what was the basis for this decision? In an era of intense environmental activism, investment decisions about new facilities are never purely economic decisions. They are also decisions about the political risks inherent in these investments. The successful corporation is one which manages and/or controls those risks. In the case of the Crandon project, it became increasingly clear to Exxon's top management in Houston that the multitude of risks inherent in this project could not be managed or controlled.

Top management's concern with the Crandon project was evident in 1984 when Robert Russell, longtime Crandon project manager, was replaced by Donald Achttien, formerly vice-president of operations for Exxon Minerals. Russell had not successfuly managed a project facing growing local opposition and significant delays in the permiting process. This prevented Exxon Minerals from beginning mine construction in 1985, as they had announced. Donald Achttien, however, immediately went on the political offensive and organized a vocal pro-mining constituency among local government officials, local and state business organizations, the press, and the governor's office. As a result, the DNR came under increasing criticism from State Senator Lloyd Kincaid (D-Crandon) and Governor Earl for "holding up" the permiting process. When the DNR released its draft environmental impact statement in May 1986, it was clear that the agency had given in to pressures for speeding up the permiting process and had ignored major environmental issues.

This strategy of accommodating Exxon backfired on the DNR. When the U.S. Department of the Interior responded to the draft, they criticized the DNR for "a consistent pattern of failure to deal with the long-term potential impact of this project on the biota and natural resources of the area. In most instances, the planning horizon does not extend past getting the operation to a steady level of production."[43] The Department of the Interior took the DNR to task for not addressing the question of the long-term contamination of the Wolf River watershed, the impacts on Indian water resources, and the lack of any kind of a performance guarantee from Exxon that the conditions of the permit would be met. All of these criticisms simply reinforced and legitimated what the environmental opposition had been saying all along. Even the *Milwaukee Journal,* which had refrained before from taking a position on the proposed mine, suggested in a September 1986 editorial that "there are already enough danger signals to make one wonder whether this enormous, $540 million project, can ever be made environmentally acceptable. And if it can, would the mine be economically viable?"[44]

This wave of public criticism of the project alone would not have convinced Exxon Minerals to withdraw from the permit proceedings, however. In October 1986, Exxon approached the town of Nashville for the zoning permits required before mine construction could begin. Local residents turned out in large numbers and grilled Exxon representatives about numerous issues affecting all aspects of the operation. Several Exxon representatives from Houston flew in to observe these proceedings. The Crandon project staff was unprepared to give the kind of specific answers that would address the broad range of local concerns about the mine's impact. The town decided to withhold zoning approval until after the DNR master hearing on Exxon's permit application was over.

In the absence of local zoning approvals, Exxon Minerals faced the possibility of going through the enormous time and expense of a master hearing only to be denied permission to mine by the township. By the time Exxon announced its withdrawal from the Crandon project in December 1986, they confronted a powerful Indian-environmentalist alliance that had strong support in the local area, among other tribes, within the tourist community downstream from the mine on the Wolf River, and among the state's largest and most influential environmental organizations. Rather than admit defeat due to a grassroots organizing effort, Exxon blamed their decision on weak metal prices.

While Chippewa treaty rights were not the only, or even the decisive, factor in Exxon's withdrawal, they did figure prominently in the minds of the project's major supporters. From the perspective of ex-governor Anthony Earl, who actively promoted the Exxon-Crandon project while he was governor (1982-86), the Chippewa treaties proved to be a frustrating defense against potential environmental damage from the proposed mine. "The implications of that mine on the Wolf River and the people who live downstream were among the most serious questions raised about that mine," he said. "And that was on account of the treaties."[45]

The struggle was not over, however. While the Menominee tribe welcomed Exxon's withdrawal from the Crandon project, they believed that if market conditions improved, Exxon would reapply for mine permits. As the Menominee Tribal Mining Impacts Committee noted after Exxon's announced withdrawal from the Crandon project, "We will continue to assert tribal concerns regarding the proposed mine." The delay would give the tribe additional time to seek funding from the Bureau of Indian Affairs to get technical help to analyze the volumes of reports prepared by Exxon. "Faced with the real danger of pollution of the Wolf River we cannot accept Exxon reports at face value," said Gordon Dickie, Jr., a member of the committee. "We believe the Secretary of Interior has a trust responsibility to protect the resources of the Menominee tribe. We also feel the federal government in the past has failed much too often to properly protect the water resources throughout the nation. We cannot allow this to happen to the Wolf River. The work of the mining impacts committee must continue."[46]

The first indication that Exxon might revive its Crandon project came in May 1988 when James D. Patton, Exxon Minerals' manager of regulatory affairs, wrote to Wisconsin DNR Secretary Carroll Besadny opposing the DNR's classification of the upper Wolf River as an "Outstanding Resource Water" under the provisions of the federal Clean Water Act. Patton warned that DNR's proposed classification of the Wolf River "could create a significant potential roadblock to any future resumption of the Crandon project."[47] In response, Hilary Waukau, chair of the Menominee mining impact committee, told the Wisconsin Natural Resources Board, which oversees the DNR, that it didn't make any sense to have different classifications for separate parts of the Wolf River. The lower portion of the Wolf River, which runs through the Menominee reservation, already has federal recognition as a wild and scenic river. "You can't just take a portion here and preserve it. You have to preserve the whole thing."[48]

But the Wisconsin Natural Resources Board was reluctant to approve Outstanding River status for the upper Wolf River. Three members of the board, all appointed by pro-mining Governor Tommy Thompson, consistently blocked Outstanding classification for the Wolf river. The Indian-environmentalist coalition that had come together to oppose Exxon's proposed mine now focused their political energies on the Natural Resources Board. The groups organized a massive letter-writing campaign to the board and appeared at every single meeting of the board between May and November 1988, when the board finally granted Outstanding status for the upper Wolf River. This was a major victory for the Menominee tribe and the Wolf River Watershed Alliance, which had led the campaign for Outstanding status. If Exxon decided to resurrect its Crandon mine project, it would have to prove that its proposed discharge to any tributary of the Wolf River would not lower the water quality of the river.

In August 1992, however, Exxon officials did announce that they would resume efforts to construct an underground zinc-copper mine next to the Sokaogon Chippewa reservation.[49] A number of conditions had changed since Exxon had abandoned the project in 1986. First, the price of zinc, which is the primary metal in the deposit, had risen from 41 cents a pound in 1986 to about 69 cents a pound in 1992. The price of copper had similarly risen, from 61 cents a pound in 1984 to $1.25 a pound in 1992. The market value of just the zinc and copper, not including the trace amounts of gold and silver, had increased the value of the deposit from $4.6 billion in 1984 to $7.6 billion in 1992.[50] Secondly, Exxon now had a partner to share the financial risks of the project and also provide considerable experience in the copper mining and smelting business. Phelps Dodge Mining Co., of Phoenix, Arizona, is the largest nongovernmental copper producer in the world.[51] The company also knows something about how to deal with tribal sovereignty over natural resources. Much of the southern Arizona copper belt, where Phelps Dodge has mining operations, is on lands that used to be part of the Papago Indian reservation. Once copper was discovered on Papago lands, pro-mining interests convinced the U.S. Congress to pass legislation that deprived the Papago of all mineral rights on their own land.[52]

Finally, the political "investment climate" had considerably improved under the pro-mining administration of Wisconsin Governor Tommy Thompson and Secretary of Administration James Klauser. By the time Exxon made its announcement, the hotly contested Ladysmith copper mine was under construction, and Noranda Minerals of Toronto, Canada, was lobbying hard to persuade the Wisconsin DNR not to grant "Outstanding Resource Water" status to any bodies of water that might receive mine waste water. Noranda's long-range objective was to challenge the whole process of identifying and providing protection to valuable, high-quality waters.[53]

While the international mining industry has achieved some notable successes with the help of the Thompson administration, the Indian-environmentalist coalition that blocked Exxon's first proposal has not disappeared. Today, this coalition has considerably more experience in fighting mining companies and a much broader base in the state's environmental community. The Wolf River Watershed Alliance immediately urged its members to send letters to Exxon's board of directors warning the company not to revive the permit process. The issues of Chippewa treaty rights and the Outstanding status of the Wolf River have the potential to make the mine permiting process a political quagmire for Exxon and Phelps Dodge. Raymond McG-eshick, Sr., tribal chair of the Sokaogon Chippewa, responded to Exxon's announcement by noting that the tribe has been, and continues to be, in litigation with Exxon over the company's violation of the tribe's off-reservation hunting, fishing, and gathering treaty rights. As for Phelps Dodge, the tribal chair assumed "that the Phelps Dodge management and shareholders have been informed of the current litigation, and that, should the company choose to buy into the controversy, its shareholders will not claim surprise if it encounters opposition."[54]

Apparently, this was enough to persuade Phelps Dodge to withdraw from the joint venture with Exxon. On December 14, 1992, Phelps Dodge Vice-President Thomas M. Foster announced that the company had decided to invest elsewhere.[55] Just a month earlier, the Exxon and Phelps Dodge study team had met with the DNR and announced that they would recommend that the project go ahead. This recommendation meant that the project was technically feasible and financially sound. The fact that Phelps Dodge withdrew from the project after this study lends support to the idea that top management perceived the political risks inherent in the project and decided that withdrawal was the safest choice. Now that Phelps Dodge has evaluated the Crandon project and decided against it, Exxon will have great difficulty trying to find another partner for this extremely risky project. In the meantime, the Midwest Treaty Network has brought together more than a half-dozen tribal mining committees and an equal number of environmental organizations to discuss a unified response to the revival of the Crandon project. If Exxon decides to go it alone, it can expect the same kind of protracted struggle that Kennecott/RTZ encountered at Ladysmith, as discussed in Chapter Four.

Chapter 4

Kennecott's Best Laid Plans

A year before Exxon first tried to set up shop in Crandon, Wisconsin, Kennecott Copper Corporation began laying plans to construct a small open-pit copper mine in the town of Grant, one mile southwest of the city of Ladysmith, between the Flambeau River and State Highway 27. Backed by the British-owned Rio Tinto Zinc (RTZ) corporation, its new parent and the world's largest mining company, Kennecott seemed to face only a minor hurdle rounding up local and state permits for its mine in the heart of dairy farming country. This was a welcome relief after Kennecott's struggle to retain control of its Chilean mining operations after the 1970 election victory of socialist President Salvador Allende.

Kennecott's exploration for copper in northern Wisconsin exemplifies the shift in multinational corporate mining investment from "politically unstable" Third World mineral suppliers to more "secure" resource areas within the advanced capitalist countries. From 1915 to 1970, Chilean copper formed a highly profitable part of Kennecott's worldwide low-cost copper reserves.[1] However, in 1971, the Chilean Congress voted unanimously to nationalize all foreign-owned copper mining operations and to pay compensation to the companies. Kennecott responded by undertaking an "economic destabilization" campaign against the democratically elected government of President Allende.[2] As Robert Haldeman, executive vice-president of Kennecott's Chilean operations, explained, "Nobody expropriates Kennecott without upsetting customers, creditors, and governments on three continents."[3] By September 1973, the destabilization campaign had contributed to the conditions that led to the overthrow of the Allende government and the imposition of one of the most brutal military dictatorships in Latin America. From Kennecott's perspective, Chile was an object lesson for other Third

World countries who dared to contemplate taking control of their own natural resources.

At the same time, Kennecott was taking steps to develop new domestic sources of copper. The presence of copper in the dairy farming region of northwestern Wisconsin had been known since 1914, when the Wisconsin Geological Survey reported the discovery of a rock sample containing 1 percent copper. Although Kennecott had initiated geological investigations in the Ladysmith area of Rusk County through its Bear Creek Mining subsidiary in 1953, it was not until the mid-1960s that it invested in exploratory drilling. By this time, their higher-grade copper reserves (averaging 3-4 percent copper) were becoming exhausted, and Third World supply sources were demanding a greater voice in the decisions about the exploitation of their nonrenewable resources.

In 1970, Kennecott announced the discovery of a six million ton copper deposit of 4 percent copper, known as the Flambeau deposit, near Ladysmith, Wisconsin.[4] While the Flambeau deposit would not be a significant proportion of Kennecott's total production, company officials stressed that it was "an important part of the total effort to increase domestic supplies of copper."[5] Indeed, if Kennecott/RTZ is allowed to go ahead, it will open the doors to at least a half-dozen companies that hope to mine identified ore deposits across northern Wisconsin. "Discovery of the Flambeau deposit," wrote Kennecott geologist Edwarde May, "far exceeds in importance the size of the orebody as it has opened the way to the development of a new domestic mining district."[6] In 1974, Noranda, a Canadian mining company, announced the discovery of a 2.3 million ton zinc-copper orebody in Oneida County. Other companies, as we have seen with Exxon, were also sitting on ore-rich lands in the region, hoping to profit from mining operations in the near future.

The Ladysmith mine has another special significance for the international minerals industry. Kennecott/RTZ has portrayed this as a "green" mine project, where environmental protection measures will account for at least 70 percent of the $20-30 million that Flambeau Mining will spend to develop the mine.[7] The success of the Ladysmith mine would be a welcome signal to the industry that the "growing anti-mining lobby" in North America and Australia may not be powerful enough to drive multinational mining companies out of heretofore "politically safe" areas: "For years North America and Australia have attracted most exploration spending," observes the *Mining Journal*, "but the growing anti-mining lobby and the coincident introduction of new and improved mining and investment codes in many developing countries could soon shift the balance in the latter's favour."[8]

Kennecott/RTZ's desire to resist this shift from the advanced capitalist countries to the risky political environment in the Third World accounts for its desire for a quick victory in establishing its mine at Ladysmith. At the beginning, it had few doubts about its success. For the nation's largest copper company, the development of a relatively small copper mine near Ladysmith was not seen as a major problem. Kennecott's 1973 annual report suggested that a mining operation would be underway in Rusk County by 1976.

When Kennecott first started buying land in Rusk County, there was hardly anyone who knew enough about mining to have any objections to the proposed mine. The town of Grant, just south of Ladysmith, liked the idea so much that it sold Kennecott its town hall, an old building on land the company needed for its mining operation. Through its fully-owned subsidiary, Flambeau Mining Corporation, Kennecott planned to construct an open-pit mine covering 55 surface acres and descending to a depth of 285 feet. A concentrate mill to be constructed at the site would upgrade the ore before it was shipped out of state for smelting and refining. The tailings, which are finely ground powdered waste rock left behind during the concentrating stage, would be piped as a slurry to a 186-acre tailings settling pond on the edge of a marsh. During its 11-year life, the mine would generate a total of 2.6 million tons of tailings at an average rate of 840 tons per day.[9]

"At first, most of us thought a copper mine would bring prosperity to this area," said Roscoe Churchill, a retired school principal, part-time farmer, and Rusk County supervisor.[10] During this early honeymoon period, Kennecott also worked to establish a favorable legislative framework for mining at the state level. When the company began collecting data for its mine permit application the state of Wisconsin had no mining taxation code or regulatory framework for mining. Kennecott lawyers quickly filled the gap by drafting a mining tax that levied a low 1.1 percent production tax on copper. The tax was approved by the Wisconsin Department of Revenue and then rushed through both houses of the legislature in a period of less than two weeks between first consideration and final vote. Representative Midge Miller (D-Madison) attributed the swift passage of the bill to the fear that if the legislature did not act quickly it would be killing the prospect of mining jobs in economically depressed Rusk County.[11]

Despite these successes, public doubts about the future of mining in Wisconsin were beginning to surface. Before the bill was passed into law, for example, Representative Miller added two amendments. The first raised the tax levy from 1.1 to 1.5 percent. The other amendment called for a study committee to review the tax and determine if the legislature had made a big mistake. Even with the slight tax increase, William Bateson, a University of Wisconsin economist at the Institute for Environmental Studies, calculated that if Kennecott were to mine a deposit in Arizona identical to the one in Ladysmith, it would be paying three times the taxes. He estimated that the Ladysmith mine could provide the company with $20 million worth of copper and $5 million worth of gold and silver each year. For each $25 million worth of minerals taken from the mine, Kennecott would pay $375,000 to the state. The town of Grant's share would be $10,312; Rusk County would get a mere $4,688. Kennecott's after-tax profits, by comparison, were conservatively estimated at $5 million annually. "We ought to wake up," said another University of Wisconsin economist. "We're getting plucked like a banana republic when we could be acting like an oil sheikdom. Not that we should act like an oil sheikdom, but we should start discussing what this means for the state—what stands to be gained; what stands to be lost."[12]

Early Citizen Opposition

These doubts about the future prosperity that could be expected from the mine were also increasing at the local level. Roscoe Churchill's optimism about the mine deteriorated after he received his property tax bill for 1975 and realized his taxes had soared 72 percent over the previous year. The increase was created in large part by the inflated prices Kennecott and other mining companies were paying to landowners for area farms. In Willard township, just eight miles south of the proposed mine site, one landowner reported more than 40 land transactions in one year. "That's unheard of in this area," he said.[13] Furthermore, as Churchill and others soon learned, Kennecott estimated that the mine would provide long-term jobs only for about 40 residents over its entire eight-year life. The proposed siting of the mine also raised doubts within the community about the environmental consequences from the mine. The mine would lie just 300 feet from the Flambeau River, one of Wisconsin's most pristine waterways and a prime area for walleye fishing. The site is also within the territory, roughly the northern third of Wisconsin, for which the Lake Superior Chippewa retained the right to hunt, fish, and gather after ceding the land to the U.S. government in the 19th century. The orebody is also lodged in massive sulfide-type rock. When massive sulfides are exposed to air and water during mining, they form sulfuric acid, which can contaminate both groundwater and surface waters. Contamination of this sort could devastate the dairy farming economy of Rusk County as well as the tourist trade.

These fears were increased when, in March 1976, the Wisconsin Department of Natural Resources held a hearing on the adequacy of an environmental impact statement (EIS) for the proposed mine. Under the provisions of the Wisconsin Environmental Policy Act, the state equivalent of the National Environmental Policy Act, the DNR must prepare an EIS before major development projects can be undertaken. Kevin Lyons, an attorney later hired by the town of Grant to represent the township on mining issues, describes how this public hearing was conducted: "Before testimony began, the Wisconsin Department of Natural Resources hearing examiner ruled that the only lawyer allowed to ask questions would be the Kennecott lawyer, who would be questioning his own witnesses. The examiner also ruled that there would be no cross-examination of the Kennecott witnesses by anyone. The Kennecott lawyer then called and examined his witnesses, all of whom supported the EIS...At the end of the hearing, the examiner ruled that the EIS was adequate."[14]

At one point in the hearing a farmer dressed in coveralls got up and asked if the hearing examiner could ask the Kennecott representatives to raise their hands. Then he asked if the DNR representatives could raise their hands. "Thank you sir," he said, "for a while I had a hard time figuring out who was who." "The mining company wanted to railroad something, we could see that," said Roscoe Churchill. "They were some pretty high-powered people, and they had expectations of getting the mine started. They were treating us like a bunch of peasants who were just in the way. Let me tell you, there are not a bunch of dumb farmers around here."[15]

One of the few community groups that was able to testify at the EIS hearing was Northern Thunder, an environmental action group from nearby Eau Claire, Wisconsin. They offered testimony about the problems of acid mine drainage and groundwater contamination from sulfide mining. After listening to such testimony, Roscoe Churchill and other concerned citizens called a meeting. "We decided that we were very much in need of support because each one of us that was concerned about the mine felt like we were alone," said Churchill. Out of that meeting came the Rusk County Citizens Action Group (RCCAG). "It grew rapidly from that point on," recalls Churchill, "because we had enough interested people who knew we had to do something to protect our community."[16] The immediate objective of the group was to slow down the development of the mine until there was adequate environmental legislation to control mining and to put a higher tax on mine operations.

The group began educating themselves about the pollution problems associated with copper mining. Roscoe Churchill and his wife, Evelyn, visited several operating copper mines in the western United States and in the Sudbury mining district of Ontario, Canada. They reported their findings throughout the county through public meetings and through the "Letters to the Editor" column of the *Ladysmith News*. "In my own travels to metallic mines in Canada and the United States," wrote Churchill, "I have not seen one site that has not poisoned the rivers and streams adjacent to the mining activities. And, of course, areas with heavy rainfall, such as Wisconsin, would find the mining pollution most difficult to handle."[17]

Sitting around the Churchill's dining room table, 13 members of RCCAG prepared a legal appeal of the DNR's approval of the EIS for the proposed mine. They filed their appeal with the Dane County Circuit Court in Madison and asked for a judicial review of the agency's decision. They argued that the EIS "does not meet the meaning of the word 'reclamation' because the land will not be restored to its original usable condition, but will be left a waste area and a possible source of pollution to the area surrounding the proposed mine and disposal area forever."[18] At the preliminary hearing on the appeal, Judge William Sachtjen gently reprimanded the group for failing to follow proper legal form. "I could have thrown this out" the judge said, "but I'm not going to. I'm going to give you 30 days to get some legal help so you can resubmit this to the court."[19]

The group then sought legal help from the public intervenor in the Wisconsin Department of Justice. The public intervenor is an assistant attorney general who represents the public in all environmental matters. By November 1976, as the final permit hearing on Kennecott's mine application approached, the RCCAG had put together a legal defense team consisting of Kevin Lyons, attorney for the town of Grant; and Frank Turkheimer, attorney for the Natural Resources Defense Council (NRDC), a highly respected national environmental organization which combines legal action, scientific research, and citizen education to protect natural resources. Public Intervenor Peter Peshek represented the citizens of the state in the proceedings.

During investigations preceding the permit hearing, it became clear that the DNR had accepted Kennecott's own environmental impact report without verifying critical interpretations of groundwater quality, soil permeability, seepage of toxic metals, etc.[20] At the beginning of the final hearing on Kennecott's mine permit, Public

Intervenor Peshek asked that the DNR's EIS on the Kennecott mine not be admitted as evidence because it was "a mere unverified parroting of data and statements originally appearing in the previously-written environmental impact report drafted by the Flambeau Mining Company, a subsidiary of Kennecott."[21] While the hearing examiner said he did not have the authority to decide the adequacy of the EIS, he said there would "not be a presumption that everything in the document is true."[22] The effect of the ruling was that Kennecott would be forced to produce evidence in support of each mine permit request to the state, rather than simply refer to sections of the EIS.

One of the critical issues in the hearing was the question originally raised by the RCCAG about post-mining pollution to the Flambeau River. At the conclusion of mining, Kennecott proposed to pump water from the Flambeau River into the abandoned open pit to create a small artificial lake some 300 feet from the river. The water near the top of the pit lake would flow westerly toward the Flambeau River. Kennecott alleged that there would be no potential danger of pollution to the river because the heavy metals and other toxic materials would only occur at the lower levels of the lake; in other words the lake would become meromictic—a lake that does not turn over seasonally.

The EIS stated unequivocally that "regardless of the method of filling the pit, the lake would eventually become meromictic."[23] The EIS did not provide any information about how this conclusion was reached. However, University of Wisconsin consultants told Kennecott, as early as 1973, that there was no way to state with certainty that the lake would be meromictic. Public Intervenor Peshek later obtained access to an April 21, 1977 letter sent by Kennecott which said, in part, "Our recent investigations indicate that the lake would *not* become meromictic [emphasis added]."[24]

In the end, however, it was not the DNR's inadequate and misleading EIS which brought the permit proceedings to a halt, but the public education efforts of the RCCAG. Between the March 1976 hearing on the EIS and the November permit hearing, the group had convinced large numbers of Rusk County residents that the mine would provide little economic benefit to the community while the pollution could destroy the ecological basis of the county's main industry—dairy farming. On the second day of the hearings, the Rusk County Board of Supervisors had their monthly meeting. As a member of the board, Roscoe Churchill introduced a resolution to "stop the issuance of county mining permits" until adequate laws were in place to protect the environment and sufficient tax revenues were available to pay for all the costs of mining to local communities. The 21-member board passed the resolution unanimously. Since Wisconsin law requires that mine applicants show that the project would comply with local zoning requirements, the hearing examiner had no choice but to adjourn the mine permit hearings indefinitely. Eighteen months later, the applications were dismissed. "A handful of citizens beat a multinational corporation," said Peshek. "They whomped the living tar out of 'em. There were eight legal proceedings and the people won every one of 'em that ever ended." A grassroots citizen's movement convinced the town of Grant and Rusk County boards to deny Kennecott's mining application. And, to further safeguard the community from future mining projects, the county passed a tough mining code in 1984.[25] The whole experience moved one Kennecott corporate vice-president to describe the state in an internal corporate letter as "the People's Republic of Wisconsin."[26]

Kennecott Rethinks Its Strategy

The defeat of Kennecott's proposed mine and the emerging Indian resistance to Exxon's proposed mine in Crandon necessitated a reevaluation of corporate strategy to gain access to new resource supplies in Wisconsin. This effort became even more urgent as Kennecott reevaluated the economics of the project in 1986 and discovered that the rich copper lode, originally estimated at 500,000 tons, was actually two million tons of 10.6 percent copper, an extraordinarily rich deposit.[27] The multinational corporation could no longer afford to ignore the social and political dimensions of its desired access to resources. The new corporate strategy involved, among other things, coopting and splitting the opposition and building an alliance between mining corporations and the state of Wisconsin to neutralize potential opposition to mining.

How was this new strategy to neutralize environmental opposition to mining to come about? A Kennecott official gave a preview of a new cooptation strategy when he wrote to his superiors two days after the company's mine permit hearing was adjourned: "Getting into bed with environmentalists might rub raw with many of our colleagues, but in this day and age I cannot recommend a better course of action for expedition of our project."[28] In the aftermath of Kennecott's defeat, the company went to work first on lobbying the Wisconsin public intervenor. In response, after conferring with mining company executives, lawyers from Wisconsin regulatory agencies, key legislators, and environmental lobbyists, Public Intervenor Peshek announced a new "consensus decision-making process" to facilitate the beginning of mining in northern Wisconsin.

The essence of this process involves local citizens, Indian tribes, and environmentalists in negotiations with mining companies and the state about the ground rules that would allow mining companies to proceed with their projects. The assumption underlying the consensus process is that mining is inevitable no matter what the social and environmental costs may be. And if it is inevitable, in the intervenor's view, it is better to have the state effectively regulate the social, economic, and environmental effects of such projects. Participants in this elite planning group included lawyers for Exxon, Kennecott, and Inland Steel; the DNR; Wisconsin's Environmental Decade; the public intervenor; and lawyers for three of the affected townships. Exxon assumed a leadership role and provided major funding to the group from the very beginning.

From the state's perspective, the consensus approach provides important legitimation for the state's regulatory role. According to Public Intervenor Peshek:

> The state of Wisconsin has neither the personnel nor the financial resources necessary to allow northern Wisconsin communities to feel comfortable with new mining operations. The mining companies who wish to develop

major mining enterprises in northern Wisconsin can provide major personnel and cash contributions to the process. For example, I estimate that Exxon has spent well in excess of $400,000 participating in the development of administrative rules for the protection of the environment from metallic mining waste. Kennecott has also spent a considerable sum of money doing similar things. The kind of expertise, both internal and external, that Exxon, Kennecott, and Inland Steel have been able to bring to bear on the process for writing appropriate regulations are not available to citizens or local and state government in Wisconsin. The consensus approach maximizes utilization of the companies' resources in helping to formulate public policy.[29]

Rather than address the real problem of unequal access to information and organizational resources between the mining companies and the public in the formulation of public policy, the consensus process simply legitimates this political inequality. The mining companies retain their dominant role in the shaping of mining rules and regulations while diverting potential opposition from independent political organizing, public education, and protracted legal battles. A key feature of the consensus process is that disagreements among consensus participants are not brought to the public's attention through the mass media.[30] This strategy of consensus decision-making is in reality a subversion of democratic decision-making whereby potential conflicts which may otherwise arise between corporate and community interests are either suppressed or neutralized in the legislative and regulatory processes.

The suppression of conflict about groundwater contamination from mining is a good illustration of this process.[31] More than two-thirds of Wisconsin residents and up to 500,000 private well owners depend upon groundwater for drinking water. The possibility of mining-related groundwater contamination from Kennecott's proposed mine in Rusk County was a major impetus to the mobilization of public opinion against the mine. And the Rusk County Board made it clear that they would not reconsider Kennecott's application for a mining permit until adequate groundwater protection legislation was enacted.

In April 1981, the Natural Resources Board, whose members are appointed by the governor, gave the DNR until June 1982 to propose draft rules for groundwater protection. Exxon and Kennecott objected to this timetable because it would interfere with their plans to apply for mining permits by the spring of 1982. So, at a closed meeting on July 31, 1981, lawyers for Kennecott and Exxon met with lawyers for the DNR, the public intervenor, the town of Grant, and Wisconsin's Environmental Decade to decide on a comprehensive package of groundwater rules. Although members of the RCCAG had participated in earlier discussions of the consensus group on groundwater rules, they were not notified of the July 31 meeting. Two members of the group learned about the meeting at the last minute and demanded to be included in the final drafting session. They made the five-hour car trek from Ladysmith to Madison, but when they arrived at the office of Kennecott's lawyer they were presented with the final draft of the rules. The actual drafting had taken place the night before.

Under the consensus groundwater rules, the mining companies would be allowed to contaminate groundwater to federal maximum contaminant levels for drinking water, as specified in the Safe Drinking Water Act. During public hearings on the DNR's adoption of these rules, Thomas D. Brock, the chair of the Department of Bacteriology at the University of Wisconsin at Madison, testified that it was not the intent of Congress to allow high-quality waters to be degraded to the levels specified by the Safe Drinking Water Act, and that this act should not be used as an excuse for allowing the degradation of Wisconsin groundwater. Brock's testimony was particularly noteworthy because he was a member of the National Academy of Science's Safe Drinking Water Committee and a co-author of a report made in conjunction with the Safe Drinking Water Act. Brock concluded that the consensus groundwater rules were not only inappropriate but unenforceable: "There can be no conclusion other than that the mining companies, with their superior legal and technical resources, will be able to do virtually whatever they want to the groundwater quality of Wisconsin."[32]

The DNR's acceptance of these groundwater rules was a complete reversal of a previously existing policy of nondegradation of groundwater that had been unanimously approved by the Natural Resources Board just a year earlier in October 1980. During public hearings on the proposed new groundwater rules in the fall of 1981, the majority of those who testified spoke in opposition not only to the rules but to the consensus decisionmaking process that led to the rules. "The groundwater of the northwoods is the basis for the economy," said Jim Wise of the Northwoods Alliance, an environmental action group in Tomahawk, Wisconsin. "To compromise for an industry as big as mining is wrong."[33]

While most of the newspaper accounts of the hearings mentioned the majority opposition, they emphasized that the rules were a needed compromise between mining companies, state agencies, town governments, Indian tribes, and the state's leading environmental organizations.[34] The *Milwaukee Journal,* the state's largest circulation newspaper, gave prominent coverage to Exxon lobbyist James Derouin, who characterized the opposition as a "vocal minority" who "are absolutely ignorant of what they are talking about."[35] Because naming the decisionmaking process "consensus" gives the strong impression of all parties participating equally in these decisions, it may, as one political scientist observed, "only serve to hide the fact that powerful interests and their legislative partners are using the process to force their will upon weaker interests."[36] The groundwater rules were not substantially modified as a result of public criticism during the hearings. They were officially adopted by the Natural Resources Board in March 1982.

The first organized resistance to the rules and the consensus process came from the town of Grant. At their annual town meeting in April 1982, they fired their lawyer, who had been representing them in the consensus process. The town also voted overwhelmingly in favor of an indefinite moratorium on mining. Dianne Bady, president of the RCCAG, called Public Intervenor Peshek "our own James Watt" and demanded his resignation. In June 1982, leaders from six environmental organizations and three township mining impact committees supported the demand for Peshek's resignation because he was no longer representing the environmental concerns of northern Wisconsin residents.[37] Nine months later, Peshek announced he was leaving his post as public intervenor to take a job with DeWitt, Sundby, Huggett & Schumacher, the Madison law firm that had represented Exxon during the consensus rulemaking.[38]

Among the many lessons the mining industry drew from the Kennecott defeat in 1976 (and Exxon's withdrawal in 1986), one was paramount: any future mine proposal would have to find a way around the intractable problem of democratic veto power over controversial mine projects at the grassroots level of government. Thus, when Kennecott announced that it would revive its mine permit for the Flambeau deposit in May 1987, its first order of political business, as outlined in a company position paper, was "to obtain relief from onerous existing local approvals."[39] These included both county and township zoning regulations pertaining to mining and the mining moratorium resolution in the town of Grant. Kennecott's corporate counteroffensive against local environmental activism involved three key components: (1) a divide-and-conquer approach to local politics using sophisticated mass media promotions, behind the scenes political influence, and "gifts and donations" to community groups; (2) legal threats; and (3) pressuring the DNR into putting the mine permit application on a "fast track" for approval.

All of these initiatives received the enthusiastic support of Republican Governor Tommy Thompson, who came into office in 1987 pledging his support for mining in northern Wisconsin. Thompson's campaign manager and chief political adviser was James Klauser, principal lobbyist for the Exxon Minerals Company when that company was seeking permits to open a mine at Crandon, Wisconsin. In 1982, Klauser told the Wisconsin Manufacturers and Commerce Association that the state could host up to ten major metal mines by the year 2000, the Ladysmith mine being one of them.[40]

In one of Kennecott's "issue papers," the company identified "a small vocal opposition group" whose concerns about mining impacts could be "neutralized" if local leaders and company officials could negotiate a "local agreement" addressing some of these concerns.[41] Governor Thompson facilitated this process by appointing a Governor's Ad Hoc Task Force on Mining. Heading up the task force was Stanton Helland, a close Thompson friend and the current chair of the Natural Resources Board, the "citizens' board" that oversees the DNR. The governor also invited Roscoe Churchill to be on the task force. Churchill accepted, but was then surprised to learn that the "Findings and Recommendations" had been written without his input. The task force's report said that "state laws were sufficiently comprehensive" and recommended that the state take action to "legitimize" the local agreement process.[42] Churchill wrote a dissenting report and warned that "Unless the state adopts a new attitude, so that we in potential mining areas, feel we have an ally in Madison rather than two enemies—the mining company and the state, there is small chance that the current situation in this area will change much."[43]

Kennecott convinced some Ladysmith businesspeople that a scaled-down version of the defeated mine project would be a boom to downtown businesses. Officials of the city of Ladysmith then invited the town of Grant and Rusk County to join them in a united effort to negotiate an agreement for mining with Kennecott. After a very informal selection process, two elected officials from each of the three governments began meeting in December 1987. The negotiation meetings were held in closed session. Kennecott lawyers attended some of these sessions, but the public was excluded. The bottom line of the negotiations, from Kennecott's perspective, was that "the local communities must agree to provide Kennecott with relief from the local approvals such as the Rusk County ordinance."[44] It mattered little to Kennecott that the local impact committee had no authority to negotiate with Kennecott. Committee members did not have the benefit of legal counsel familiar with mining agreements. And, since the DNR had not yet prepared an EIS on the proposed mine, committee members had very little information about the social, economic, and environmental impacts of the project.

Kennecott had anticipated the possibility of continued resistance from both Rusk County, where Roscoe Churchill was vice-chair

of the board, and the town of Grant, which had passed a mining
moratorium by a two-thirds vote in 1982. "If an agreement cannot be
worked out which would provide for local approvals, there appear to
be only two potentially viable alternatives to satisfy the local approval
requirements," stated the company's strategy paper. "These are
either to have the entire parcel annexed by the city or to initiate
litigation challenging the existing local law."[45]

If Ladysmith were to annex the mine site—located in the town
of Grant just south of the city—it would deprive Grant of any tax
proceeds from the mine. At the very beginning of the negotiating
committee's deliberations, William Thiel, the lawyer for the committee, reminded committee members that Kennecott's lawyers were
ready to submit a petition to annex the entire Kennecott properties
to the city of Ladysmith.[46] And, if the annexation threat were not
sufficient to compel the committee to reach an agreement acceptable
to Kennecott, Thiel told the committee that Kennecott probably
would have legal grounds to sue if they didn't alter tough local zoning
laws.[47] Thiel said the company could claim "deprivation of economic
use of its property" if mining were not allowed. Ladysmith Mayor
Martin Reynolds acknowledged the intimidating effect of such a
threat: "Any time you've got a small city and an economically poor
county, the threat of a big-time lawsuit is always scary."[48]

Although the Governor's Ad Hoc Task Force on Mining encouraged the formation of the negotiating committee, the state was
not prepared to provide either financial or technical assistance to
such a committee. Mayor Reynolds and other committee members
complained that the lack of assistance from the state left the communities in an uncomfortable and dangerous situation. "We're little and
the mining companies are big," said Ladysmith administrator Alan
Christianson. "That's the bottom line."[49] Instead, the governor's task
force suggested that the committee seek reimbursement for their
negotiating expenses from Kennecott. The company agreed to pay
up to $60,000 in negotiating costs, but only after the negotiations were
completed and the local agreement signed.

Once Kennecott had intimidated the local negotiating committee with threats of annexation and a lawsuit, the only remaining

obstacle to implementing the local agreement was the passage of enabling legislation. A Kennecott lawyer drafted the legislation and had a pro-mining state senator introduce the bill as an amendment to the state budget bill. There were no public hearings, and very few legislators were even aware that it was part of the budget bill. Kennecott lobbyist James Wimmer requested Administration Secretary James Klauser's help in getting the budget amendment passed. "Without enabling legislation," wrote Wimmer, "there can be no local agreement and without a local agreement the timetable for the mine project will be seriously delayed."[50] In May 1988, Governor Thompson signed the bill into law with hardly any public notice. Flambeau Mining Company Vice-President Larry Mercando later thanked the governor for establishing the task force which was "the catalyst" in the successful negotiation of the local agreement.[51]

At public hearings on the local agreement in the town of Grant and in Rusk County, the overwhelming majority of the citizens testified against it. Many citizens felt it was premature to give permission for a mining project before the DNR had even issued a draft EIS on the project. Despite the vocal opposition, the local agreement was signed in July 1988. Once the local agreement took effect, local officials were prohibited from criticizing the mine. Article 31 of the agreement, under the heading "Local Governments Will not Oppose the Mine," states: "Except as provided herein, the participating local governments and parties negotiating this agreement agree not to oppose the mine or to take any action which would serve to unreasonably delay the construction of the mine." Kennecott was well on the way to creating a political climate in Ladysmith where criticism of the mine was unthinkable.

To further minimize the environmental controversy which led to the company's defeat in 1976, Kennecott also publicly announced in May 1987 that it would pursue mine permits for a scaled-down version of its original mine proposal. The new proposal called for only a 32-acre open pit, with the ore being shipped out of state for processing.[52] This eliminated the need for a concentrating facility and a tailings dam at the mine site. In light of this, Kennecott's consultant reminded the DNR when forwarding the "Scope of Study" report for the new proposal that the project was on an "accelerated schedule."[53] The scaled-down version did little to allay local concerns, however. The new proposal placed the edge of the open pit within 140 feet of the Flambeau River (instead of the 300 feet in the original proposal) and still involved the storage of sulfide-bearing waste rock in two rock piles. The high-sulfur waste rock (greater than 1 percent sulfur) would cover 27 acres and be 70 feet high. The low-sulfur waste rock pile (less than 1 percent sulfur) would cover 40 acres and be 60 feet high. The high-sulfur waste rock pile would also receive 124 tons daily of "metal and sulfur-enriched sludge" from the waste-water treatment plant.[54] All of this posed environmental problems from sulfuric acid runoff and leachate from the waste rock piles.

Nevertheless, time was of utmost concern for Kennecott management. Shortly after announcing the revival of its mine proposal, company executives met with Governor Thompson and dis-

---

Diagram 1
Mine Permit Process

1. Company submits notice of intent (NOI) to collect data for mine application.	2. Company submits plan for scope of study. Public hearings are held.	3. Company prepares and submits necessary permit applications
4. Company prepares environmental impact report (EIR).	5. DNR prepares draft environmental impact statement (EIS). Public hearings on draft EIS.	6. DNR prepares final EIS.
7. Department of Administration conducts master hearing on final EIS and mine permits.	8. Hearing examiner approves or denies permit.	9. Appeals considered.

cussed their proposal for securing DNR permits in record time. They reminded the governor that "The 33 months from project announcement to the issuance of permits required under the DNR-based schedule for a mining project as small and simple as the Flambeau project will not encourage other mining companies to explore for ore or plan to develop any known deposits in Wisconsin."[55] The earliest that the DNR estimated that permits could be issued was March 1990. Kennecott's schedule called for permits to be issued by September 1989. The eight-month difference, according to the company's position paper, was partially "due to the fact that the DNR is not fully reflecting the simplicity of the Flambeau project."[56] Among the specific recommendations Kennecott made to speed up the permiting process was that the DNR should cut down the time for public comments on the draft EIS "on the anticipation that the public comments will not substantially change the draft EIS and minimum time will be expended on comments which will have no significant effect on the project plans for protecting the environment."[57]

Ironically, in their rush to meet deadlines in their accelerated schedule, Kennecott occasionally tried short cuts that created new delays. In December 1988, for example, Assistant Attorney General and the new public intervenor, Kathleen Falk, announced that Kennecott's study plans contained serious discrepancies relating to groundwater flow in Rusk County. In a letter to local project manager Larry Mercando, Falk wrote that "The contour water table maps currently have serious errors." Mercando explained that state officials had been given some outdated information from a study the company had done in the mid-1970s.[58] Having to go back and redesign the groundwater study with the correct information created additional delays in the company's accelerated timetable.

Shortly afterwards, in February 1989, Larry Mercando and company lobbyist James Wimmer met with Governor Thompson "to suggest to the governor where his office could possibly help to prevent major delays to the proposed schedule."[59] With the delay in getting the groundwater study underway, the company was concerned that "the DNR will be issuing its draft EIS without incorporating the results of the July 1, 1989 groundwater modeling report" and that the public intervenor "has raised some concerns with this EIS procedure."[60] Following the meeting, Thompson Chief-of-Staff Bruce Hagen sent a letter to DNR Secretary Carroll Besadny: "The governor requested that I seek what information you may have regarding Kennecott and their proposed timetable for the Flambeau project."[61] Kennecott later noted the DNR's willingness to issue the draft EIS without incorporating the groundwater report as long as the information was presented in the final environmental impact report.[62] Thus, while the DNR officially encouraged "public participation" in the review of the draft EIS, some of the critical information necessary to evaluate the project was only available in the environmental impact report, which was not readily available for public review. From the perspective of both the DNR and the mining company, public comments on the draft EIS are more usually seen as a chance for the public to "let off steam" rather than an opportunity for the agency to substantially modify its conclusions before releasing a final EIS.

An essential component of Kennecott's corporate response to environmental activism is the management of local public opinion. The success of the Churchills and RCCAG in mobilizing public opinion against the mine prompted one Kennecott executive to recommend to his superiors that "We must get back to the residents of the town if we are going to erode the building base of opposition which this [environmentalist] is fostering."[63] The company's pro-active strategy was outlined by another Kennecott executive as follows: "It is necessary now for us to take the initiative and establish an offensive position, rather than finding ourselves in a defensive excuse-making situation as it seems we, as an industry, are in so often. We must go to them before they come to us."[64]

This responsibility was delegated primarily to Larry Mercando, Kennecott's local project manager, who is also a vice-president for Flambeau Mining Company, the Kennecott/RTZ subsidiary. As Kennecott's manager of mining projects, Mercando has been involved in developing new ventures on the world's resource frontiers. He was coordinator for the development of a master plan for establishing a mining, metals, and minerals industry in Saudi Arabia and is currently chair of Kennecott's "Ocean Nodules" consortium, which would extract minerals from three miles under the Pacific Ocean.[65]

In announcing the opening of the company's new office in the heart of downtown Ladysmith, Larry Mercando said: "Flambeau Mining is going to be a part of the community, and we see this move as another opportunity to reaffirm our intention of being good neighbors." At churches and civic clubs, he touted the proposed mine as "environmentally safe." "I consider myself an environmentalist" he proclaimed, pointing to his membership in the World Wildlife Federation. He eagerly showed a newspaper photograph of two whales— Patches and Silver—that he and his wife had adopted.[66]

Mercando's ultimate goal in Ladysmith, however, is to use the overwhelming economic and political power of RTZ to make the mine seem inevitable and to divide neighbor against neighbor in the town of Grant (pop. 970) and the city of Ladysmith (pop. 3,800). His efforts have often been successful. Grant town chair Bob Plantz, for example, had been a vocal opponent of the mine when it was first proposed in 1974. Now, he feels, "You can't fight big corporations." As he put it, "They know all the loopholes and have the best lawyers. Sometimes you have to see the light of day and realize that some things are going to happen whether you want them to or not."[67] Other local residents who have not seen the light have been made to feel like outsiders in their own community. After a number of well-publicized anti-mining demonstrations, Mercando got local pro-mining business owners to distribute free campaign buttons which said "Rusk County Yes/Protestors No." Despite the large numbers of local residents who have spoken out against the mine at numerous public hearings, Larry Mercando continues to refer to the environmental opposition as "outsiders" who are "un-American." It would appear that to be patriotic in Ladysmith, one must be in favor of the mine.

To help get the word out, the company also hired Wood Communications Group of Madison, a public relations firm, to publish the *Flambeau News*. The newsletter appears weekly as a supplement to the *Ladysmith News*. The company has also paid out thousands of dollars to local charities, schools and governments. The most criticized "contribution" was a $60,000 payment for the purchase of a water tanker truck for the Ladysmith Fire Department to replace the department's leaking tanker. Mercando was quoted in *The Flambeau News* as saying that "the truck would be ordered as soon as the company gets the permits it needs to build the mine."[68] Mine opponents made it clear what they thought about Mercando's offer when they distributed a flyer with Mercando's water tanker truck announcement on one side and a page out of Wisconsin's criminal statutes on the other side—the section on "Bribery and Official Misconduct."

Other notable company contributions included a $30,000 grant to sponsor a Junior Achievement program for four area school districts, and a $4,500 loan for a second-hand forklift to be used in a workshop for the developmentally disabled.[69] During the U.S. war against Iraq, the company wrapped itself in the U.S. flag. It made a $4,000 contribution to pay for the postage for the cookie packages that were sent to local soldiers serving in the Persian Gulf. Copies of the *Flambeau News* and the *Ladysmith News* were offered to all Rusk County residents in the armed forces. Week after week, the *Flambeau News* featured a front page "Rusk County Honor Roll" listing the names and addresses of those serving in the Persian Gulf.

And Flambeau Mining isn't the only mining company spreading money around the community. County Supervisor Stanley Kromrey has a prospecting lease with Ernest K. Lehmann & Associates, a mine exploration company with headquarters in Minneapolis. The prospecting lease allows the company to prospect for mineral deposits on his land in Flambeau. Kromrey stands to make more than $662,000 if the company decides to buy the land under the existing purchase option. He is also a member of the county board's Land, Forestry, and Zoning Committee, which is responsible for agreements with mining companies on exploration and prospecting leases.[70] The Ladysmith district attorney said there was no evidence that Kromrey did anything illegal by casting votes on issues that involve the interests of both himself and Lehman's company.

The Limits of Kennecott's Best Laid Plans

By taking the initiative and establishing an offensive position, Kennecott had hoped to quickly preempt, coopt, and generally intimidate the environmental opposition. But, as we will see in Chapter Five, the company miscalculated both the depth and extent of environmental activism in the local area. It also had not at all anticipated the involvement in the permit process of the Lac Courte Oreilles (LCO) Chippewa tribe, whose reservation is just north of the proposed mine. Indeed, throughout the negotiation of the local agreement and the gathering of information for the EIS, neither Kennecott nor the DNR had consulted the Lake Superior Chippewa tribes. As far as Larry Mercando was concerned, Indian treaty rights were irrelevant. "We own the land," he told a reporter, "and we own the mineral rights."[71] Such short-sighted logic ignored the fact that the off-reservation treaty rights to hunt, fish, and gather in the ceded territory of Wisconsin, including the Flambeau River downstream from the mine site, gave the Chippewa legal standing to intervene in any state permiting activity that might endanger treaty-protected resources. Federal courts have frequently found that treaty-protected Indians have "an environmental right" to preserve fishing habitats.[72]

When LCO tribal chair Gaiashkibos (pronounced "gosh-ki-bosh") showed up at the October 1989 prehearing permit conference and registered the Chippewa's opposition to Kennecott's mine permit, company officials were taken by surprise. "The company is saying it will be here for six years," said Gaiashkibos. "Their liability goes for another 30 years. We're going to be here forever."[73] The prospect of the Chippewa treaty rights issue being joined to the already heated environmental controversy over the Ladysmith mine was anathema to Kennecott's parent company, RTZ. International anti-RTZ activist Roger Moody has noted that "it is indigenous land claims which have been the bane of RTZ's expansionist policies for two and a half decades."[74] Among RTZ's mines which have displaced native people, or risked their lives are the north Queensland, Australia bauxite stripmine at Weipa, the Bougainville copper mine in

Papua, New Guinea; and the Elliot Lake uranium mines in Ontario, Canada.

The Bougainville copper mine was forced to close in May 1989 as a result of a guerrilla insurgency organized by the Bougainville Revolutionary Army.[75] According to an account in the *Engineering and Mining Journal,* the mine came under attack "from rebellious local inhabitants whose motives appear to be a mixture of objection to the mine on environmental grounds, demands for a bigger local share of revenues and massive compensation, and a desire to secede politically from Papua, New Guinea."[76] The repercussions of the revolt are still being felt throughout the region: "The term 'to bougainville' is now common currency among indigenous people in the Pacific region: it is synonymous with the increasingly militant stance being adopted by traditional landowners in the face of multi-national mining and natural resource corporations, and what they see as the collusion of their central governments."[77]

In May 1990, Gaiashkibos announced that he would travel to London to attend RTZ's annual general meeting and bring the Chippewa's concerns about the Ladysmith mine directly to Sir Alistair Frame, the chair of the RTZ Board of Directors. "I intend to tell RTZ that the tribes and environmentally concerned people of Wisconsin will not accept the degradation of ground or surface water, nor the stockpiling of hazardous and toxic materials simply so a foreign company can exploit the natural resources of our region. The track record of Kennecott and RTZ in the United States, Canada, and around the world is one of pollution, dead rivers, dead fish, boom and bust economies, and displaced native peoples. That is unacceptable in northern Wisconsin."[78] It would appear that the mining wars had come to Wisconsin in earnest.

Chapter 5

A Native-Environmentalist Insurgency

Oh, Lord, the voices whisper
From other towns in other times
Don't buy what they're selling you, Mister...
Keep out the Kennecott Mine.

You've got the land of milk and honey
You've got the land of the tall dark pines
Don't sell it for the Company money...
Keep out the Kennecott Mine.

They paint a picture of greed and glory
Lord, how bright the future shines
But there's big hole in their story...
Keep out the Kennecott Mine.

If you don't want your sons and your daughters
Waking up one day to find
They can't drink their poisoned water...
Keep out the Kennecott Mine.

Oh, don't you think it's strange
All the ghost towns that you find
Up and down the Iron Range...
Keep out the Kennecott Mine.

Oh, Lord, the voices whisper
From other towns in other times

Don't buy what they're selling you, Mister...
Keep out the Kennecott Mine.

"Kennecott Mine"
Ken Lonquist, Madison, Wisconsin 1991

In 1987, when Kennecott reactivated its mine application for a scaled-down version of their defeated 1974 project, they did not expect that the siting of this proposed mine was destined to become one of the most persistent and dramatic sources of political conflict in Wisconsin over the next few years. They had thought they had taken all the necessary precautions to neutralize their opposition. Besides, they had the vast resources of RTZ, their new parent company at their disposal. RTZ's market value stood at $5.7 billion in 1988.[1] They had the sympathetic ear of Wisconsin Governor Tommy Thompson and James Klauser, his secretary of administration and a former Exxon lobbyist. They also had what they thought was a "fool proof" strategy to quickly overpower their local opposition this time around.

An impressive native-environmental resistance movement did develop, however. Exactly one year after the state groundwater rules were drafted by the so-called "consensus" group, the RCCAG sponsored a conference on mining and groundwater in Ladysmith. The keynote speaker was Phil Tawney, one of the founders of the Northern Rockies Action Group, a citizens' organization which had succeeded in extracting economic and environmental concessions from coal mining companies in Montana. At the conclusion of the conference, the group voted to organize a statewide environmental organization to focus on mining and groundwater issues. In October 1982, the group announced the formation of the Wisconsin Resources Protection Council (WRPC). Included in the group's membership were grassroots environmental organizations like RCCAG, Indian tribes, elected officials in potential mine areas, anti-nuclear organizations, and resort owners. The first test of the new native-environmentalist coalition was defeating Exxon's proposed zinc-copper mine at Crandon.[2] The second test was blocking the newly proposed construction of the Kennecott copper mine near Ladysmith.

Perhaps the most significant factor in this second mobilization effort was the presence of the Lac Courte Oreilles (LCO) Chippewa. In 1989, the LCO Chippewa formally intervened in the Kennecott mine permit process, arguing that Wisconsin "cannot issue a permit [to mine] unless and until Kennecott can prove that its mining activities will not degrade the plant or animal resources in the ceded territory." Shortly thereafter, treaty-rights support groups and grassroots environmental organizations formed *Anishinaabe Niijii* (an-ish-i-naw-bee nee-gee), Friends of the Chippewa, to support the tribe's decision to exercise its rights and oppose Kennecott. International anti-RTZ activist Roger Moody called this movement "one of the most resilient coalitions of environmentalists, farmers, and Indians that I am aware of."[3]

One of the strategic benefits of the Chippewa joining the anti-mine struggle was the international treaty rights contacts they brought with them. Lac Courte Oreilles Chippewa chair Gaiashkibos was able to attend RTZ's 1990 annual meeting with the help provided by People Against Rio Tinto Zinc and its Subsidiaries (PARTIZANS), a London-based group that "networks with other campaigns around the issues of multinational mining, indigenous peoples' land rights, the effects of RTZ and other mining companies on the environment and people's health."[4] The group was set up in 1978, at the request of aboriginal communities in north Queensland, Australia. PARTIZANS has brought the concerns of native peoples to the attention of RTZ directors by buying shares of RTZ stock, which allow them to attend the company's annual meeting. At the 1982 annual meeting, PARTIZANS protestors took over the platform and, for the first time at a British company's public meeting, the police were called to eject an aboriginal delegate and 30 supporters. The event was headline news around the world the next day.

Other communities that could become the victims of land dispossession and environmental contamination from RTZ's mining activity in the remote corners of the world took note: their appearance at the annual meeting would be one very effective way of communicating their concerns to those who exercise the real power in the corporation. And as PARTIZANS has emphasized, "If you don't actually SEE how this power is concentrated and misused, how can you get worked up about it?"[5]

With hopes of heading off a possible confrontation at the 1990 annual meeting, Larry Mercando obtained Governor Thompson's help to arrange for a messenger from the governor's office to hand-deliver a letter to Gaiashkibos from Mercando. The letter asked Gaiashkibos to meet with Mercando so they could discuss the tribe's concerns about the Ladysmith mine. Gaiashkibos declined. As the head of a sovereign nation, Gaiashkibos preferred to meet with the head of RTZ to discuss his concerns, not some local representative.

At the London meeting, when Gaiashkibos asked Sir Alistair whether RTZ would respect Chippewa treaty rights in the ceded territory of Wisconsin, he was told, "We will deal directly with the federal and state government, next question." When Gaiashkibos asked for permission to ask a follow-up question, his microphone was turned off. London's *Financial Times* noted that such rude treatment of the head of a sovereign nation overshadowed the announcement that Standard and Poor's as well as Moody's (two U.S. credit-rating agencies) had awarded RTZ the top rating for its bonds.[6] "What we've observed today confirms our worst suspicions about the intentions of RTZ," declared Gaiashkibos. "We have been told firsthand that RTZ couldn't care less about our rights or concerns."[7]

This was not the first time RTZ had expressed contempt for native rights. At the 1984 RTZ annual meeting, a corporate officer, Sir Roderick Carnegie, said, "The right to land depends on the ability to defend it."[8] Native peoples have increasingly taken Sir Roderick's advice and have had a few successes in halting RTZ's expansion on resource frontiers. During the mid-1980s, for example, international support for the land claims of Panama's Guaymi Indians, combined with opposition from Panamanian bishops, forced RTZ to back off from its huge Cerro Colorado copper project.[9] RTZ's new chair, Sir Derek Birkin, now faced a growing native-environmentalist coalition in Wisconsin.

Guerrilla Media in Ladysmith

Shortly after Kennecott started publishing the *Flambeau News,* the Rusk County Citizens Action Group, along with the help of *Anishinaabe Niijii,* started publishing a look-alike newsletter, the *Real Flambeau News,* as an insert to the town shopper. The war of words went into high gear. "Kennecott Makes 'Top 10' Polluters List," proclaimed the first issue of the *Real Flambeau News.*[10] Countering Kennecott claims that the mine would be safe, the paper reported that the National Wildlife Federation had listed Kennecott's Bingham Canyon Copper mine as one of the nation's most polluted sites.[11]

Larry Mercando immediately went on the offensive, running ads on Ladysmith radio station WLDY charging that the National Wildlife Federation "misused" federal Environmental Protection Agency data when it listed Kennecott's Utah mine as perpetrator of the ninth largest toxic release in the United States. The RCCAG contacted Dr. Gerald Poje, the environmental toxicologist who had co-authored the National Wildlife Federation report, and ran a radio ad on WLDY featuring his response to Mercando's charge: "Communities need to carefully assess the track record of companies," said Poje, as he called on Mercando to debate him on the topic. They must "look at what companies have *actually done* elsewhere, rather than simply take their word that they will operate a safe, clean business." Mercando refused the challenge to debate. The next Kennecott newsletter said: "The First Amendment protects RCCAG's Fake News' right to ignore the truth, but it doesn't mean the people of Rusk County have to like RCCAG's abuse of the basic rules of honesty, fair play and decency."[12]

With extremely limited financial resources, *Anishinaabe Niijii* and RCCAG decided to develop a series of radio ads which highlighted critical environmental issues and suggested how citizens could become more involved in the mine permit process. The ad on regional environmental effects of mining said:

Ladysmith is standing with it's finger in the dike. Kennecott Copper wants to mine in Ladysmith…which might be okay. But, it may also be the beginning of the end of our way of life. More than 500,000 acres of northern Wisconsin are under lease to mining companies. Exxon wants to mine Rice Lake's Blue Hills, Union Carbide has its sights on Hayward. Bruce, Catawba, Cameron, and many more communities will be next. Our farms, tourism, and our way of life are in danger. Before Kennecott mines in Ladysmith we need to know what the impact of regionwide mining will be…not just the local impact of Kennecott. As citizens we can demand that the DNR make a regional environmental study…so far they haven't. If you want a regional impact study, come to the DNR environmental impact hearing on October 6th, 6:30 pm at Mt. Senario College in Ladysmith. Exercise your right to be concerned about your community.

The ads were broadcast over WLDY in Ladysmith and WJMC in nearby Rice Lake. Larry Mercando responded immediately with a desperate letter to all the Rusk County board supervisors except Roscoe Churchill. "Recently," he wrote, "those who oppose the Flambeau Mine have adopted a new strategy that relies not upon a rational presentation of the facts, but rather upon using the airways, flyers, letters to the editor, and the U.S. Mail to spread half-truths, distortions, and outright lies. Having been proven wrong on the facts, this small, but vocal, opposition group has obviously become desperate, and in their desperation have initiated a campaign that is a disservice to the people of Rusk County and to the worthwhile cause of environmental protection. As you know, I have avoided a blow-by-blow rebuttal because I have faith that you and the people you represent will base your judgement about the mine on the facts, not upon untruthful statements."[13]

Mercando's plea to the Rusk County board had little impact in swaying public opinion in favor of the mine. The overwhelming majority of those who testified at the October 1989 DNR hearing on the draft EIS spoke in opposition to the mine. Just before the July

1990 master hearing on the final EIS and mine permits, *Anishinaabe Niijii* placed a quarter-page ad in the *Wisconsin State Journal* calling public attention to RTZ's corporate track record of pollution and disregard for indigenous peoples around the world. The headline to the ad read: "One of the World's Most Notorious Polluters Wants to Set Up Shop in Wisconsin!" The ad was signed by 30 groups representing labor, the environment, treaty rights, farmers, and social justice religious constituencies. The adamant refusal of the DNR to address this corporate track record in either the EIS or the master hearing became a focal point for widespread public opposition to the mine.

The Politics of the Mine Permit Hearing

One of the potentially explosive issues in the contested case hearing was the fact that the state agency that was conducting the proceeding and would make the permiting decision for Kennecott/RTZ was headed by former Exxon lobbyist James Klauser. Public perception of the conflict of interest was clearly of some concern to hearing examiner David Schwarz. He passed on newspaper articles about Gaiashkibos's criticism of Klauser's role in promoting the Ladysmith mine and opposing Chippewa treaty rights to the deputy secretary in the Department of Administration: "While the Lac Courte Oreilles tribe seems to be emphasizing Jim's previous lobbying activities, I have not seen or heard any other specific reference to this in my handling of the case."14

Attached to Schwarz's memo was a copy of his order denying LCO's motion to extend the date for submission of its witness list for the contested case hearing. Larry Leventhal, the Chippewa's attorney, argued that the extremely short period for public comment made it difficult for groups with limited funds, such as LCO, to properly respond. The company had had three years to complete its multi-volume environmental impact report, its 13 permit applications, and more than two dozen technical reports supporting its permit applications; the tribe wanted 30 days after the close of the public comment period on the final EIS to prepare its response. The additional time was needed to study the comments made by members of the public and federal government. "We'd like to look at everything that comes in and see how it affects treaty rights," said Leventhal.[15] Leventhal appealed Schwarz's denial at the final pre-hearing conference, and Schwarz, with the reluctant consent of Kennecott's legal counsel, granted the Chippewa an additional ten days to submit its list of witnesses for the contested case hearing.[16]

The dilemma of how to effectively participate in the contested case proceeding with limited resources was not limited to the Chippewa; none of the citizen and environmental groups were able to undertake the entire legal process of discovery, interrogatories, pre-filed testimony, etc., prior to the actual hearing. The cost of full participation can easily run into tens of thousands of dollars. The prohibitive cost is not accidental. The rules for the conduct of the master hearing were developed by the industry-dominated "consensus group."

Arrayed against the well-financed lawyers for Kennecott/RTZ were the Rusk County Citizens Action Group, the Flambeau Valley Peace Coalition, the Wisconsin Greens, the Wisconsin Resources Protection Council (WRPC), and the Chippewa. The Flambeau Coalition and RCCAG were represented by non-attorney volunteers from each organization. The attorneys for the other environmental groups and the tribe worked for a fraction of their normal fees or pro bono. None of these groups could afford to pay expert witnesses to review the numerous technical reports, permit applications, etc., be available for depositions by the company and the DNR, or travel to Ladysmith to attend 21 days of testimony and cross-examination of witnesses.

While the Indian-environmental coalition did offer some expert testimony, the hearing examiner sustained the objections of the company and the DNR regarding the admissibility of evidence relating to the consideration of Chippewa treaty rights, the need for a comprehensive regional environmental impact statement, the consideration of the corporate track record of RTZ, and the company's disregard for local zoning and township moratoria on mining. From the perspective of the mine opponents, the most critical issues of the project were not allowed to be discussed or to become part of the record.

The domination of the contested case hearing by highly paid expert witnesses and the restrictions on admissible evidence meant that much of the environmental opposition to the mine had to be expressed outside the formal proceeding. The day before the Ladysmith hearings, 150 Native American and white canoeists paddled down the Flambeau River to protest the mine. After the canoes reached the proposed mine site, speakers from Earth First!, Greenpeace, and several treaty rights groups pledged their determination to stop Kennecott/RTZ. Wisconsin Greens' lawyer Waring Fincke told the crowd: "The next time we're here it's going to be to put our bodies in front of those bulldozers!"[17]

The spirit of the rally carried over into the public testimony portion of the permit proceeding. The company had planned to put its expert witnesses on the stand after the first day, but there were so many people who wanted to testify that the public comment period had to be extended to three days. Even then, there were dozens more who were unable to testify because of the long wait. Of the 180 people who spoke, only one supported the mine. The people testifying represented a broad cross section of the community, from farmers to high school teachers to housewives. Several times, the hearing examiner tried to limit people to ten minutes, but the audience shouted: "The only one in a hurry is Kennecott."

One of the more remarkable aspects of the hearing was the presence of large numbers of Indians in the audience and among those offering testimony. Tribal members from Lac Courte Oreilles, Mole Lake, Red Cliff, Bad River, and Lac du Flambeau testified in opposition to the mine and protested the way in which the state had proceeded without consulting the Lake Superior Chippewa tribes. The hearings were also broadcast in their entirety over the Chippewa-owned and -controlled radio station WOJB-FM.

Gaiashkibos spoke about canoeing down the Flambeau River with his father and gathering sacred medicines. He also noted that the Flambeau is the home of the eagle, the highest symbol of Indians. "It's not only RTZ-Kennecott-Flambeau," he said. "It's Exxon,

Noranda, and other mining companies."[18] Because of the possibility of widespread mining, he repeated the Chippewa's request for a comprehensive regional environmental impact statement before any mine permits were given.

While the Chippewa and sportfishing groups had been in conflict over the exercise of spearfishing treaty rights, they found some common ground at the Ladysmith hearings. "When the time comes that you can't eat fish out of the Flambeau River," said Kermit Benson, speaking for the 6,000 members of the sportfishing group, Muskies Inc., "we don't want someone coming to us and saying, 'Where were you when they had this public hearing.' We want it on record here and now that we oppose this mining project. Mining is the real long-term threat to the environment and the fishery in northern Wisconsin. It has the potential to make the Indian spearfishing controversy look like a piece of candy."[19] Benson's comments were greeted with cheers and applause from the Chippewa and their environmental allies.

The dramatic and moving testimony of ordinary citizens and tribal members was complemented by two women dressed in Grim Reaper costumes who walked up and down the aisles. Cassandra Dixon held a dead fish in an outstretched palm; Nancy Peterson held a large chunk of native copper. After Dixon placed the fish on the stage in front of hearing examiner David Schwarz, he ordered Ladysmith Police Chief Norm Rozak to arrest her. When Rozak approached Dixon and informed her she was under arrest she "went limp," unwilling to leave the auditorium under her own power. A crowd of about 40 mining protestors then surrounded Rozak and Dixon in a tight circle, holding hands and chanting: "The people united will never be defeated." As the crowd pushed closer to Rozak, he fell down into a row of auditorium seats. Additional Ladysmith police came to Rozak's aid and then dragged Dixon and Wisconsin Greens spokesperson Jeff Peterson out of the auditorium. Peterson had sat down in the aisle and was arrested for allegedly obstructing an officer.

Dixon was released outside the auditorium but Peterson was placed in a squad car. Some protestors sat in front of the car in an attempt to prevent Peterson from being taken to jail. The squad car backed out and Peterson was taken to jail, charged with obstructing an officer, and then released. Dixon summed up the reason for her protest very simply: "I think death is what we're talking about here. Living organisms will die if that mine is built."[20]

The dramatic confrontation and arrests made headlines in Madison, Milwaukee, and Minneapolis newspapers and, for the first time, focused statewide public attention on the controversial environmental issues surrounding the Ladysmith mine. It also focused the attention of the mining industry on the political risks associated with this activity. Minnesota mining executives "shuddered" as they watched Grim Reapers and dead fish being used to protest efforts to get mining underway in Ladysmith: "The street theater and alarmist conduct by opponents of the proposed Flambeau Mine push the debate beyond a calm review of the facts and make it more difficult for proponents to make their case for environmentally safe mining."[21]

But for longtime mining opponents like Roscoe Churchill, "environmentally safe mining" has yet to be demonstrated. The ability of powerful multinational mining corporations to revise the state's mining laws so that pollution is legal does not constitute proof of "environmentally safe mining." "Why do I fight the mining in Rusk County?" asked Churchill rhetorically at the public hearing. "Because I looked at mining in so many places both active and abandoned; and I have seen so much devastation in every case. I do not believe there are many people in our area who really want RTZ's proposed mine. I believe most people are overwhelmed at the prospect of fighting the multinational monsters, so they do not know what to do." Roscoe concluded his testimony in a defiant note that brought the 200 people in the Ladysmith high school auditorium to their feet in a standing ovation: "My ancestors fought the British exploiters through many generations; so I am just following tradition. But I do not want Wisconsin to be a resource colony to *any* mega-corporation, be it British, Canadian, Dutch, or U.S.-based! We must not stop no matter what lengths we have to go to stop these corporate invaders intent on plundering our countryside."[22] By the end of the public-hearing portion of the master hearing, David Schwarz had to admit that he had never presided over such a dramatic outpouring of public opposition to a project. This was not lost on the politicians in the state capital in Madison.

"Smoking Guns" and Mining Moratoria

No sooner had the contested case portion of the mine permit hearing begun than the Ladysmith mine controversy assumed center stage in the gubernatorial race. Tom Loftus, the Wisconsin Assembly speaker and Democratic Party candidate for governor, announced his support for a moratorium on all metal-ore mining in Wisconsin. "Northern Wisconsin's resources were exploited by the robber barons of the 19th century, who stripped the land and recklessly destroyed a priceless resource," Loftus said. "Now multinational mining companies are knocking on the door. The promise is jobs, but the reality may be environmental damage and economic disappointment." Before any mining is allowed, Loftus said, the state should study whether laws and regulations are adequate to protect the environment from mining. Loftus emphasized that mining companies have bought or leased hundreds of thousands of acres of land in northern Wisconsin and that the proposed mine at Ladysmith was just the first in a series of mines that might operate in Wisconsin if the state allowed it. "Once we open the door and put out the welcome mat for mining, we won't be able to close it again."[23]

One area that needed particular scrutiny was the state's water pollution rules. "Right now, mining operations are covered by the same wastewater regulations which allow other industries to increase their discharge of toxic pollution over time," Loftus said.[24] The candidate also criticized Governor Tommy Thompson for aggressively pursuing mining. He noted Thompson's approval of the Local Agreement Act, which allows local anti-mining ordinances to be overridden by local mining impact committees. The law, Loftus reminded voters, was drafted by attorneys for Kennecott. Loftus released a copy of a 1988 memorandum in which Senator Walter Chilsen (R-Wausau) directed a legislative researcher to contact

Kennecott attorneys about help in drafting the "local agreement" law. "This is the smoking gun that opponents to the Ladysmith mine have long suspected to exist."

Loftus also attacked Administration Secretary James Klauser. "As the man Governor Thompson calls the deputy governor, Jim is now in a position to make his prediction of six to ten major mines operating in northern Wisconsin by the 1990s come true," Loftus said. "This is the governor, after all, who brags that he likes to be the one to close the deal with corporations. Now, with Jim Klauser at his side, he's moving to close another one."[25]

Although Loftus was unsuccessful in his bid to unseat Governor Thompson, he did succeed in placing the issue of a mining moratorium on the Wisconsin legislative agenda. Representative Harvey Stower (D-Amery) joined the call for a moratorium and drafted a bill that would: place a two-year moratorium on all metal mining; require a regional environmental impact statement before any single mine permits are granted; repeal the so-called "local agreement" provision of the current mining law, which essentially grants mining companies a short-cut through the permit process; extend liability for any mining problems to the mining company and its parent company; and prohibit uranium mining in the state. Stower said his bill was designed to protect northern Wisconsin from "a kind of Third World treatment."[26]

By the time that the master hearing on Kennecott/RTZ's mine permit ended on August 7, 1990, the battle lines were already being drawn for future confrontations. The native-environmentalist coalition was not going to wait for what it saw as the inevitable go-ahead decision from the hearing examiner, expected in January 1991.

The Protect the Earth Survival Gathering

Anishinaabe Niijii organized a Protect the Earth Survival Gathering and Pow Wow over Labor Day weekend in 1990. This was an opportunity for the Indian-environmentalist coalition to evaluate its participation in the master hearing and plan its future strategy for blocking the Ladysmith mine. The gathering also marked the tenth anniversary of the International Survival Gathering held in the Black Hills of South Dakota, where thousands of Indians and their supporters gathered under the banner of the Black Hills Alliance to stop uranium mining in the Black Hills.

The "talking circles" at the Protect the Earth Survival Gathering focused on legal, legislative, and civil disobedience strategies for fighting Kennecott/RTZ in Ladysmith. All these tactics were considered necessary in the struggle to stop the mine. A Flambeau Defense Fund was also organized to raise money for the legal fees that the Chippewa already had incurred during the master hearing as well as for those anticipated in a likely federal court challenge based on Chippewa treaty rights. One of the honored guests at the Protect the Earth Survival Gathering was Roger Moody, founder of the London-based PARTIZANS and host to Gaiashkibos when the tribal leader went to London to address RTZ's annual meeting. Roger Moody shared his plans for a new organization called Minewatch that would link together communities affected by specific types of mining or the operations of particular corporations. Through the gathering and dissemination of information about mining impacts and multinational mining corporations, activist groups and communities could "strengthen their ability to negotiate with, or oppose mining plans."[27]

Many individuals who came to the gathering had become interested in the Ladysmith mine controversy as a result of listening to the master hearing over WOJB-FM. One such person was Linda Craemer, an elementary school teacher living in Bruce, a few miles from Ladysmith. What she heard on the radio terrified her. "They're going to come in and lay the land to waste," she said. "It's real easy not to know what mining companies do, but once you do know, it's awful hard not to fight it."[28] Craemer and several other individuals who came from Rusk County heard Roger Moody and decided to form a Wisconsin chapter of PARTIZANS.

Restoring Democracy in Ladysmith

The first task for this expanded native-environmentalist coalition was a petition drive to overturn the "local agreement" in Rusk County. In the fall of 1990, the battle of words had shifted from the state's regulatory proceedings to the Rusk County board. RCCAG circulated petitions asking citizens to urge the Rusk County board to rescind the "local agreement" with Kennecott/RTZ. The petition mentioned Kennecott's threats of annexation and court suits to pressure Rusk County and the town of Grant into negotiating with the company for a start-up of its proposed mine. The petition also charged that the "local agreement" ignored the 1982 and 1988 bans on mining in the town of Grant. Finally, the petition pointed out that Kennecott/RTZ had gone so far as to prohibit local officials from criticizing the mine as a condition of the agreement.

Over 2,000 people from Rusk County signed the petitions asking the Rusk County board to: rescind the local agreement with Kennecott; and delay consideration of any applications for mining until a thorough study had been made of the cumulative effects of a series of mines across northern Wisconsin. When Larry Mercando learned about the petition drive, he reacted with a letter to every home in Rusk County and a series of radio ads on WLDY. In his letter, Mercando accused RCCAG of "an effort to mislead, frighten, and stampede citizens into encouraging the Rusk County board to pass a moratorium on mining." Despite the 2,000 local petition signatures, Mercando insisted upon characterizing the opposition as "a small, but vocal opposition" who offered "only opinions and fear." Just in case the Rusk County board might allow itself to be influenced by the opinions of its constituents, Mercando made it clear that the board might be subject to a lawsuit if it overturned the local agreement: "The Local Agreement is a legally binding contract...Consequently, those who are calling for a moratorium are, in effect, asking everybody to violate a contractual agreement."[29]

On September 25, 1990, Rusk County board supervisors Roscoe Churchill and Phil Schneider introduced the resolution to rescind the local agreement and postpone any further mining decisions until a comprehensive regional environmental impact statement had been completed. Over 100 supporters of the resolution were on hand to speak in favor of the resolution. But before any public testimony was allowed, the county's attorney, William Thiel, read a letter from Kennecott's legal counsel suggesting that the company would sue if the board voted in favor of the resolution. Rusk County supervisor Stanley Kromrey who has mineral leases with E. K. Lehman Exploration Company, immediately introduced a motion to table the resolution. His motion passed by a two-to-one ratio. Kennecott's threat had proved effective once again.

Many local residents left the board meeting more determined than ever to overturn the local agreement. RCCAG immediately sent out a fundraising letter to support a legal challenge to the agreement because it denies freedom of speech to local residents. At the same time, RCCAG and the newly-formed Wisconsin PARTIZANS began organizing a "Freedom March" on Ladysmith for November 10, 1990. Local organizers advertised the march as an event "to honor our veterans and our forebearers who fought to protect our democratic freedoms and to protest the inaction of elected officials who do nothing as control over our community's future is taken away from us by RTZ."[30] Larry Mercando responded with a front page "Open Letter" in the *Flambeau News,* in which he portrayed the opposition as "outsiders" who "may not appreciate how we normally conduct ourselves here in Ladysmith" and may "seek confrontation." While he recognized "the rights these marchers will be exercising, we are also reminded of another of the basic tenets of the American way of life: government that governs closest to the people governs best. Local issues should be discussed and decided on a local level."[31] Mercando's use of the imperial "we" in his letter was doubly offensive to those whose voices had been silenced as a result of Kennecott's threat of legal action.

Despite a cold and windy day, over 500 men, women, and children marched from the DNR ranger station on Highway 8 to the Rusk county courthouse in Ladysmith to demonstrate their opposition to Kennecott/RTZ's proposed mine. En route to the courthouse, marchers stopped at the Flambeau Mining office to deliver petitions from area citizens. No one from Kennecott/RTZ was in the office, so petitions were taped to the door and window of the firm's office. Later, a mock wedding between the state of Wisconsin and RTZ was held on the Rusk County Courthouse lawn. Speakers included Tom Maulson, a treaty rights activist from the Lac du Flambeau band of Chippewa; John Detloff, Chippewa Flowage resort owner; Roscoe Churchill; and Marilyn Benton, a Lac Courte Oreilles tribal member. Benton told the crowd: "I am a representative of the Ojibwa Nation—our people have been living to protect the earth. We are told as long as we take care of the earth, the earth will take care of us. If we don't take care of the earth, we will stop living. My purpose here today is to tell you that you are doing the right things. The Indian people will join hands with people of other colors—fulfilling an Ojibwa prophecy."[32]

While protestors marched in Ladysmith, Kennecott lawyers in Salt Lake City, Utah were busy preparing their responses to potential lawsuits from LCO and RCCAG. In a status report to James Klauser, they discussed the merits of LCO's treaty rights claim and noted, "We have briefed many of these issues before the Hearing Examiner and believe that we will be on solid ground should such a lawsuit ensue. As a legal matter, we do not believe that the current law of treaty rights provides the Indians with the type of co-management rights being asserted." They concluded that: "While none of these lawsuits appear to represent a substantive risk to the project, they do create the potential for additional lengthy, burdensome, and costly delays to the project."[33]

Kennecott Gets the Green Light

The state of Wisconsin's approval of Kennecott/RTZ's open-pit copper mine in Ladysmith was announced on the same day that the United States went to war against Iraq. The war for oil overshadowed the war for Wisconsin's mineral resources. In issuing the permit, the hearing examiner granted Kennecott six variances, including permission to construct a mine less than 300 feet from a river.[34] "Not only did the DNR approve the project," said Wisconsin Secretary of State

Douglas La Follette, "they had to bend over backwards to grant special variances."[35]

"This is a black day for the people of Wisconsin who share our reverence for the natural beauty and value of the northern woodlands," said Gaiashkibos, LCO tribal chair.[36] The Chippewa's attorney, Marie Butler, immediately began work on an appeal to the DNR for a review of the hearing examiner's decision. Butler argued that the potential environmental damage from the mine could hinder the tribe's right to hunt, fish, and gather food in the ceded territory of Wisconsin.[37]

On February 13, 1991, however, DNR Secretary Besadny refused LCO's request to review the hearing examiner's decision. "I do not believe that further proceedings in this matter would produce relevant substantive evidence that was not available at the time of hearing or not already in the record," wrote Besadny. Representative Spencer Black (D-Madison), a leading environmental legislator and chair of the state assembly's Natural Resources Committee, responded to Besadny's decision by noting that "A lot of people in the North feel the decision was made before the hearing even took place...I don't think the DNR has done a very thorough job."[38]

The Chippewa had planned to file a federal treaty rights lawsuit against the DNR to stop the mine but had to drop the idea when they learned they would have had to put up a surety bond that would cover all financial damages that Kennecott/RTZ would sustain if its permit was delayed. This bond would have been determined by the company and run into the millions of dollars. Tribal adviser and WOJB-FM station manager Dick Brooks called the surety bond an "economic subversion of democracy. The tribe still has treaty rights and property rights issues that have not been resolved. If you don't have the resources of the mining companies, your opportunity to get a fair hearing is substantially reduced."[39]

While LCO's legal options were blocked for the moment, a class-action lawsuit against the local agreement was still in Rusk County Circuit Court. On December 20, 1990, 18 opponents of the Ladysmith mine had filed suit in Rusk County Circuit Court, charging that the local agreement with Kennecott/RTZ was unconstitutional because it violated opponents' First Amendment rights of free speech.[40] As long as the constitutionality of the local agreement was in doubt, the 18 citizens who filed the suit could go into court and request a temporary restraining order against mine construction until the suit was settled. This possibility undoubtedly influenced Kennecott's decision to delay groundbreaking for two months, until July 1991.[41]

In the meantime, legislative opposition to mining was growing. Representative Harvey Stower scheduled public hearings on his mining moratorium bill for March 1991. And Representative Spencer Black announced his co-sponsorship of a bill with Senator Russ Decker (D-Schofield) that would deny mining permits to companies with poor environmental records. Black said that if more stringent state background checks had been required, approval of the Ladysmith mine would have been "much less likely." Black noted that Kennecott was ranked as one of the nation's top ten polluters by the National Wildlife Federation and recently had been fined nearly $100,000 for killing more than 1,000 birds at its Alligator Ridge gold mine in Utah in 1988. Black said that current law "makes it easy for an environmental outlaw to receive a mining permit."

Larry Mercando blasted as "half-truths" accusations that Kennecott and its parent RTZ are "environmental outlaws" undeserving of state mining permits. "I think Spencer's getting his information from people who are biased," said Mercando. "Generally, Kennecott has a fine record. So does RTZ. We have nothing to hide."[42] For a corporation with nothing to hide, Kennecott's lawyers had strenuously objected every time during the previous summer that the Chippewa or the Wisconsin Greens attempted to introduce evidence about the company's environmental track record into the master hearings. In response to its problems on the legislative front, Kennecott launched a major public relations campaign that included glossy brochures, press packets, and meetings with the editors of the state's major newspapers. Secretary of State Douglas La Follette said that the company's campaign "attacking mine critics" proves the company "clearly is running scared."[43]

Between January and June 1991, Kennecott, Noranda, Exxon, and the Wisconsin Manufacturers and Commerce Association spent approximately $160,000 lobbying state government against rules and proposed laws seen as harmful to the mining industry. "As with so many environmental issues, the environmental community's rhetoric strikes a populist and popular chord," said James Buchen, an industry lobbyist. "Because so much of the rhetoric is inaccurate, industry has to try to set the record straight," he added. "They hire professionals to do that and that costs money."[44]

A New Phase of Environmental Resistance

After the state of Wisconsin gave Kennecott/RTZ the go-ahead for mining, many environmental activists realized that the legal avenues for opposing the Ladysmith mine were becoming exhausted. The DNR's refusal to review the hearing examiner's decision and the financial obstacles which prevented the Chippewa from pursuing their treaty rights lawsuit simply reinforced this belief. More importantly, there was a widespread public perception that the mine was inevitable and that there was nothing anyone could do to stop it. The time was ripe for some new and creative tactics to shatter this "psychology of inevitability." The result was Flambeau Summer.

Inspired by the success of Earth First!'s "Redwood Summer" campaign to save the old growth forests in the Pacific Northwest, several groups within *Anishinaabe Niijii,* including the Wisconsin Greens, Nukewatch, the Midwest Headwaters chapter of Earth First!, Wisconsin PARTIZANS, and Northern Thunder, decided to plan a series of nonviolent civil disobedience actions. "Our first objective," said Jan Jacoby, a spokesperson for Flambeau Summer, "is to stop the Kennecott mine through whatever creative tactics we can dream up." Kicking off Flambeau Summer was a July 6, 1991 rally at the town of Grant town hall, followed by a march to the mine site and an occupation of the site by all those who were willing to risk arrest for trespassing on mining company property. "If you ever wanted to do anything against the mines, now is the time," said Jan Jacoby. "Construction begins three days after this event."[45]

Letters were sent out to everyone who testified in opposition to the Ladysmith mine at the master hearing to invite them to attend nonviolence training sessions in Ladysmith, Madison, Milwaukee, and Stevens Point. Press releases, letters to the editor, and opinion pieces were sent out to local, state, regional, and national media as well as to the alternative press. Speakers went out to promote Flambeau Summer among other environmental groups, on college campuses, church social action committees, peace groups, and treaty rights groups. The Madison Treaty Rights Support Group and the University of Wisconsin Greens organized a fundraising concert featuring John Trudell, a Native American poet and performer, and Floyd Red Crow Westerman, a Native American actor and singer. Francene Hart, a well-known local Wisconsin artist, drew a Flambeau Summer poster featuring a large eagle flying over the Flambeau River and a hand gripping a sign which said "Take Back the Site!" Organizers also met several times with the Rusk County sheriff and Ladysmith police to inform them of the group's plans and assure them that the protest would be peaceful and nonviolent.

The focus of the demonstration was the old town hall which had been sold to the company, a fitting symbol of the decline of local democracy. The town hall was on Highway 27, two miles south of Ladysmith and now directly across from the site of the proposed open-pit mine on the banks of the Flambeau River. It had been jacked up and moved across the highway after Kennecott had bought the land of the original site. It was the perfect site for a reaffirmation of Rusk County citizens' rights to control their own future.

As the date for the rally drew near, however, the town of Grant passed a new ordinance requiring groups seeking to hold rallies or demonstrations on town property to first obtain a permit. The group would also be required to obtain liability insurance coverage "of the same type and in like amounts [$2 million] as those carried by the town."[46] Robert Plantz, chair of the town board, predicted that mass arrests would occur if Flambeau Summer organizers violated the ordinance. "We have a pretty big jail, and I expect we will have that jail full."[47]

Cheryl Barker, a member of RCCAG, had informed the township authorities of the plans for the rally in early May. The first indication that there were any problems came when the township passed the new ordinance on June 11, 1991. "All of a sudden this ordinance springs up," said Jan Jacoby, a spokesperson for Flambeau Summer. "This is a blatant attempt to stop us. What can we do except assemble anyway? We do have a right to assemble unless they have changed the U.S. Constitution in the last couple of weeks."

The group made an attempt to comply with the ordinance, but after several attempts to obtain liability insurance Cheryl Barker concluded that such coverage was simply not available. "After Lloyd's of London said no, I didn't call State Farm," she noted. Meanwhile, the American Civil Liberties Union (ACLU) offered to assist the group in challenging the action of the town board. Chris Ahmuty of the Milwaukee ACLU office said that the ordinance was unconstitutional because it posed impossible-to-meet criteria and was drawn up specifically to stop the rally. "We would hope that the town of Grant will recognize that everyone would be better off if constitutional rights were upheld," said Ahmuty.[48]

A week before the planned rally, the town reluctantly gave Flambeau Summer its permission to use the town hall property. The threat of an ACLU lawsuit was a major factor in the town's decision to suspend the ordinance. "There were some errors in the ordinance, I guess," said town board chair Plantz.[49] Meanwhile, the Rusk County Board passed a trespassing ordinance and raised the maximum fine from $500 to $1,000, and the maximum jail sentence from 30 to 90 days. Larry Mercando sent a letter to all Rusk County residents warning them that "a small group of people...who just hate to admit that they're wrong and don't know what else to do...will carry out their threat to disrupt our community."[50] He also released a slick booklet printed on recycled paper detailing and rebutting 83 alleged "misrepresentations, distortions and half-truths" used by opponents of the Ladysmith mine.[51]

But the most serious effort to sabotage the rally came from Rusk County Sheriff Dean Meyer and Ladysmith Police Chief Norm Rozak. Just five days before the rally, they issued a press statement saying that they had received death threats through the mail warning them not to help the mining company.[52] In light of the death threats and the possibility of violence, they urged "both opponents and supporters" of the mine to stay away from the July 6 rally. Flambeau Summer organizers were highly suspicious of the "death threats" because of the timing of the announcement. According to Meyer and Rozak, the death threats had been received the previous May, but they did not make them public at the time. They also failed to do any further investigation of the threats or to notify the FBI of a potential federal felony crime.

Despite the political atmosphere of fear and intimidation created by local authorities and the mining company, over 500 people assembled at the Grant town hall on July 6, 1991. Jan Jacoby gave tobacco in traditional Chippewa fashion to a tribal elder, Eugene Begay, and asked him to open the rally with a pipe ceremony. Begay pointed his carved wood pipe to the north, south, east, and west asking the spirit in each direction "to help us in our cause" to prevent the construction of the Ladysmith mine. As he spoke, a bald eagle flew overhead and was joined by a second eagle as the crowd broke out in applause. Said Begay:

> I asked the spirits to acknowledge us, because we are a part of the movement that all humanity should be involved in, and that is the preservation of our land and our environment and all the things that were given to us originally for the life of the human beings, and of the birds, and of the fish, and of the animals, and of the vegetation. My people tell me from a long time ago that everything was created to be in balance, that one should not overpower the other, and that we should all live together in harmony, and that creation was definitely a purpose to be of great diversity. That's why we are of different races of people, that's why there are different

animals and fish and birds. That's why there are different types of vegetation, because creation, life, was made to be a diverse life. And we need to preserve that. The earth upon which we stand is Mother Earth.

And so when I performed the pipe ceremony this day I offered, to the spirit in the earth, the tobacco, and told the spirit that we are here today to protect this land. We are here today to protect all life that is a part of this land. Not only here in Ladysmith, Wisconsin but in the surrounding area, because my people say that everything is to be in balance in order for life to survive, in order for life to be good, in order for people to be happy and healthy, there must be a balance in life. And that's why we are here today—to stop the destruction to Mother Earth, the removal of these things they want out of it, so that we can preserve life for ourselves and our children, and our children's children and the children yet to come.

If it does not happen we will all cease to be. And there will be another *moosh-ka-nong,* what the Indian people talk about, another third creation will have to take place again. And so I am here today, ladies and gentlemen, because I too believe in life. I too believe in the goodness of life. I too believe that we must be in harmony with each other, to stand up for each others' rights, to be alive, and to practice our life the way we want to do it, the way that is good for all of us.

Earlier in the day, a rally and news conference in support of the mine attracted fewer than two dozen people to Falge Park on the edge of Ladysmith. Linda Lybert, executive director of the Ladysmith Area Chamber of Commerce, said: "It's not the Rusk County residents fighting about this. It is the outsiders coming in."[53] However, at the "Take Back the Site" rally, Al Barker, a Rusk County supervisor and member of RCCAG, called Ladysmith "a mining town that has been bought and paid for by the Flambeau Mining Company to silence critics." Longtime local mine opponent Roscoe Churchill then received a standing ovation when he told the crowd that "The only outsiders here are working for the mining company." At about 2:00 pm, Bob Kaspar of Earth First! climbed up the hay wagon that served as a speaker's platform and urged the crowd to march to the mine site. "It's time to take back the site. It's time. Its' time. Remember, be happy. We're celebrating the site. We're making a statement about the protection of that spot on the planet."[54] The protestors marched in a long, slow procession down Highway 27 toward the mine site. They sang "This Land is Your Land" and carried large, colorful banners that read "RTZ—Go Mine in Hell" and "People Act Now—Claim Your Power."

Over 100 demonstrators marked their arrival on mining company property with chants, drumming, and a prayer. The entire event was broadcast live over WOJB-FM. The announced purpose of the action was to "reclaim" the site for the local citizens whose democratic rights had been eroded by RTZ. In London, PARTIZANS arranged to have a 15-foot-long, five-foot-high and four-feet-wide aluminum dragonfly land on the steps at RTZ's corporate headquarters. A large sign, attached to the dragonfly, said: "I will remain here, on the steps of the world's most powerful mining company, until it announces the closure of the Flambeau mine. At that point I will fly to Rusk County, Wisconsin and celebrate on the steps of the Grant town hall."[55]

After a successful overnight occupation, the protestors, having achieved their tactical goal, decided to leave of their own accord. "We now call upon Kennecott/RTZ to postpone construction at the site until adequate studies have been done," said Jan Jacoby. "If the company ignores this call for a postponement, we will take further action to prevent mine construction." The peaceful rally and festive mine site occupation made headlines in all the state and regional press, radio, and television. The coverage emphasized the proximity of the proposed mine to the Flambeau River, the growing coalition between Indians and environmentalists, and a recent discovery of endangered species near the mining site (discussed further in Chapter Six). None of the company's dire predictions about violence and community disruption occurred. From RTZ's perspective it was a public relations disaster. Larry Mercando responded with a radio and television ad campaign spending about $10,000, primarily on television stations in northern Wisconsin.[56]

This did little to slow the momentum of the direct action movement against the mine. Once it became clear that Kennecott/RTZ was not going to delay mine construction, Flambeau Summer activated its phone tree and asked for volunteers to block mine construction. On July 10, 15 activists assembled at the entrance to the mine site and unfurled a large black banner with white letters which read: "Stop! Wait! Endangered Animals Here. DNR, Where Are You?" Declaring the day an "environmental holiday," nine activists blocked vehicles entering the gate and sat in front of a mobile generator, thus ending work for the day. Rusk County sheriff's deputies waited patiently until all newspaper reporters had left, then quickly arrested the nine people. However, Luciano Matheron and Todd Price, two camera-operators for Madison public access cable television station WYOU, caught the arrests on videotape. Sheriff Dean Meyer and another deputy asked them for their tapes. When they hesitated, they were threatened with arrest. At one point, a deputy wrestled with Matheron for his camera. The tapes were seized but later returned to the reporters when the ACLU threatened to get involved.

Tom Starr, acting Rusk County assistant district attorney, said copies of the tape would be kept as possible additional evidence in the prosecution of the nine on trespassing violations. "If I had been with a news team from the network, I don't think they would have done that," said Matheron. "It is very easy to push us around because we are not like a network."[57] The seizure of the videotapes made headlines, along with the arrests, and focused public attention on the police-state mentality in Rusk County. The editor of the *Superior Evening Telegram* called the sheriff's actions "the best imitation we've yet seen of a storm trooper." The Madison-based *Capital Times* was equally outraged: "There would be no free press in this country if a reporter's work automatically became property of the local police department. If that's the way the sheriff and the district attorney operate in Rusk County, then there is no free press there…The Rusk County sheriff's action would be welcomed in many of the world's totalitarian regimes. But it flies in the face of everything that our Constitution stands for and protects."[58]

Sheriff Dean Meyer admitted that the protestors offered no resistance to arrest. Yet, the nine were handcuffed and taken to the Rusk County jail in Ladysmith where they were fingerprinted, photographed, and issued jail uniforms, a highly unusual procedure for a civil offense. Bail had been set and they planned to remain in jail overnight, when they were suddenly recharged on state, rather than county, trespass charges. This resulted in substantially higher bail, but a call from the ACLU to the Rusk County district attorney resulted in the surprising, unconditional release of all nine protestors on that same Wednesday afternoon. "We're going back Friday, and we'll keep going back in a series of these confrontations until we can get the company to suspend operations," said Jeff Peterson, a spokesperson for Flambeau Summer.[59]

Larry Mercando responded to the arrests with an angry press release. He said that construction would continue at the mine site and that "neither the Flambeau Mining Company nor the people of Wisconsin are going to turn their backs on the truth just because a handful of malicious, uninformed people…now decide to resort to a last-ditch campaign of threats and intimidation." Despite the testimony of the arresting officers and numerous eyewitnesses about the peaceful nature of the protest, Mercando insisted that mine opponents harassed workers and attempted to seize and destroy construction tools. "Obviously we had hoped that the protestors would abide by their promise to engage only in nonviolent activities, but I can't say that I am surprised the promise wasn't honored," Mercando said. "They're frustrated that they can't win, and that frustration seems to have persuaded them they're entitled to ignore the law, threaten other people, and destroy private property."[60] Subsequent newsreports quoted eyewitnesses about the peaceful nature of the protest, but no reporter ever confronted Mercando about his blatant misrepresentation of the protest.

After the first arrests, there was increased interest in the next protest. About 30 Flambeau Summer activists staged another protest two days later at the company's Ladysmith office. They had planned to occupy Larry Mercando's office, but when they found the door locked they sat down in front of the office instead. They hung a "Going Out of Business" sign on the company logo above the doorway and turned away United Parcel Service and Federal Express deliveries.

Two protestors were arrested when they climbed on the roof and hung a banner. Five more protestors were arrested when they refused to move away from the doorway. As the protestors were handcuffed and put into squad cars, the chief of police personally escorted Larry Mercando to a car where his personal security guard was waiting. All seven of those arrested were charged with disorderly conduct, fined $150, and released on signature bond. "We're not giving up," said Jan Jacoby. "We'll be back until we run out of people to do this."[61] Joyce Melville, a spokesperson for the Wisconsin Greens and one of those arrested, said the protest was necessary because "Our watchdog agency in the state, the Department of Natural Resources, doesn't seem to be doing what it's supposed to do. Every year the fish advisory list grows longer. There are more fish that more categories of people—kids, pregnant women—can't eat because they're poisoned. At some point it has to stop."[62]

Flambeau Summer did not stop, however. In an effort to garner national media attention, Earth First! member Bob Kaspar of Madison showed up at the company's corporate headquarters in Salt Lake City, Utah on August 7, 1991. He went directly to the 16th floor and asked to speak to Kennecott's top management about the Ladysmith project. A spokesperson told Kaspar that Larry Mercando was the only one who speaks for the company on that issue. "Yes, I know," said Kaspar, "that's the problem." As he was being escorted out of the building by security guards, the local press was there to record the protest and ask some questions. Kennecott's pollution problems at its Bingham Canyon open-pit copper mine in Salt Lake City had been headline news the week before. The company had agreed to pay the state $12 million for its decades of contamination of western

Salt Lake County water as a result of its mining operations.[63] Kaspar seized the moment to call upon the company to suspend operations at the Ladysmith mine site while the DNR completed its studies of the endangered species that had recently been discovered near the site. The one-person press conference made the headlines in Salt Lake City and was picked up by the wire services and reported nationwide. The event was planned to coincide with a Flambeau Summer informational picket outside Kennecott headquarters in Ladysmith.

The promising direct action efforts of Flambeau Summer kept the struggle against the mine alive and in the public eye. Yet direct action strategies were also coupled with a promising new legal strategy based on endangered species and Indian treaty rights. This new strategic element offered renewed energy to the native-environmental movement against the mine. It also sparked the interest (as well as the financial and legal resources) of the Sierra Club, thus breaking the long-standing hands-off attitude toward the anti-mine effort held by the state's mainstream environmental organizations. Where they once had seen the struggle against the mine as unrealistic, they began to see that the rise of a regional mining district was not inevitable. Clearly, Kennecott had not achieved its goal of neutralizing its opposition.

Chapter 6

Endangered Species and Treaty Rights

Just as the publicity campaign for Flambeau Summer was beginning to move into high gear, two purple wartyback clams were found less than a mile downstream from Kennecott's proposed Ladysmith mine. This opened the possibility of an effective legal challenge to the mine. The clams, or mussels, were found in the Flambeau River by a DNR survey crew working on a Federal Energy Regulatory Commission relicensing application for the Thornapple Dam. The purple wartyback mussel, between two and three inches in diameter, had been placed on the state's endangered species list in August 1989. "These things turn up," said DNR mine project manager Robert Ramharter. "Trying to survey for things that are very rare is difficult to do." Mine opponents saw the discovery quite differently. "It seemed like everything was going against us," said Cheryl Barker, a member of RCCAG from Glen Flora. "All that testing they said they'd done...and the EIS said there were no endangered species."[1]

So why should anyone care about the discovery of a tiny mussel in the Flambeau River? Because mussels "tell us something about the health of our rivers. If you have fresh-water mussels, you know you have good-quality water," according to Marian Havlik, a malacologist, or mussel expert, from La Crosse, Wisconsin.[2] The purple wartyback mussel also revealed how the integrity of the DNR environmental review process had been corrupted by mining industry pressure.

The Clamgate Memo

In their 1990 EIS for the proposed Ladysmith mine, the DNR said there were no threatened or endangered species near the mine site. Yet, an internal DNR memo dated July 5, 1989, eight months before the DNR released the final EIS, revealed that the DNR was withholding information about the likely presence of endangered species in the Flambeau River. The memo from Ronald Nicotera, director of the State Bureau of Endangered Resources was obtained by Democratic representatives Frank Boyle and Harvey Stower in an open-records request. Nicotera notes within the memo the absence of mussel surveys, at any time, upon the section of the Flambeau River closest to the project site: "Comprehensive endangered re-source surveys may not have been completed for this project area. As a result, our data files may be incomplete. The absence of known occurrences does not preclude the possibility of their presence. Specifically, no mussel surveys have ever been performed for this part of the Flambeau River."[3]

Nicotera's memo goes on to identify three endangered mussels which were known to occur in the nearby Chippewa River and might be present in the Flambeau. These included the purple wartyback mussel. He recommended that: "Due to the lack of existing aquatic species information, especially with respect to mussels, we recom-mend that all areas of potential impact be surveyed for endangered species."[4] Robert Ramharter, Ladysmith project coordinator, ignored Nicotera's warnings and did no studies. Neither the draft EIS nor the final EIS mentioned DNR staff concerns about the lack of surveys of endangered species. Quite to the contrary, the final EIS states that "No threatened or endangered plant or animal species are known to inhabit the project area of the Flambeau River adjacent to the mine site."[5]

In a June 17, 1991 memo to DNR Executive Assistant Linda Bochert, Ramharter attempted to rationalize the failure of the DNR to follow up on Nicotera's recommendation to survey the Flambeau River for mussels. Ramharter explained that the decision not to conduct the surveys had been based upon his belief that "the project would have little impact on aquatic organisms." But this speculation is contradicted by his own admission in the same memo that "the body of scientific knowledge on mussels and the DNR's expertise in the area is still in an early stage of development. At the time the field surveys for the mine were designed and conducted, the DNR had very limited programs and capabilities to deal with rare mussel species." If the DNR did not have the capacity to do the surveys, state law provides that the DNR could have contracted some other agency to do the work and charged the cost to Kennecott/RTZ. "In retrospect," Ramharter wrote, "it obviously would have been desirable to conduct the recommended mussel surveys."[6]

Subsequent DNR surveys in the Flambeau River downstream from the mine site discovered three additional threatened and/or endangered species—the bullhead mussel, the pygmy snaketail dragonfly, and the gilt darter minnow. An additional study was done to determine if the threatened red horse minnow was in the river. It had been found last in a 1972 survey. After the discovery of the bullhead mussel, mining opponents asked that the DNR put the Ladysmith mine on hold. "If the clam goes today, the walleyes may go next year and the muskies may go the year after that," said Secretary of State Douglas La Follette. But Robert Ramharter said the discovery of the clams did not affect the DNR's conclusions in its EIS on the project. "The EIS states that all aquatic organisms are afforded a high degree of protection, and that's the case," he said.[7]

At the same time, the DNR issued a gag order on David Heath, the DNR's mussel expert. Linda Bochert, executive assistant to DNR Secretary Besadny, said that until the DNR issued a statement regarding the endangered species, Heath could not talk on the subject. The gag order reinforced the belief of mine opponents that the DNR was engaged in a coverup of the scandal. "I think it's outrageous that a state agency, which is supposed to protect the environment, which belongs to the people of Wisconsin, has forbidden a state employee to talk about environmental problems that they are clearly trying to cover up," said Secretary La Follette.[8]

The credibility of the DNR's mine review process came under intense scrutiny at the precise moment that the Wisconsin Assembly

was debating Representative Harvey Stower's mining moratorium
bill. In announcing the existence of the clamgate memo in DNR files,
Representative Frank Boyle (D-Superior) asked "What else don't we
know about? What else has been convenient or inconvenient to
release in relation to the development of the mine in Ladysmith?"[9]
Boyle suggested that the DNR is a political agency that may have
been moved by intense lobbying to issue a permit for the Kennecott
mine.

The revelation of the DNR's clamgate memo surprised and
shocked many legislators who would never have considered voting
for a two-year mining moratorium. Stower's bill passed 54 to 44. It did
not get enough votes to automatically send it on to the Senate,
however. That would have to wait until the fall 1991 session of the
legislature. The passage of the bill was nonetheless a powerful
political statement on the eve of construction of the Ladysmith mine.
"Even if the moratorium is eventually defeated, it has been a victory
for environmentalists," said Robert Fassbender, director of environmental policy for the Wisconsin Manufacturers and Commerce Association. "If they make enough noise, mining companies might
conclude that it is politically too unstable to invest in Wisconsin," he
said.[10] A few weeks earlier, NDU Resources of Vancouver, Canada,
had pulled out of a joint venture with E. K. Lehman of Minneapolis.
They had been seeking a permit for a proposed underground gold
and copper mine in the Chequamegon National Forest in Taylor
County, in north-central Wisconsin. Company President James Stephen said he was wary of mining opposition and "the perception of
environmental concerns in Wisconsin."[11]

LCO Demands a Supplemental EIS and Suspension of Mine Permits

On July 9, 1991 Gaiashkibos sent a letter to DNR Secretary
Besadny suggesting that the DNR had failed in its responsibility to
inform the public about the likely effects of the proposed Ladysmith
mine. "It is now clear," said Gaiashkibos, "that the action by your

Department was taken without due regard to the full environmental impact of the project and that the parties and the public were misinformed as to potential impacts upon endangered and threatened species due to the inadequacy of the Final Environmental Impact Statement [FEIS] in this area. Further, the determination by the hearing examiner that the FEIS was adequate was made upon a record burdened with deliberate omissions within the FEIS and attendant testimony." In light of the failure of the DNR to carry out its responsibility, the Lac Courte Orielles Chippewa demanded that the DNR prepare a supplemental environmental impact statement (SEIS) to consider the potential impact on threatened and endangered species of the proposed project. The Chippewa requested that such a study be done immediately, "and that the 11 project licenses and permits previously issued, be suspended during the pendency of this process."[12]

By the time the Chippewa had put these demands in writing, the DNR had come under considerable criticism from environmental groups, legislators, and Secretary of State Douglas La Follette. The DNR was now ready to do further testing on the wastewater discharge from the proposed mine to determine the effect on the threatened and endangered species. Robert Ramharter had abandoned his earlier position that all aquatic organisms were afforded a high degree of protection under the existing mine permit conditions. Now the official agency position was that the new tests were being done "because the clams may be more sensitive to some mine pollutants than originally thought."[13]

However, the DNR was not prepared to reopen the permit process by conducting a supplemental EIS, as requested by the Chippewa. Secretary Besadny said the DNR was not legally required to supplement its impact statement with information on endangered species that had been discovered in the river since the original document was written.[14] The department was most emphatic about its refusal to delay the beginning of mine construction while the studies were being done. In a particularly revealing comment, Robert Ramharter said he was confident that the mine wastewater could be cleaned enough to protect the clams "while not changing *the economics of the project for the mining company* [emphasis added]."[15] Mine critics immediately attacked this new study, calling it "whitewash" and "window dressing" as long as the mine was allowed to open. Secretary La Follette said the DNR was "irresponsible" in letting the mine open while important environmental testing was being done. "If they want these tests to be more than window dressing to cover their political decisions, they should delay the project," he said.[16]

On July 15, the Flambeau Summer coalition took its protest directly to DNR Secretary Besadny in Madison. About 15 protestors assembled outside the state office building in downtown Madison during lunch hour when many DNR employees were enjoying their lunch outside. Protestors distributed copies of a brochure entitled "Is the DNR telling us the truth?" which featured the "clamgate" memo. Several protestors wore pictures of endangered clams; one wore a Carroll Besadny mask and held a sign which read: "Kennecott's profits are certainly worth a couple of white lies and a couple of dead clams."

The protest then moved to the door of Besadny's office where Sean Guilfoyle, a coalition spokesperson, read a press statement which called upon the DNR to: (1) conduct a supplemental EIS on the endangered species; (2) stop all activity at the mine site until the supplemental EIS was completed; and (3) if the species could not be adequately protected, require changes in the conditions for the operation of the mine, including possible revocation of the permits. In return for not attempting to enter, and possibly to occupy, the secretary's office, the security guard promised that the secretary and his executive assistant, Linda Bochert, would meet with representatives of the coalition and exchange views before the press.

During the meeting, Secretary Besadny said he would take 30 days to respond to Flambeau Summer's request for a supplemental EIS. "We take this very seriously," he said.[17] He also said that halting construction was not necessary because Flambeau mining officials told him that it would be at least a year before wastewater from the project was discharged into the river. Sean Guilfoyle responded that the mine wastewater discharge was not the only concern. Site preparation itself had the potential to discharge sediments into the river that could harm the clams and the dragonflies. Furthermore, the longer the DNR allowed construction to continue, the more money would be invested and the harder it would be for the agency to order a halt to the project.

At the Natural Resources Board meeting on July 25 in Ashland, Wisconsin, Flambeau Summer spokespeople Jeff Peterson, Sean Guilfoyle, and David Skrupky repeated the coalition's three demands. The board refused to take any action on the coalition's demands. By this time, the Lac Courte Oriellles Chippewa and the John Muir chapter of the Sierra Club in Madison had agreed to file a joint lawsuit asking for a supplemental EIS and a halt to mine construction. "We were waiting to see if the Natural Resources Board would do anything," said Roger Buffett, attorney for the state Sierra Club. As soon as the national Sierra Club board in San Francisco approved the lawsuit, the state Sierra Club took the issue into Dane County Circuit Court. The suit charged that the DNR had failed to comply with state law in issuing permits for the mine. In particular, the permits were based upon an inadequate EIS which did not disclose the potential impact of the mine upon endangered and threatened species in the project area. Larry Mercando dismissed the lawsuit as "a gimmick to stop an environmentally benign mine. I don't think a judge that looks at the scientific evidence will ever dream of doing that. Every time you find an endangered species doesn't mean you have to do a new study."[18] In contrast, LCO Chippewa Vice-Chair Al Trepania argued: "We should not allow endangered species to perish because we did not have the time to look for them. The DNR shows such contempt for the chain of life that it does not even look for endangered species."[19]

Carl Zichella, regional director of the Sierra Club, explained why his organization was joining the Chippewa in their lawsuit:

> Since the contested Master Hearing it has appeared to many of us that the DNR has become increasingly hell bent to permit this mine regardless of any environmental considerations that might arise. We simply cannot trust the DNR to do what's right. They misled the public in the

EIS process. They have refused LCO's request to suspend the permits. They've told us to be patient and wait for a response to our own request, while they allow the mining company to begin their site preparation. Site preparation for the open-pit mine involves removing all vegetation on the site, erecting fences, and building roads. The DNR hasn't a clue what endangered resources may be on that site. They've never looked. We can't trust them to act expeditiously or in good faith.[20]

DNR spokesperson Linda Bochert defended her agency's actions, however. "When we found the endangered species there, we told people," she said. "They will be protected."[21] In fact, it was the *Wausau Daily Herald*, not the DNR, which first brought the discovery of the clams to public attention.[22] The clams were discovered on May 24, 1991, but the DNR waited 11 days, until June 4, to issue a press release. The DNR issued its press release on the same day that the *Wausau Daily Herald* story appeared. Robert Ramharter has stated that this is not an unusual delay, but mine critics wonder how long the DNR would have waited before making the discovery public.

While attorneys for Kennecott/RTZ promised rapid court intervention, construction activity was proceeding at an accelerated pace in anticipation of a possible court-ordered halt to further construction. Flambeau Summer responded immediately. In early August, 13 Flambeau Summer activists visited Kennecott's downtown Ladysmith office and served Larry Mercando with a citizens' injunction. "Kennecott/RTZ's frenetic construction activity next to the Flambeau River has created a state of environmental emergency in Ladysmith," said Jan Jacoby. "We are here today to present you with a citizens' injunction to halt all activity at the mine site until the courts have ruled on the merits of the case against the DNR. To deliberately accelerate the pace of construction activity while these critical legal and ecological issues are unresolved is eco-terrorism."[23] Mercando met with the protestors and told them, "We feel it's an environmentally safe project," adding that because of that, he saw no reason to stop the project now.[24] When two police officers arrived to clear the office lobby, all but two of the protestors left voluntarily. Ray Starrett and Phyllis Hodgson were arrested and charged with disorderly conduct. The latest arrests brought the total to 18 arrested since mine construction began. Five of those arrested had entered pleas of not guilty and would appear in Rusk County court in October 1991.[25]

Meanwhile, in Madison, the DNR announced that it would order a supplemental EIS to assess the effects of the mine on several endangered species. However, they found no reason to halt mine construction activity while the study was being conducted. Carl Zichella, the spokesperson for the Sierra Club, immediately characterized the announcement as a move designed to relieve pressure from the lawsuit filed earlier in the week. The first hearing on the suit was scheduled for the following Monday, August 5, 1991. "I think this one's a no-brainer for the DNR," said Zichella. "They had to do a supplemental [EIS]. I'm just surprised it took them so long." George Meyer, a top DNR official, said the announcement was "clearly not" a reaction to the suit because the staff analysis had been in the works for six weeks. He said the DNR's information didn't show the current clearing of land at the site to be environmentally damaging, given a strict erosion control program. Zichella said that the Sierra Club had no intention of dropping its lawsuit, which sought to stop work on the project while a new EIS was done. "In order for the EIS to mean anything, you have to stop the work," he said. "Why in God's name doesn't the DNR pull the permits. What's the rush?"[26]

At the preliminary hearing on the suit, Dane County Circuit Court Judge George Northrup allowed Kennecott/RTZ to join the suit, in part, to protect the $19 million it claimed already to have spent on the project. Sierra Club attorney Roger Buffett then asked for an immediate restraining order to halt work at the site until the suit was settled. "We're concerned that by the end of this week all the vegetation on the site will be gone," Buffett told the judge.[27] Attorney John Koeppl, representing the company, and Assistant Attorney General Lisa Levin, representing the DNR, both argued that the Sierra Club and the Chippewa were not entitled to a temporary restraining order because no factual showing of irreparable harm had been made. The judge refused to grant the restraining order at the preliminary hearing but set a formal hearing on the order for August 23.

As preparation for the suit against the DNR, malacologist Marian Havlik recruited a dozen volunteers—a kind of "citizens' DNR"—to conduct a survey of clams in the Flambeau River both above and below the mine site. Havlik, who holds three federal and four state permits to collect endangered species, had been retained by the Chippewa to provide expert testimony for their lawsuit against the DNR. "We shouldn't have to do this," said Havlik. "The DNR should have seen that this was done before they issued the environmental impact statement."[28] Before entering the river on August 17, Havlik had notified both the DNR and the mining company of her survey plans. On the Saturday morning of the survey, Northern States Power Company, the operator of the dam on the Flambeau River, unexpectedly released a large amount of water which raised the river level two feet above normal and made survey work difficult and dangerous. As the two survey boats were navigating under a bridge, the swift-running current capsized one of the boats, endangering lives and resulting in a loss of expensive camera and diving equipment. No one was injured, but a wrecker had to be called to dislodge the capsized boat from where it had been wrapped around the bridge's concrete support by the force of the current. The survey had to be called off. Normally the dam operator does not change the water level on the weekend because it may endanger those who use the river for recreation. Flambeau Summer activists suspected, but could not prove, foul play.

Meanwhile, in Madison, Assistant State Attorney General Lisa Levin filed for dismissal of the lawsuit because the time to challenge an EIS on the project had long passed. She argued that the 1989 memo from the director of the agency's Endangered Resources Bureau was in DNR mine project files available to both LCO and the Sierra Club before the 1990 master hearing on the EIS. As a result, Levin's brief said, any challenge to the EIS based on that memo should have been made last year, before the permits were issued.[29] The logical implication of the state's motion is that the public should not assume that the EIS is a truthful document and should take responsibility for verifying every statement in the EIS by examining DNR files in detail.

On August 23, however, Judge Northrup held a daylong hearing on a temporary restraining order against further mine construction. The judge said a fundamental issue of the hearing would be: "Did the public have any meaningful opportunity to participate in [the environmental impact statement], if the public was led to believe that there were complete surveys of endangered species in the area, and if the public was led to believe there was no reason for concern in that regard."[30]

The first witness called by the Chippewa and the Sierra Club was Ronald Nicotera, director of the DNR's Endangered Resources Bureau. State law describes endangered species habitat as "unsuitable for mining" unless the species can be relocated.[31] Nicotera testified that no endangered species surveys were performed by the DNR during its environmental review of the Ladysmith mine project. Expert witnesses called by Kennecott and the DNR testified that development and operation of the mine would not affect the river or the endangered species. They also suggested that all three endangered species could be relocated into similar waterways elsewhere in the state.

Marian Havlik, testifying on behalf of the Chippewa, said that the mussels in the area of the mine "appear to be already stressed by environmental pollution which may be coming from towns, cities, and factories above the proposed mine site."[32] Moreover, scientists don't know what fish species hosts the larvae of the purple wartyback clam, Havlik said. Lacking that knowledge, it would be difficult to relocate the species. She also said that site preparation, including alteration of the flood plain, clearing the woods, and using heavy machinery along the river might be just enough damage to push the clams in that area to extinction.[33] Greg Busacker, a Minnesota Transportation Department aquatic biologist, said that the mine's slurry wall and flood control dike were inadequate and would not stop large amounts of sediment from entering the river during a heavy rain, smothering the clams.[34]

Arthur Clarke, the malacologist who testified on behalf of Kennecott, shocked the court when he said that the rare bullhead clam may have been "planted" to further confuse the mine permit process. "I feel it was planted in the river for someone to find," Clarke said. "It's the best way to cause trouble."[35] Chippewa attorney Larry Leventhal asked Clarke why he didn't say anything in his report about the potential planting of the clams. Clarke replied, "I didn't know I was going to be retained [by Kennecott]." Leventhal then asked him how mine opponents would have known exactly where to plant the clams, and all the other dead bullhead clam shells, so that he could find them. At that point, some of the courtroom spectators could hardly contain their laughter and Kennecott attorney John Koeppl objected to continuing this line of questioning. The judge dismissed the witness.

In his closing argument Larry Leventhal noted, "The fact is that the public was grossly misled. There was no proper environmental impact statement done regarding threatened or endangered species. If they're allowed to do it here, they'll do it again."[36] A decision had been expected at the end of the hearing, but Judge Northrup said he needed more time to consider the numerous records, arguments, and affidavits filed in the case. He would announce his decision on August 29.

Judge Orders Halt to Mine Construction

In the first restraining order decision in a Wisconsin court against a project failing to meet the standards of the Wisconsin Environmental Policy Act, Judge Northrup ordered Kennecott/RTZ to suspend work on the Ladysmith mine. The preliminary injunction required that "All permits issued which relate to either site preparation or mining operations and activities shall be suspended pending completion of a Supplemental Environmental Impact Study (SEIS) by the Department of Natural Resources."[37] This preliminary injunction would remain in effect until 30 days after the DNR issued a supplemental EIS on endangered species in the area. "The dangers are so great that the facts support the order," Northrup said.[38] The restraining order was not a complete ban on construction activity, however. In response to a motion by Kennecott attorney John Koeppl, the judge gave the company permission to proceed with erosion control and environmental protection measures at the mine site. This attempt to subvert the intent of the injunction was not unexpected. "As soon as they knew we filed the lawsuit, they started stripping away the soil," said Caryl Terrell, spokesperson for the Sierra Club's John Muir chapter. "If we have another big rainstorm like we did this spring we're going to have real problems."[39]

Judge Northrup said he could not specify what erosion control measures the company should take, but he made it clear he wanted the river protected. However, when John Koeppl suggested that the activity at the site consisted primarily of environmental protection measures, the judge made it clear that "anything that is going to involve a substantial investment is under the injunction. Given the size of the project and what is involved in it, the further along it goes, the more rationale there is for not stopping the project because of all that's invested in it," he said. "The more that's invested in this project, the more that's going to weigh against environmental interest groups and in favor of the mining company."[40] He added that he did not want to give Kennecott the opportunity to argue in a few months: "You can't stop it now." He denied another request from Koeppl that he delay his order to give the company time to appeal. He likewise denied Koeppl's request to require the Chippewa and the Sierra Club to put up a surety bond to cover the company's financial losses if the lawsuit were unsuccessful. Kennecott said the injunction would cause it to lose $650,000 each month that construction was suspended.

Lac Courte Oreilles chair Gaiashkibos declared Northrup's ruling a victory for the natural world. "The clams won—temporarily," he said. He also expressed satisfaction that the Chippewa had the courage to initiate the action that had brought the construction to a halt. "I'm satisfied to know that we just didn't roll over on this thing. Just the dollars alone involved in taking on this huge conglomerate was a challenge," he said.[41] Roscoe Churchill of Ladysmith exclaimed: "We are all cheering up here. It has taken a lot of years for a judge to come along and make a decision as good as this one." When asked about the likely appeal of the decision by Kennecott, he said: "Maybe the litigation will make the company's owners tired of the fact that they can't ramrod this down the throats of the people of Wisconsin."[42] While the Chippewa and the Sierra Club had successfully challenged the world's largest mining company and the Wisconsin DNR, bringing the project to an abrupt halt, Larry Mercando had no comment for the press.

Despite Judge Northrup's injunction, however, Kennecott continued clearing the site and constructing settling ponds on August 30 and 31. When all of the parties to the lawsuit met on September 4 to negotiate a formal written agreement about what activities would be permitted to protect the river, each side accused the other of misinterpreting the judge's ruling. Carl Zichella, Sierra Club spokesperson, accused the company of going beyond stabilizing what's already been done and undertaking major new expenses, such as installing a large plastic liner for the waste stockpile area. Larry Mercando complained that the company had already ordered the liner and would have to bear additional costs that were unrelated to long-term stabilization of the site if they were not allowed to install it.[43] With the threat of being held in contempt of court, the company reluctantly agreed to a site revegetation plan as an alternative to the plastic liner. At the same time, the company announced plans to appeal Judge Northrup's order. John Koeppl said that he thought the judge had neither the legal right to take the case, nor grounds to stop the project.[44] Larry Mercando told a reporter that there was a "reasonable chance" that an appellate court would overturn the August 29 order. And, he said, the restraining order could be lifted by the appeals court judges before they made a decision.[45]

Over the weekend of September 6, a rainfall of less than two inches washed away the erosion control structures on the site. Prior to the injunction, the company had accelerated its topsoil removal activity with insufficient attention to erosion control measures. Despite the company's claim that environmental protection was a critical element of site preparation, aerial flyovers of the site by Chippewa consultants and photographers revealed minimal erosion control measures until several days before the August 23 court hearing on the temporary restraining order. At that hearing, Kennecott construction manager Robert Sinclair produced maps and photographs purporting to show a sophisticated system of straw bale dikes, silt fences, and settling ponds. According to Sinclair, this system was designed to manage runoff from a rainfall of 4.6 inches in 24 hours. After the two-inch rainfall, however, Ladysmith residents photographed a plume of mud in the Flambeau River, stretching a mile downstream from the mine site. The news release issued by Larry Mercando suggested that "over six inches of rain" had fallen, in contrast to the 1.78 inches reported by the DNR ranger station at Ladysmith. The company's press release also blamed Northrup's injunction for "preventing completion of some key components of the erosion control and surface water management plan."[46]

The company's accelerated pre-injunction construction activity not only had serious environmental consequences, it had social and political ones as well. Additional workers were hired while the judge was taking time to make his decision about the injunction. By the time Judge Northrup issued his order, 75 employees were working at the site and five state construction firms were contracted. The layoffs that followed the judge's order created an opportunity for the Ladysmith Chamber of Commerce to focus local resentment against "outside protestors" and the mass media, which had given prominent coverage to the environmental issues involved in the mine controversy. "It's never been a secret that the majority of people here in Rusk County are supportive of the Flambeau Mining Company and the mine," said Tom Pynch, president of the Ladysmith Area Chamber of Commerce.[47]

The mine support group organized a half-mile-long caravan of heavy equipment and cars from the Grant town hall to the Rusk County courthouse where a state legislative mining committee held hearings on September 20, 1991. The following week, the group took out a full-page ad in the *Ladysmith News* which said that the court injunction imposed by Judge Northrup would result in "over 100 jobs lost in the next six weeks," including ten Rusk County contractors. The ad concluded: "It is not right that oppositionists who are not Rusk County residents and are not being affected by the recent injunction, impose their views on the people of the county who live, work, pay taxes, and want the further growth and economic development of the area."[48] This carefully orchestrated political campaign did not escape Judge Northrup's attention. In a letter to all the parties in the lawsuit, the judge encouraged the parties "to try the issues in Court, not the news media. If the news media in northern Wisconsin is accurate, the public is intentionally being misled about the legal issues and Court ruling in a massive public relations effort. This unnecessary expense is contrary to orderly resolution of the issues in a legal proceeding."[49]

The Politics of the Supplemental EIS

The outcome of the Ladysmith mine controversy depended, in large part, on how the DNR handled the study of endangered and threatened species. In a status report issued prior to the court order, the DNR made a number of recommendations indicating their approach to the studies:[50]

- Although not legally required, the Department should prepare a supplement to the EIS documenting the results of the endangered resource studies.
- Identification of the host fish species for the purple wartyback clam is not necessary to provide protection to either the host fish or the clam.
- Toxicity testing on the purple wartyback's host species or the pygmy snaketail dragonfly is probably not possible and is not necessary for protecting these species.

In response, the Sierra Club had made it clear to the DNR that such an approach, relying primarily upon a literature search and short-term bioassay and toxicity studies, was not sufficient "to determine the effects of construction and operation at the mine on endangered and threatened species." In a letter to Secretary Besadny, the Sierra Club outlined five areas that should be covered in any supplemental EIS:[51]

- Survey for all terrestrial and aquatic endangered species which may be present at or near the mine site;
- Determine the life cycles of the endangered and threatened species already discovered;
- Identify existing threats to the endangered and threatened species, and how mine activities might cause synergistic and/or cumulative detrimental effects;
- Identify the host species of the known endangered clams and invertebrate species, and any existing, mine-related and synergistic or cumulative threats to the host species; and
- Identify all toxic chemicals presently in the river, their sources and concentrations, and their likelihood to produce synergistic or cumulative negative effects on the known endangered and threatened species, or any others subsequently discovered.

Obviously this kind of study would take longer than the three months the DNR had anticipated. However, as Zichella emphasized, "it would take more time to litigate an inadequate attempt to supplement the original EIS." The DNR's initial response to the Sierra Club's suggestions indicated that the mine permit process was still on the "fast track." Steven Ugoretz, acting director of the DNR's Bureau of Environmental Analysis and Review, wrote that "the Department believes the SEIS has no legal basis and has, therefore, no mandatory process, content, or scoping requirements associated with it." Furthermore, "basic scientific research is not normally considered appropriate for EIS or regulatory purposes."[52]

The lengths to which the DNR was prepared to go to get this mine underway became clear in the aftermath of the September 1991 failure of Kennecott's erosion control system. Glenn Miller, the DNR diver who discovered the purple wartyback mussel in the Flambeau River, was denied permission to survey the river for possible damage to the endangered mussels. Now a staff biologist for the Great Lakes Indian Fish and Wildlife Commission (GLIFWC), Miller maintained that his ex-superiors didn't want him to interfere with the DNR's accelerated schedule to complete the supplemental EIS on the endangered species.[53] In classic bureaucratic doublespeak, the DNR stated that the "temporary erosion control structures functioned as designed...While there were two failures of structures during these storms [one straw bale barrier and a short segment of filter fabric fence], these failures represent *a very small fraction of the site's overall erosion control system* [emphasis added]."[54] The critical issue, however, is not the magnitude of the failure, but the impact of the sedimentation upon the endangered species. In the absence of any surveys of the river, the DNR had no scientific basis for evaluating the possible harm to endangered species.

In their rush to complete the SEIS as quickly as possible, the DNR also ignored the advice of their own mussel expert, who strongly urged the DNR to use the purple wartyback mussel, rather than the more readily available paper floater mussel *(Anodonta imbecillis),* for the toxicity tests. "As I understand it," said DNR mussel expert David Heath, "the purpose of doing bioassay tests is to ensure protection of endangered mussels. *A. imbecillis* is a very common, ubiquitous, environmentally generalized, and tolerant species. I am afraid test results using this animal *may not translate into usable information for the goal of listed species protection* [emphasis added]."[55]

The DNR's rush was also evident in the way they went about asking for public comments on the proposed scope of study of the endangered species. The announcement was made so quietly that most environmental groups that had been following the issue did not learn of the three-week public comment period until the Sierra Club issued an emergency action bulletin. The DNR's original announcement was not labeled "urgent news" and was not distributed to newspapers around the state. "They pretend they're going to listen to what the public has to say, but in actuality they've made up their minds to do a half-baked job," said Sierra Club regional director Carl Zichella. "It's essentially a fraud. The decision has been made, and now they're trying to justify their decision before it comes out. The most important thing to Tommy Thompson and the DNR is to allow the mine to proceed." While disagreeing with Zichella's characterization of the DNR's political motivation, George Albright, chief of the DNR's environmental review section, did agree that the key issue was a procedural one: "They want to open the entire process to public debate and that isn't appropriate in our view."[56]

Just as the DNR was getting ready to release its SEIS, the DNR's Bureau of Endangered Resources announced that a rare dragonfly found near the minesite the previous summer (1991) had just been identified and would be recommended for protection as an endangered species. The new dragonfly brought the total number of endangered species found near the proposed minesite to six. Bill Smith, of the Bureau of Endangered Resources said that the agency would recommend that the new dragonfly, informally called the St. Croix dragonfly, be included on state and federal endangered species lists. Although the dragonfly found near the St. Croix, Chippewa, and Flambeau rivers is so exclusive to those rivers that it hasn't been officially named yet, Robert Ramharter, DNR mining coordinator, said that the discovery of the new dragonfly should not affect the project. "The protection we already have in place is applicable to all species of dragonflies," he said. Larry Leventhal, attorney for the Lac Courte Oreilles Chippewa, disagreed, arguing that the specific requirements of the new species needed to be considered before mining could be allowed. "To say that because of unique conditions this [dragonfly] only exists in two or three rivers in the world, and then to say this species doesn't need to be studied to see what unique conditions it requires—I doubt if [Ramharter] said that with a straight face," said Leventhal.[57]

On April 15, 1992, the DNR officially released its whitewashed supplemental study which assured the public that the operation of the mine would not harm the endangered species near the minesite. While reassuring the public, the DNR admitted that they had not done surveys to determine which species were present at the minesite: "Additional sampling would be necessary to verify that the species [six different species of dragonflies identified in a literature search] do actually exist at this location in the Flambeau River. If all of these species actually occur at this site, it would be considered an unusually diverse dragonfly community which includes several species considered rare or uncommon in the state."[58] Dr. Ken Parejko, the aquatic biologist whose biological monitoring proposal for the Flambeau River had been rejected by the Rusk County board, asked the obvious question about the DNR's scientific logic: "How can we know what effect the mine might have on endangered or threatened species without even knowing what those species are?"[59]

Before the Chippewa and the Sierra Club had a chance to respond to the DNR study, Larry Mercando announced plans to resume mine construction on May 14, 1992. But the DNR had not scheduled a public hearing on the study until June 3, 1992, almost three weeks after mine construction would have begun. Having decided that the study was not legally required, the DNR argued that it had no legal authority to stop Kennecott/RTZ from proceeding on May 14. By emphasizing that the "supplement" to the EIS on the mine project "does not necessarily have any legal status or function" the DNR could also avoid compliance with the public participation requirements that would normally govern the SEIS process.[60]

In response to this ducking of public comment prior to mine construction, Flambeau Summer called for a "citizens' hearing" at DNR headquarters in Madison on April 29, 1992. More than 40 people took over the public area of the DNR's Bureau of Environmental Review and stated their objections to the SEIS. Secretary of State Douglas La Follette joined the protestors and called the SEIS a "fairly slipshod study" that lopsidedly cited only certain experts' opinions.[61] Flambeau Summer also announced that the coalition was planning civil disobedience when mine construction resumed on May 14. When asked about the resumption of civil disobedience at the minesite, project manager Larry Mercando told a reporter for London's *Financial Times* that "we are ready and prepared for more attacks by environmentalists. They never give up."[62]

Defending One's Homeland

Resistance to the mine reached a new level when Anishinabé treaty rights activist Walt Bresette climbed over a ten-foot security fence carrying a war club once used by Black Hawk and "counted coup," a symbolic scoring of victory against one's enemies, on some earth movers. Bresette, a member of the Red Cliff band of Lake Superior Chippewa and a founder of *Anishinaabe Niijii* and the Wisconsin Greens, hit the machines with his war club but did no physical damage. With the help of three other Flambeau Summer activists—Jan Jacoby, Sean Guilfoyle, and Sharon Gulseth—he then removed, and respectfully folded, a U.S. flag flying high above a 50-foot pile of topsoil at the site being cleared for mining alongside the Flambeau River. The activists planned to hold the flag hostage until RTZ agreed to postpone further mine construction until a proper public hearing on the SEIS was held. Rusk County sheriff's deputies charged the protestors with trespassing and theft. Linda Craemer, an outspoken local critic of the mine, was also charged with theft when she caught the flag thrown to her over the security fence by one of the protestors. Craemer, who lived in nearby Bruce, was the first local activist to be arrested in connection with opposition to the mine. "It's obviously an illegal permit," said Walt Bresette, "so I don't recognize the authority of this mine to move forward." Bresette added:

> There's no proper environmental impact statement com-
> pleted on this. The DNR is a rogue government. The State
> of Wisconsin, has, in this permiting process, failed to
> protect the legal interests of the Lake Superior Chip-
> pewa...Wisconsin, under Governor Tommy Thompson,
> has a legal responsibility to protect the interests of the
> Lake Superior Chippewa. Instead he acts like a modern
> day Andrew Jackson who said, after the Cherokee of the
> 1830s won their rights, "Chief Justice Marshall has made
> his ruling, now let him enforce it." Shortly thereafter,
> despite being armed with the protections of the U.S.
> Constitution, the Cherokee were marched from their
> homelands; many died in what has been termed the "trail
> of tears." There will be no trail of tears from northern
> Wisconsin. It is time to stay and fight for our rights. I ask
> others to search their hearts and review the facts which

bring us today to these crossroads. This mine can only go
in if we all allow it. If it does go in then the entire region
will be opened up as a resource colony. Like Native
Americans of a century ago, whose land was "opened" to
homesteaders, now all who live in northern Wisconsin
will experience similar displacement. These resource
homesteaders will not care if you're Indian or white,
farmer, fisherman, or resorter. So, today, I stand with
those citizens who too have faith in doing what is right,
even having lost all optimism. I too am revolting against
a rogue government and a rapacious corporation. This
mine as proposed is bad for democracy, bad for the
economy, and ultimately a threat to the environment. I
call upon other tribal members to defend their home-
land.[63]

Within days of the arrests, the Lac Courte Orielles Chippewa
and the Sierra Club filed a new lawsuit, asking the court to order the
DNR to follow the Wisconsin Environmental Policy Act and conduct
public hearings on the supplemental EIS before allowing mining to
proceed. On June 3, 1992, two more Flambeau Summer activists were
arrested in Ladysmith as they tried to enter the building where the
DNR was conducting an "open house" hearing on the SEIS. John La
Forge, dressed as a large pig in a suitcoat and tie and identified as
RTZ, and Cassandra Dixon, once again dressed as the Grim Reaper
and carrying dead fish, were both arrested for their choice of clothing
and dragged from the hearing. Ladysmith police refused to say what
charges were being brought against the two. The Associated Press
story erroneously reported that they were charged with disorderly
conduct and had posted a $150 bond.[64] In fact, both were held in the
Rusk County Jail for 20 hours and then released without bail and no
charges were ever filed.[65] While the DNR was trying to suppress
dissent in Ladysmith, the Chippewa and the Sierra Club were in Dane
County Circuit Court in Madison presenting experts on toxicology,
biology, and endangered species to show that the DNR's study was
inadequate to provide protection of the endangered mussels,

dragonflies, and fish in the Flambeau River. It was a preview of the evidence that would have been aired in a well-advertised public hearing if the DNR had followed the state Environmental Policy Act rules.

Despite evidence of DNR's failure to comply with the Act's requirements, and its disregard for the public's right to participate in the mine permiting process, Dane County Circuit Judge Angela Bartell dismissed the Chippewa/Sierra Club lawsuit on June 13, 1992. Among the reasons for dismissal in her 26-page decision was that citizens had had 30 days to appeal the January 1991 decision and had failed to do so. At the time the permits were granted, however, DNR studies claimed that "no threatened or endangered species are known to exist at the mine site." It was not until May 1991 that two endangered mussels were discovered in the river. And it was not until June 1991 that an internal memo was leaked from the DNR that revealed that agency scientists were aware during the permiting process that endangered species were probably present at the site. Chippewa attorney Larry Leventhal said Bartell's ruling "essentially says if an agency hides information from the public, it won't be held accountable for it."[66]

This setback did not end the opposition to the project, however. On Saturday, July 25, 1992, more than 60 concerned citizens and tribal members joined a canoe flotilla down the Flambeau River past the mine site to protest ongoing construction in an area "unsuitable for mining." At the same time, the Rusk County Citizens Action Group announced the formation of a "citizens' monitoring committee" to ensure that Kennecott/RTZ's mine construction activities did not violate the conditions of its mine permit. If violations occurred, as with the failure of the mine's erosion control system in the fall of 1991, RCCAG could ask the DNR to impose penalties or to revoke the permit altogether.

On August 7, 1992, Walt Bresette went on trial in Ladysmith for trespassing on mining company property during his May 14 action. Acting as his own attorney, Bresette used his trial as a forum to argue that the failure of the state of Wisconsin to do an adequate EIS on the endangered species in the Flambeau River was a violation of the "fiduciary responsibility of the state of Wisconsin to defend my [treaty-ceded] property. If the state will not defend my roperty, I must defend it myself. There was growing evidence that the activities that were going on at the mine construction site posed a threat to my ability to hunt, fish, and gather. Those are my treaty rights and those rights are the Supreme Law of the Land." Rusk County Circuit Court Judge Frederick Henderson complimented Bresette on the eloquence of his defense but still found him guilty of the county ordinance violation and fined him $153. Meanwhile, mine opponents discussed future legal challenges, as well as other forms of resistance, at the seventh annual Protect the Earth Community Gathering over Labor Day weekend on the Lac Courte Oreilles Reservation near Hayward, Wisconsin. On September 9, 1992, Bonnie Raitt and Lyle Lovett donated part of their Milwaukee concert proceeds to *Anishinaabe Niijii*. Bonnie Raitt also addressed the issue from the stage. When she said we had to stop copper mining in Wisconsin, nearly 20,000 people cheered.

The New Face of Corporate Mining?

In September 1992, Survival International listed RTZ as one of the top ten companies who were doing serious damage to tribal peoples' lands in the Americas. Among the many places where the world's largest mining company was "operating in the face of strong opposition from the people whose lives are being affected" was Ladysmith, Wisconsin.[67] Whatever the eventual outcome, the Ladysmith mine controversy has become a microcosm of the complex social and political forces driving the new resource wars. On one side are the large multinational corporations trying to adapt their traditional resource acquisition strategies to new realities of Third World economic nationalism, native land rights, and a heightened environmental awareness about mine pollution. On the other side are environmental and citizen action groups who have broadened their concerns to include alliances with native peoples, international networking, and strategies of direct action and civil disobedience, as well as an increasingly complex understanding of the relationships among environmental protection, social justice, and sustainable economic development.

Over the 17 years of the Ladysmith mine controversy, Kennecott has been in the forefront of mining companies that have used the enormous economic and political clout of their parent companies to shape the policies of both state and local governments in accord with their long-range corporate planning for a new mineral and energy resource colony in northern Wisconsin. Along with Exxon, Noranda, and Inland Steel, these companies have revised Wisconsin mining regulations, overridden local zoning authority, and used their economic power to divide neighbor against neighbor in small, rural communities. It is precisely this fusion of corporate and state political power to promote controversial mining projects that is the hallmark of the new resource wars.

Arrayed against this formidable alliance of corporate and state power are a variety of both grassroots and mainstream environmental organizations, citizen action groups, and Indians. From the first Ladysmith mine controversy in 1976, to the Exxon-Crandon battle from 1976 to 1986, to the ongoing battles, this native-environmentalist coalition has developed leadership skills, organizational resources, and a mass political constituency that has often effectively stalled the resource colonization process. With extremely limited financial resources, this coalition has placed the mining issue in the forefront of public political debate in the state, challenged multinational corporations before their own stockholders, and called into question the legitimacy and integrity of the Wisconsin DNR's mine permit process.

The *Anishinaabe Niijii* coalition has demonstrated that the incessant drive of the multinational mining corporations to create new resource colonies need not come at the expense of small rural communities and Indian tribes. Quite to the contrary, this coalition has shown that through a careful evaluation of the strengths and weaknesses of multinational corporate power, it is possible to develop long-range political strategies for negotiating with, or opposing the plans of the multinational mining corporations. Robert Wilson, the chief executive officer of RTZ, recently paid a backhanded compliment to the Chippewa-environmentalist alliance in Wisconsin when he noted that "the greatest political risk today" for new mining projects no longer comes from the developing countries, but from the United States and Australia, where opposition movements, as at Ladysmith, have resulted in costly project delays.[68]

Given the increasing power of mining opponents, new corporate weapons must be found. As Chapter Seven shows, corporations and state governments like Kennecott and Wisconsin are not above fostering a climate of race hatred in an effort to weaken and divide potential coalitions active against their multinational corporate vision of industrial development. In their arsenal of weapons used to attempt to crush and manipulate the native-environmental alliance, fanning the flames of white racism is too useful to ignore.

Chapter 7

The Corporate/Government Appeal to Racism

> The attacks on our sovereignty and treaties are really attacks on our way of life, our way of viewing things. The environment is critical to our being. The same tactics to separate us from our resources and land are being used in Brazil, Alaska, and elsewhere. It's really racism, with many different names and faces.
>
> Ed Bearheart
> St. Croix Chippewa tribal council member[1]

In surveying the recent resource wars in Wisconsin, we should not ignore the relevant political fact that Wisconsin has also been, in recent years, the site of intense racial conflict. This conflict has bitterly divided many northern communities ever since off-reservation treaty rights for Wisconsin Chippewa Indians were reaffirmed by a court decision in 1983. Chippewa seeking to exercise their lawful right to spearfish outside reservation boundaries have been met at the boat landings by angry white protestors, who have hurled rocks, fired shots, and yelled racial slurs like "Timber Nigger" at Chippewa spearfishers. Posters advertising the First Annual Indian Shoot have been found in northern Wisconsin bars.[2] None of this is unrelated to the new resource wars.

In 1983, the U.S. Supreme Court refused to hear the state of Wisconsin's appeal of the Voigt Decision, which reaffirmed Chippewa treaty rights. While the U.S. Constitution says that treaties are the supreme law of the land, the state administration of Governor Tommy Thompson has criticized the Chippewa for exercising their treaty rights. Indeed, as the so-called Strickland report on the situation notes, the state of Wisconsin has acted as if its "problem" in northern Wisconsin is the result of Chippewa behavior.[3] The racial hostility that has been directed at Chippewa spearfishers who take approximately 3 percent of the walleye fish harvest is almost beyond belief. This 3 percent is subject to more DNR attention and observation, monitoring, press coverage, and political manipulation than the entire other 97 percent.[4] Every study that has been done on the impact of Chippewa spearfishing, from the Wisconsin Department of Natural Resources, to the Great Lakes Indian Fish and Wildlife Commission, to the most recent report commissioned by the U.S. Congress, has failed to find any evidence that the Chippewa are threatening the fish resource.[5] Why then the hysteria?

The mass media has assisted the anti-Indian movement by narrowly focusing public attention and discussion on the more sensationalistic aspects of the treaty controversy while virtually ignoring the economic and political contexts of the issue. As we have seen, the state of Wisconsin, especially the executive branch, has been actively promoting plans for a mining district in the ceded territory of the Wisconsin Chippewa that has the potential to cause serious long-term damage to the resource and economic bases of northern Wisconsin. Underneath all the racist rhetoric of the spearfishing controversy lies the essential and inseparable connection between the political assault against Indian treaties and the corporate assault on the environment in the 1990s. By focusing on the issue of resource control in the ceded territory, it is possible to see the convergence between the anti-Indian movement, represented by groups like Protect Americans' Rights and Resources (PARR) and Stop Treaty Abuse (STA), and the pro-mining policy of the Thompson administration in Wisconsin. This convergence between anti-Indian sentiment and mineral interests is best understood as the most recent episode in the long history of Indian dispossessions outlined in Chapter Two.

More specifically, the historical origins of the anti-Indian movement can be traced to the federal government's General Allotment Act of 1887.[6] This act provided for the division of communally held reservations into individual parcels or allotments to be transferred to individual Indians, with remaining "surplus" land to be made available to white settlers. Lands suspected of containing valuable minerals were often closed to Indian selection.[7] The result was the movement of non-Indians onto Indian reservations and the creation of checkerboard land ownership patterns on every allotted reservation. The inevitable jurisdictional mess between tribal, federal, and state governments provided a ripe environment for the emergence of an anti-Indian movement: "Resident and absentee non-Indian landowners and businesses objected to the growing exercise of general governmental powers by tribal governments. This was particularly true in the areas of taxation, zoning, construction, and land-use ordinances."[8]

Organized reactions to the exercise of tribal authority first began in the western states of Washington, Montana, and Wyoming in the early 1970s with the formation of such groups as the Quinault Property Owners Association, Montanans Opposed to Discrimination, and Wyoming Citizens for Equality in Government. In 1976, many of these groups came together in the Interstate Congress for Equal Rights and Responsibilities. This organized anti-Indian network "linked on-reservation non-Indian landowner opposition to tribal governments with off-reservation non-Indian sport and commercial fishermen opposed to tribal treaty protected fishing rights."[9]

Scapegoating the Chippewa

Conveniently, while multinational mining and energy corporations were exploring, drilling, leasing, and preparing to mine the region's mineral resources, the leaders of Protect Amercians' Rights and Resources and Stop Treaty Abuse were blaming the Chippewa for the economic decline of the tourist industry. Anti-treaty groups found a receptive audience in northern Wisconsin, where per capita income has lagged behind the rest of the state and where unemployment rates are higher than the state and national averages. Has northern Wisconsin tourism suffered as a result of Chippewa spearfishing activities, as the anti-treaty groups claim? The director of the Wisconsin Division of Tourism, Dick Matty, has stated that there has been no real negative impact on tourism as a result of Chippewa spearfishing. Chamber of Commerce officials in northern communities like Minocqua and Boulder Junction report that tourism is booming.[10]

There have been significant changes in Wisconsin's tourism economy that were having negative economic effects prior to the favorable Voigt decision on off-reservation spearfishing, however. A 1981 Wisconsin tourism industry study concluded:

> Resort problems were shown to increase with the age of the resort. Those that appear to be having the most significant problems, however, were built prior to 1930. Twenty-five percent of these resorts were shown to have declining occupancy trends. This may be attributable to the declining quality of these resorts due to their age and the fact that over 60 percent of their owners have not made any improvements or done upkeep since the resort was built.[11]

As newer and more modern resorts attract tourists away from the antiquated ones, the Chippewa have become convenient scapegoats for the failure of these older mom-and-pop resorts.

The Wisconsin Department of Natural Resources has also contributed to the scapegoating of the Chippewa by the way it has manipulated the bag limits on non-Indian sportfishing. The DNR's own studies have shown a steadily decreasing walleye fish population for decades due to habitat destruction and pollution. At the same time, sportfishing demands have risen. In 1979, a DNR report recommended decreasing bag limits as an option, long before the spearfishing controversy.[12] However, as the Strickland report has noted, the DNR has only reduced the bag limit on those lakes speared by the Chippewa, making it appear that the Chippewa are responsible for the reduction in bag limits. Although the bag limit reduction has been long in coming, the state refuses to acknowledge that the lowering of the bag limit is due to other factors and not to Chippewa exercise of reserved rights. Resort owners, already feeling the pinch of changing vacation planning, fear that these lower bag limits will decrease tourism and, thus, blame the Chippewa.[13]

By scapegoating the Chippewa for the economic problems of northern Wisconsin, anti-treaty groups and the state have diverted attention from the significant environmental threats to the economy and culture of both Indian and non-Indian communities in the northwoods. The Chippewa, along with the other Indian nations in northern Wisconsin, already suffer a disproportionate environmental risk of illness and other health problems from eating fish, deer, and other wildlife contaminated with industrial pollutants like airborne polychlorinated biphenyls (PCBs), mercury, and other toxins deposited on land and water. "Fish and game have accumulated these toxic chemicals," according to a 1992 U.S. Environmental Protection Agency study, "to levels posing substantial health, ecological, and cultural risks to a Native American population that relies heavily on local fish and game for subsistence. As the extent of fish and game contamination is more fully investigated by state and federal authorities, advisories suggesting limited or no consumption of fish and game are being established for a large portion of the Chippewa's traditional hunting and fishing areas."[14] To suggest that the treaty rights of the Chippewa are a threat to the economy of northern Wisconsin is to promote the most cynical sort of victim-blaming. Sooner or later, says Anishinabé activist Walt Bresette, "people in northern Wisconsin will realize that the environmental threat is more of a threat to their lifestyle than Indians who go out and spearfish. I think, in fact, that we have more things in common with the anti-Indian people than we have with the state of Wisconsin."[15]

Sadly, as Lac Courte Oreilles tribal chair Gaiashkibos has noted, PARR and STA members have been all but absent from efforts to protect Wisconsin's environment from mine pollution:

> There won't be any tourism business—or any industry—should this mining activity occur throughout the ceded territory. We're going to see a degradation of the water quality we're accustomed to; we're going to see a disruption in our lifestyle. We're going to see a degradation of

the air quality; the winds will blow the tailings. You're going to see more and more acidity in our lakes and streams. You're going to see a greater number of fish advisories than we have now. I think that's a shame, because I hear that the Great Lakes is one of the seven wonders of the world. You can't drink the water out of Lake Superior. There's young children that will never be able to taste the fish out of those lakes. There's advisories that women of childbearing age and pregnant mothers cannot consume certain species of fish out of the Great Lakes. You're going to see more of that in northern Wisconsin. The question I ask today is where the hell are these hellraisers? Where's PARR and STA that are saying they're concerned about the environment, concerned about the resources? Yet I have heard not one peep out of them about the proposed mines that could devastate the whole northwoods. Not one word from these people.[16]

As we have seen in the last chapter, the Wisconsin Department of Natural Resources has been found to be negligent in its responsibility to protect endangered species at the Ladysmith minesite, and the Lac Courte Oreilles Chippewa have taken primary responsibility for seeing that the six endangered species that have been found in the Flambeau River receive adequate protection. Indeed, the Chippewa's identification of mining-related problems has been consistently more reliable than that of the DNR. After the prodding of the Chippewa/Sierra Club lawsuit, the DNR's own supplementary environmental impact statement on the endangered species in the river showed that the current mine license threatens these species. Thus, in September 1992, the DNR held public hearings on permit modifications to limit the discharge levels for cadmium and nickel from Kennecott/RTZ's wastewater treatment plant.

The Chippewa continue to pressure the DNR into providing greater levels of protection for the endangered species in the Flambeau River. Al Baker, Jr., speaking on behalf of the Chippewa, put the matter quite simply:

The license conditions of the mining operation should recognize that the protection of endangered species is of paramount importance, not the property interest of a licensee. Accordingly, the license should be amended to state that if discharge levels need to be adjusted to protect endangered or threatened species, they will be. If this is not acceptable to Flambeau Mining, it need not construct the project.[17]

The fact that the Chippewa have been in the forefront of the struggle to protect the endangered species in the Flambeau River is hardly coincidental. In 1921, the Lac Courte Oreilles Chippewa Reservation lost much of its historical wild rice acreage because of an off-site dam and flooding that the Federal Power Commission forced upon the tribe.[18] The Ladysmith mine is yet another colonial imposition that will accelerate the poisoning of the remaining land base of the Chippewa. Tribal member Ron Winters made this point most dramatically: "We have got to stop poisoning our land, and our air, our water, and rain. One time the rain used to bless us, now it poisons us because they are mining and putting things in the air and they are endangering my children. They are putting me on that endangered species list. Whatever that bureau is that makes that list, I'd like to be on that list. I'm part of the land here. I'm part of the trees, the water, I'm part of that. I'm Anishinabé"[19] This sense of urgency has not disappeared even as mine construction begins at Ladysmith. Again and again, native efforts to preserve treaty rights have served as an obstacle to environmentally destructive resource projects. The persistence of the Chippewa and their environmental allies in educating the public about the environmental threats posed by mining and oil drilling, for example, has had a major effect upon the outcome of environmental battles against Noranda Minerals and Terra Energy.

The Fight Against Noranda Minerals and Terra Energy

Directly to the east of Ladysmith, in Oneida County, Noranda Minerals of Toronto, Canada, has discovered a six million ton deposit of zinc-lead-silver, with copper and gold, in the town of Lynne. The company wants to construct an open-pit mine, up to 60 acres wide and 500 feet deep, with on-site mineral concentration and tailings disposal. Most of the proposed mine would be located in wetlands. The site is one-half mile from important walleye spawning areas of the Willow River. Directly downstream from the site are the Willow and Rice flowages, several lakes, and the Willow, Little Rice, Tomahawk, and Wisconsin rivers. If Noranda is allowed to proceed with its mine plans, the extraction of sulfide-bearing rock could result in acid mine drainage and toxic contamination of the fish. Many of these lakes have seen major confrontations between Chippewa spearfishers and non-Indians over the exercise of Chippewa treaty fishing rights.

Shortly after Noranda's public announcement of the Lynne discovery, Wisconsin Administration Secretary James Klauser invited Noranda's project manager, Michael Donnelly, to "exchange our perspectives on the project's status."[20] After attempting to assist Kennecott/RTZ in overcoming local opposition to the Ladysmith mine project, Klauser was now ready to assist one of Canada's largest mining companies, whose aim is to become the "premier diversified natural resource company in the world," with interests in minerals, forest products, energy, and manufacturing.[21] Noranda is part of the Brascan corporate group and owns over half the shares in a number of mining companies, including Falconbridge, Kerr Addison Mines, Hemlo Gold, and Brunswick Mining and Smelting Corporation. It has direct and indirect ownership of 28 mines and ten metallurgical plants.[22] Noranda is also a partner in the Kennecott deep-sea Ocean Nodules consortium, controlled by RTZ.[23] Noranda had been conducting mineral exploration in Wisconsin since 1972. In the 1980 court case, *Noranda Exploration, Inc. v. Ostrom,* Noranda had won the right to keep secret from the Wisconsin public the contents of its drill core samples.[24] Noranda's successful legal challenge to Wisconsin's geology disclosure law was a major victory for the half dozen multinational mining corporations hoping to establish a foothold in Wisconsin's new mining district. The only ones that would know the full extent of Wisconsin's mineral resources were now the mining companies.

When Administration Secretary Klauser offered to assist Noranda, one of the issues that probably came up was the possibility of further Chippewa resistance to mining. The Lynne site is 25 miles from the Lac du Flambeau Chippewa reservation, but it is part of the Chippewa ceded territory where the tribes retain hunting, fishing, and gathering treaty rights. Former Lac du Flambeau Tribal Chair Michael W. Allen opposed the project, "We have too many lakes and springs and creek beds that are pure right now and we don't want to take a chance on contaminating that."[25] When asked about the company's position on Chippewa treaty rights, Noranda Project Manager Mike Donnelly told a reporter that "treaty issues haven't surfaced at Lynne but I would be surprised if it's not an issue. We are in the ceded territory. The [Chippewa's] argument is that mining disturbs the area and in turn will degrade the water and land and injure their rights to hunting and gathering. I can't imagine this disappearing overnight."[26]

Besides the possible infringement of Chippewa treaty rights, there are a number of other major environmental problems with the proposed mine. The site is directly on an open water bog. The DNR has established that the actual lakebed extends into the minesite as well as the proposed tailings disposal area. Wisconsin mining law forbids destroying or filling a lakebed. In addition, many of the wetlands at the site are classified as shoreland-wetlands, which cannot be rezoned for development if that may harm wetlands, groundwater, fish spawning, or wildlife habitat. Despite the explicit prohibition against drilling in a shoreland-wetland, a DNR district supervisor advised the Oneida County zoning administrator that the county could allow such an operation by not considering it a land use and, therefore, not subject to regulation.[27] And that is precisely what the county did. Finally, there is the issue of Outstanding Resource

Water and Exceptional Resource Water classification for the Willow flowage. More than a year before Noranda announced its plans for the mine, DNR scientists had recommended the Willow for both Outstanding Resource Water and Exceptional Resource Water status. This classification would have forbidden the discharge of mine wastewater into the river.

Noranda has opposed Outstanding Resource Water status for the Willow Flowage and has hired former Wisconsin governor Tony Earl, head of the DNR from 1975 to 1980, to lobby against DNR staff on this issue.[28] DNR Secretary Carroll Besadny caved in to pressure from Noranda and, over the objections of his own staff, created a special committee to study the classification of the Willow.[29] The 12-member committee, which included Tony Earl and Mike Donnelly, was stacked with mine proponents who were clearly opposed to such classification for the Willow Flowage. Three years after DNR scientists recommended Outstanding Resource Water status for the Willow, the decision remains in limbo. The Great Lakes Indian Fish and Wildlife Commission has requested a final decision on the Willow classification before any development of the mine site or permitting of the project. GLIFWC warned the DNR that "activity at the site might degrade these waters, making them categorically ineligible for Outstanding Resource Water and Exceptional Resource Water classification. Until a final classification decision is made, these waters should be afforded the same protection as waters currently classified as Outstanding and Exceptional."[30]

The extent and depth of local opposition to Noranda's proposed mine was dramatically illustrated when Wisconsin Representative James Holperin (D-Eagle River) announced that he was reversing his support of the mine and would seek to prevent or slow mining activities in environmentally sensitive areas. "I would say my position on mining in an environmentally sensitive area certainly has changed," Holperin said. "That change has come about through advocacy by people who live in this area, who oppose mining in areas like southwestern Oneida County, and near the Willow Flowage. I have been convinced by the people I represent that they do not want a mine here, that consequently a mine here is probably not a good idea, simply by virtue of the citizen opposition that it has attracted, and by its potential to threaten the environment."[31]

The political momentum to stop the mine was vastly accelerated when the DNR completed its review of Noranda's proposed scope of study for the mine. On July 7, 1992, DNR Project Manager William Tans wrote to Noranda Project Manager James Cahoon and told him that, based upon the DNR's survey of the wetlands within the project area, "almost all of them would be considered either lakebed, streambed, or regulated shoreland-wetlands."[32] Tans also reminded Noranda that Wisconsin mining law prohibits the destruction or filling of a lakebed. Furthermore, he noted that mining is not a permitted use under the county's shoreland-wetland zoning ordinance. Cahoon responded that the DNR's inventory of water resources would "slow us down. The scope of our project may have to change."[33]

In September 1992, Noranda announced it would halt all further exploration in Wisconsin and suspend new studies on the Lynne project until a dispute was resolved over the waste disposal site for its proposed open-pit zinc mine. "Our decision is part of an overall effort to focus our exploration activities on those states with a proven and predictable permitting environment and regions that encourage mineral development," said company spokesperson Mike Donnelly. Donnelly said that fights over the definitions of lakebeds, wetlands, and what constitutes an Outstanding Resource Water under the law had all played a part in slowing the permit process for the mining project.[34] More than 24,000 acres of mineral leases in northern Wisconsin would be dropped or optioned to other companies as Noranda shifted its exploration to "other, better opportunities elsewhere."[35]

While Donnelly's announcement holds out the prospect for a resolution of the DNR's legal objections to the project, this seems highly unlikely. Strong organizational links have been forged between the Lac du Flambeau Chippewa and a grassroots group of non-Indians called Environmentally Concerned Citizens of Lakeland Areas. Both groups have actively monitored the DNR's dealings with Noranda and have demonstrated their ability to mobilize public sentiment in favor of the strictest environmental standards for this project. The convergence between the struggle for Chippewa treaty rights and the struggle to protect the environment was further underscored by the recent election of Tom Maulson as the new tribal chair of the Lac du Flambeau Chippewa. Maulson was widely known as the Walleye Warrior during the years of conflict over Chippewa spearfishing and led the campaign to oppose the state's buyout of Chippewa treaty rights. He was also a founding member of *Anishinaabe Niijii* and feels that mining operations are "destructive to the values of Indian people. I'm dead against mining. There are other jobs that can come to northern Wisconsin without tearing up the land and polluting the water. If you don't have that clean water, all the digging in the world won't help you. We need to keep the lands pure; we have to put that at the top of the agenda."[36] Even more than was the case in the resistance to the Ladysmith mine, the Chippewa and environmentalist coalition that has developed against Noranda has expanded the terms of the debate far beyond the specific impacts of mining to the larger issues of sustainable economic development for northern Wisconsin, the integrity of the environmental laws and regulations, and the openness of the environmental review process to ordinary citizens and the Lake Superior Chippewa. While these issues do not, by themselves, constitute a radical environmental agenda, they are nonetheless seen as the elements of a hostile investment climate by multinational mining corporations. After spending $8 million on exploration and permitting at Lynne, Noranda seems to have decided that the political risks outweigh the potential profits of the project.

Yet, many companies are still attempting to make inroads in Wisconsin. Northern Wisconsin is an attractive geological frontier for oil and gas exploration for Terra Energy. Geologists believe that oil and natural gas are trapped below the surface in a billion-year-old formation of finely grained shale, known as the Nonesuch Shale. This rock formation lies within a larger geological structure known as the Keweenawan or Mid-Continental Rift, which stretches from Kansas through Iowa, Minnesota, Wisconsin, and Michigan. Oil has already been found in this formation at the White Pine copper mine in

Michigan's Upper Peninsula. As early as 1983, the Amoco Production Company, a subsidiary of the Amoco Corporation based in Houston, Texas, leased more than a quarter-million acres in the Chippewa ceded territory of northwestern Wisconsin. The lands include 170,000 acres of the Chequamegon National Forest, county forest lands, and private lands in Bayfield, Ashland, and Iron counties. Between 1983 and 1985, almost 700,000 acres of land were leased by oil companies and exploration companies interested in selling their leases to the major oil companies.[37]

In the summer of 1984, residents of northwestern Wisconsin observed convoys of special vibrating trucks crisscrossing the highways. The trucks were doing a series of seismic tests for Grant-Norpac, a Houston-based marine research corporation. Using sound waves from small explosive charges through the subsurface rock, the company was able to pick up vibrations on sensitive meters and provide a seismic picture of the rock structures below Lake Superior. According to Michael G. Mudrey, a geologist with the Wisconsin Geological and Natural History Survey in Madison, those pictures revealed rock structures that could have entrapped large pools of petroleum. Based upon the information from this survey, Mudrey predicted that up to 5 billion barrels of petroleum or 15 trillion cubic feet of natural gas could be recovered from the Mid-Continental Rift.[38] Wisconsin State Senator Daniel Theno (R-Ashland) warned that northern Wisconsin was on the verge of an oil rush. "I don't think that the state as a whole realizes what is happening up there, but oil companies are tripping over each other trying to secure leases from local governments and individuals for exploration for gas and oil. The situation has come to such a feverish pitch that I have to wonder if we are sitting on a significant deposit of oil or gas."[39]

In July 1991, Terra Energy, a Traverse City, Michigan oil firm, requested a drilling permit from the Wisconsin DNR and a conditional land-use permit from Bayfield County to drill a test well at Amoco's site near the town of Ino, in Keystone township. Prior to this, the company had leased oil rights to 30,000 acres nearby. Terra President Robert Boeve told a reporter that Amoco was Terra's passive partner in the Bayfield County venture, and could "become active if oil was found."[40]

Members of the Chequamegon Alliance, a grassroots environmental group, joined the Bad River, Red Cliff, and Lac Courte Oreilles bands of Chippewa and the Great Lakes Indian Fish and Wildlife Commission in demanding a full environmental impact statement on the drilling project before any permits were granted. "If an oil or gas industry is to gain a foothold in Bayfield County, it must not be at the expense of the Lake Superior Chippewa rights or the irreplaceable resources of the area," said Judy Pratt-Shelley, an environmental biologist with GLIFWC.[41] Frank Koehn, a Bayfield County supervisor and the first U.S. Green Party member to be elected a county supervisor, sponsored an amendment to Terra's land-use permit which required the preparation of a hydrologic study and an environmental impact statement before drilling was allowed. The amendment passed by a vote of four to three, and represented the first time an EIS was required for a drilling operation anywhere in the United States. While the EIS requirement delayed Terra's drilling plans, it did not stop them. Terra lobbied the county board and got the EIS requirement overturned and was also granted a new permit for a second test well.

The Chippewa responded by asking the DNR for a hearing on the inadequacy of its environmental assessment and on the DNR's failure to prepare an EIS. (The environmental assessment is a very abbreviated environmental review for those activities not expected to have a major impact on the environment.) The DNR denied the request and gave permission for Terra Energy to go ahead and drill a 6,000-foot exploratory oil and gas well on February 4, 1992. On March 9, 1992, the Chippewa filed a lawsuit asking a Dane County Circuit Court judge to suspend the state's drilling permits for Terra's test well. The complaint argued that oil and gas drilling, a notorious pollution-causing activity, will severely threaten the game and lake harvests of the Lake Superior Chippewa in Bayfield County and thereby subrogate its treaty rights in the ceded territory.[42] Joining their request was the U.S. Bureau of Indian Affairs, the Sierra Club, the Environmental Defense Fund, and state and local environmental groups.

Before Judge Susan Steingass ruled on the injunction, Terra Energy announced it was abandoning the Bayfield County site after reaching a depth of 4,700 feet. Before Terra could complete the abandonment, however, it had to secure the permission of its passive partner, Amoco Production Company.[43] Amoco, Shell, and other oil exploration companies retain their oil rights to hundreds of thousands of acres in northwestern Wisconsin.

Multinational corporations have unwittingly contributed to a growing tribal nationalism on the reservations through their attempt to gain control over low-cost Indian resources in the ceded territory of Wisconsin. It is not surprising, says one legal scholar, "that tribal nationalism should reemerge most dramatically in the management of reservation resources. Tribal occupancy of land has always been at the very foundation of the unique existence of America's Indian tribes."[44] Over the course of three decades, from the 1950s to the 1980s, Indian tribes had gone from being politically stable resource colonies to sovereign governments trying to assert and defend their treaty rights. Pro-mining interests have responded to this assertion of tribal sovereignty with renewed calls for Congress to terminate treaties between the United States and Indian tribes.[45] We are now in a position to understand the convergence between the anti-Indian movement and those groups interested in access to Indian resources.

The Anti-Indian Movement in Wisconsin

Anti-treaty groups in Wisconsin first organized after the 1983 Voigt decision reaffirmed the off-reservation treaty rights of the Chippewa. These groups took names like the Wisconsin Alliance for Rights and Resources (WARR) and Equal Rights for Everyone (ERFE), and tried to convince the public that the Chippewa were out to "rape the resources." Their members used slogans like "Save a deer, shoot an Indian," and "Save a fish, spear an Indian." In 1985, Larry Peterson founded yet another anti-treaty organization in

Minocqua, Wisconsin called Protect Americans' Rights and Resources. The new organization incorporated the organizational structures of both WARR and ERFE, but tried to avoid some of the overt and blatant racism of its predecessor organizations. PARR's literature also emphasized the national concerns of its members. In 1987, PARR hosted a national meeting of the anti-Indian movement in Wausau, Wisconsin, and representatives from almost all of the active anti-treaty organizations in the country attended. Out of this meeting came a national organizational effort to push the U.S. Congress to study and change federal Indian policies.[46]

With the election of Tommy Thompson as governor of Wisconsin in 1986, and his appointment of James Klauser as secretary of the Department of Administration (DOA), the anti-treaty movement went from the margins to the mainstream of Wisconsin politics. Thompson's anti-treaty sentiments were apparent when he was campaigning for governor. In June 1986, he spoke to the PARR group in Minocqua: "I believe spearing is wrong, regardless of what treaties, negotiations or federal courts may say."[47] Klauser was an important ally too. Before his appointment as secretary of the DOA, James Klauser was the chief lobbyist for Exxon Minerals while that company was seeking permits to mine at Crandon, Wisconsin. Donald Achttien, general manager for Exxon's Crandon project, described Klauser as "our eyes and ears in the Madison area."[48] Speaking before a 1981 Democratic Party meeting in Madison, Klauser said "Wisconsin has world-class mining potential. It's really hard to appreciate the mammothness and the potential impact of this industry."[49] Both Thompson and Klauser wanted to remove potential legal obstacles to opening up the northwoods to mining because of the assertion of Chippewa treaty rights in the ceded territory of Wisconsin.

Treaty Buyout, Treaty Abrogation

In December 1988, the Wisconsin Department of Justice approached the Mole Lake Sokaogon Chippewa with a ten-year pact with the state that would have required the tribe to refrain from exercising spearfishing and timber harvesting rights in exchange for a $10 million aid package. One of the least publicized provisions of the agreement was the tribe's withdrawal from the ongoing Voigt litigation over conditions of the harvest and potential economic damages owed to the tribes during the period of state preemption of the treaties.[50] If this agreement had been ratified by tribal members, it would have seriously undermined the solidarity of the Lake Superior Chippewa tribes in the Voigt litigation. Mole Lake tribal members overwhelmingly rejected the offer in January 1989 by a vote of 131 to 24.

After the Mole Lake rejection of the state's buyout offer, state leaders and anti-treaty agitators appealed to the state's congressional delegation. In an April 18, 1989 letter to the chairs of the Wisconsin Chippewa tribes, the entire Wisconsin congressional delegation threatened that, when assessing tribal requests for federal grants and projects, they would take into account the tribes' lack of cooperation and their lack of sensitivity.[51] The threatening letter was followed by the introduction of legislation by Congressman James Sensenbrenner to abrogate the Wisconsin Chippewa treaties.

Having failed to persuade the Chippewa to voluntarily give up their treaty rights, the Thompson administration then tried to get a federal court order to prevent the Chippewa from exercising their treaty rights because anti-treaty protestors threatened violence.[52] While Judge Barbara Crabb rejected the state's petition as groundless, this legal maneuver emphasized the complementary nature of the relationship between the anti-treaty protestors in PARR and STA, and the state government. Whenever the anti-Indian movement increased their agitation at the boat landings, the state could then intervene and suggest that some form of de facto abrogation of Chippewa treaties was a reasonable way of resolving the conflict. "It is a logic which defies logic," said activist Walt Bresette. "Indians win rights, whites beat up Indians; therefore, the only solution is for the Indians to *sell* rights. Whatever happened to the enforcement of laws?"[53]

The state tried to negotiate a treaty lease agreement once more, this time with the Lac du Flambeau Chippewa, the most active band of spearers. Official representatives of the band had reached a tentative ten-year agreement with the state, only to have the $35.6 million agreement voted down by tribal members by a vote of 439 to 366 in October 1989. One of the major issues of concern to the Wa-Swa-Gon Treaty Association, which opposed the tribal council's approval of the deal, was the possibility that the leasing out of treaty rights would provide a way for mining companies to acquire mineral rights on reservation lands.[54] Tom Maulson, one of the most visible Wa-Swa-Gon leaders, was singled out for special criticism by James Klauser, who called him an Indian supremacist. Klauser also referred to Wa-Swa-Gon members as confrontationists and Indian militants.[55] The conflict was very real. Dorothy Thoms, a member of the Lac du Flambeau Chippewa and Wa-Swa-Gon, said that "mining companies had already done exploration on the reservation. If our treaties are sold, those companies are ready to step in."[56]

Throughout the spearfishing controversy, both Governor Thompson and Secretary Klauser continued to meet with representatives of Protect American's Rights and Resources and the more militant Stop Treaty Abuse, headed by Dean Crist of Minocqua. Crist, who admits that his organization's goals are similar to that of the Ku Klux Klan, said he welcomed Thompson's involvement because it showed "we are not a tiny group of racists—we are indeed representatives of thousands of people."[57] The political legitimacy extended to these racist groups should not be underestimated. The Strickland report emphasized that "meeting with leaders of these groups is precisely analogous to consulting with the Ku Klux Klan regarding voting rights."[58] Both PARR and STA are member groups of the Citizens Equal Rights Alliance (CERA), a national alliance of the anti-Indian movement. Fred Hatch, a former Bureau of Indian Affairs lawyer who is now general counsel for STA and its delegate to CERA, describes CERA as "a political lobby of ranchers, doctors, lawyers, businessmen, and large corporations like Burlington Northern and Exxon. All of these companies are having problems with the federal Indian policy."[59]

In 1988, CERA joined other right wing extremist groups like the American Freedom Coalition and corporations like Exxon at a

Multiple Use Strategy Conference in Reno, Nevada.[60] The strategy conference was called in response to the attempts of a broad coalition of environmental organizations to reform the 1872 Mining Law, which gives mining companies free access to federal land without having to restore it or pay royalties. By preaching continued multiple use on public lands, the industry has appealed to ranchers, loggers, and anti-Indian groups in a backlash against emerging environmental reforms.[61] While the multiple-use conference was important in establishing organizational links between the anti-Indian movement and the right wing, CERA's ties with the Wisconsin Counties Association (WCA) has proved crucial for the legitimation of anti-Indian politics in mainstream national political debate.

The political backlash to the assertion of Chippewa treaty rights has extended to many northern Wisconsin county governments. In addition to off-reservation hunting and fishing, much of this backlash was based on the perception that the Chippewa might exercise their right to harvest timber for free on public county lands. Several northern counties derive a significant portion of their income from timber sales in county forests. While Federal Judge Barbara Crabb rejected the Chippewa's treaty claim to harvest timber on public lands, the counties continue to be concerned about questions of political jurisdiction between tribes and counties.

Mark Rogacki, executive director of the Wisconsin Counties Association, has taken a national leadership role in organizing counties which are on or near Indian reservations into a National Coalition on Federal Indian Policy.[62] According to Rogacki, the exercise of treaty rights to hunt, fish, and cut timber is "not in tune with contemporary society or the needs of local government."[63] The goals of the National Coalition on Federal Indian Policy include lobbying Congress to "modernize" Indian treaty rights and persuading the National Association of Counties to take up the issue. "All this sounds well and good," says LCO Chippewa tribal chair Gaiashkibos, "but we Indian people know what 'modernization' means." He adds:

"Modernization" means termination; "modernization" means abrogation. If you do a little independent research

you'll see that the whole master plan has been to Ameri-
canize the Indian people, to bring them into mainstream
society, and one day they would become ordinary citizens
of this great melting pot of America. The idea is hopefully
they'd leave the reservations, that they'd go off into the
cities. But I want you to know something: that our reservations are probably the only area yet today that still has
some virgin timber left on it. You go up into your state
forest that the DNR is managing for us, you're going to
see huge tracts of clear-cut areas, without any foresight.
We don't know if there are any sensitive plants in the
clear-cut areas that are dependent on certain trees, fo-
liage, or shade. We don't know these things, but they're
allowing the timber industry to go in and cut off the
timber. And then we hear the timber industry through
Mark Rogacki saying they're concerned about the eight
million acres of timber, and fearful that the Chippewa are
going to cut all that.

Again, I want to remind you of something. In the late
1890s and early 1900s, it was not the Chippewa that went
in and cut all that timber. The first trees that were cut off
were all the virgin pine. You can go back in some forest
areas today and see huge stumps. That was the first to go.
Then the second cutting was in the 1930s and 1940s when
they went in and cut off the hardwoods. And now they're
after the new growth again for the timber industry.
They're saying, "Oh, but we don't want you to come in
and cut down the forest that we've planted." To us, in all
the wisdom of the Creator, when the Creator made this
earth, the Creator didn't sit down and say, "over here, I'll
make an 80-acre bloc of aspen, and over there I'll make
an 80-acre bloc of just jackpine, and over here I'll put a
bloc of redwood." The Creator didn't do that. The Creator
had diversity in that dream. In that dream was diversity,
the force you see on the reservation. It was not the Indian
people that cut that off. That's the lie that's being told.[64]

In February 1990, in Salt Lake City, Utah, Rogacki also brought together representatives of county associations from nine other states to examine how treaty rights affect local governments. Among the dozen Wisconsin officials who attended the conference was James Klauser. Rogacki explained Klauser's participation as "a reflection of the fact that the [Thompson] administration and the county governments share the perspective that the federal government has to settle these matters."[65] While Klauser denied that the group was organized to abrogate Indian treaties, Indians from around the country protested the meeting, and three registered Indian county officials were refused entry to the meeting.[66]

Among the speakers at the conference was Robert Mulcahy, general counsel to the WCA. At a February 1991 meeting of the WCA in Madison, Wisconsin, Mulcahy noted that "timber is not the only issue. Not many understand. Mining is the real issue. Serious claims are being made against mining in the Ladysmith area. Anti-mining groups are surfacing and doing leafleting. There is even state legislation introduced for a moratorium on mining."[67] At the same meeting, a representative of the Wisconsin Counties Forest Association told WCA members that 56 percent of public land in Wisconsin is in the county forest system and that the counties would realize big profits if they could open these lands to mining.[68]

Clearly, the convergence between the anti-Indian movement and pro-mining interests at both the state and county levels of government is real. The reason, of course, is that treaty rights and environmental protection are now inseparably linked. Before multinational mining companies can transform northern Wisconsin into a resource colony, they must remove the legal obstacles that stand in the way of their access to, and control of, mineral supplies. Among the most significant legal obstacles are the treaties signed between the Chippewa nation and the U.S. government in the 19th century.

The anti-Indian movement has historically been linked to the economic expansionist needs of U.S. capitalism. When the dominant European-American society needed land and raw materials for expansion, Indians were defined as a problem or a threat and their lands and resources were taken. Now, having been left with the land nobody else wanted, it turns out that some of the last remaining energy and mineral resources are located on Indian lands or on off-reservation lands in ceded territory. Once again, there is a national hysteria about "outdated Indian treaties" and so-called "tribal misuse" of resources. Much of this hysteria is orchestrated by anti-Indian groups but, increasingly, the state itself has played an important part, as was noted in the Strickland report: "In defiance of the court rulings, the state appears to be trying to regulate the Chippewa indirectly, through the manipulation of public opinion."[69] This manipulation is apparent in the state's handling of the spearfishing issue as well as the mining issue. The Chippewa have been portrayed as the culprits on the spearfishing issue and totally ignored for their leadership role in trying to protect the resources for both Indian and non-Indian populations in the ceded territory of Wisconsin.

To counter the racist violence and hostility directed against Chippewa spearfishers, a number of religious, environmental, and treaty rights support groups came together to provide witnesses for nonviolence at the boat landings and to conduct public education about Chippewa treaty rights. These groups included Witness for Nonviolence, Honor Our Neighbors' Origins and Rights, Midwest Treaty Network, the Wisconsin Greens, Northern Thunder, and the American Indian Movement. By 1991, almost 2,000 witnesses had been trained in the philosophy and practice of nonviolence, treaty history, and environmental and cultural issues in northern Wisconsin.[70] As a result of their nonviolent activism on behalf of Chippewa treaty rights, many witnesses have joined with *Anishinaabe Niijii* in defending Indian lands against unwanted mining development.

After years of racial backlash to off-reservation spearfishing, the anti-Indian movement in Wisconsin has suffered a number of setbacks that have resulted in much smaller crowds protesting Chippewa spearfishing. In March 1991, Federal Judge Barbara Crabb issued a permanent injunction against protestors interfering physically, whether on the lake or at the boat landings, with Chippewa fishermen and women. Then in September 1991, 13 members of Stop Treaty Abuse-Wisconsin, an anti-treaty group, paid thousands of dollars to settle a lawsuit that contends they violated the Chippewas' civil and treaty rights. The Lac du Flambeau Chippewa and the Wa-Swa-Gon Treaty Association led the lawsuit with the help of the American Civil Liberties Union. Brian Pierson, an attorney for the Chippewa plaintiffs, said: "It's an acknowledgement that there is no reason to spend your time and money fighting for the right to harass Indians."[71]

Now that the immediate threat of anti-Indian violence has subsided, the important long-range resource management work of the tribes will assume greater visibility and importance. This work goes back to 1984 when the Chippewa tribes formed the Great Lakes Indian Fish and Wildlife Commission to provide coordination and services for the implementation of their treaty rights in the ceded territory and to represent tribal interests in natural resource management. An essential part of GLIFWC's mission is to provide ecosystem protection, "recognizing that fish, wildlife, and wild plants cannot long survive in abundance in an environment that has been degraded."[72] It is in this area where treaty rights have the greatest potential to protect the environment for both Indian and non-Indian communities.

Part III
A New Stage for the
Environmental Movement?

Chapter 8

Defending Indian Treaties, Defending the Earth

Cooperation between tribal groups and environmentalists is a relatively recent phenomenon. In the 1960s and early 1970s, mainstream environmental organizations and Indians were frequently at odds with each other over Indian land and water claims, natural resources, and fishing and hunting rights.[1] Even today there is still considerable tension between conservationist groups who want to preserve the tropical rainforests and the native groups who face expulsion from these areas because their land rights are not considered as part of an overall conservation strategy.[2]

Ever since the 1872 founding of Yellowstone National Park, the first national park in the world, the interests of conservationists and native peoples have frequently diverged. Once areas have been designated as parks, native peoples have been forced to move.[3] The impacts of the creation of parks on native peoples, although devastating, have rarely been taken into account by decisionmakers. Thus, when the province of Ontario created the Chapleau Crown Game Preserve in 1925, it effectively destroyed the livelihood of the Brunswick House Ojibwa Indian people by removing 60 percent of the land base, "the lands most intensively exploited by the Indian people."[4] And in Uganda there is the notorious case of the forcible expulsion of the Ik from the Kidepo Valley National Park after their traditional subsistence activities within the park were declared "unnatural." The Ik suffered starvation, disease, and cultural disintegration as a result.[5]

Nevertheless, there has been a slow but growing realization among environmentalists that Indians' assertion of treaty rights is an integral part of any environmental protection strategy. When the Sokaogon Chippewa Indians decided to oppose Exxon's plans to mine next to their reservation in 1976, they stood alone and expected no help from the environmental movement in Wisconsin. Indeed, the prevalent attitude among mainstream environmental organizations was that mining development in northern Wisconsin was inevitable and the Chippewa were fighting a hopeless battle. From the Chippewa perspective, they were fighting a battle to preserve their wild rice subsistence culture and the treaty-protected waters that flowed through their reservation. This was not simply an environmental issue for the Chippewa; they were fighting a battle for their economic and cultural survival, and that was inseparable from their efforts to protect their environment.

Over the course of a decade-long struggle against the combined resources of Exxon and the state of Wisconsin, the Chippewa were able to communicate this message to their non-Indian neighbors, the tourism industry downstream from the proposed mine, and the state's environmental community. By the time Exxon finally withdrew from the project in 1986, the Chippewa had assembled a broad-based Indian-environmentalist coalition that included every mainstream environmental organization in Wisconsin. And the coalition that developed out of that struggle was ready to be mobilized when Lac Courte Oreilles Chippewa tribal chair Gaiashkibos decided to oppose Kennecott/RTZ's plans to mine in Ladysmith, Wisconsin. While the final outcome of the Ladysmith battle is still uncertain, *Anishinaabe Niijii* (Friends of the Chippewa) has established itself as a political force to be reckoned with in the ongoing resource wars in Wisconsin.

Treaty Rights as an Environmental Weapon

"What is perhaps most important about Indian treaty rights," says Anishinabé treaty rights activist Winona LaDuke, "is the power of the treaties to clarify issues which would otherwise be consigned by nation-state apologists to the realm of 'opinion' and 'interpretation.' The treaties lay things out clearly, and they are matters of international law."[6] One of the landmark cases which clearly demonstrated the inseparable connection between treaty rights and environmental protection was the widely publicized northwestern U.S. treaty rights conflict over fishing in the late 1960s.

The case attracted considerable attention when Marlon Brando, Dick Gregory, and Jane Fonda stood alongside Native American fishermen and women who were exercising their treaty rights to fish in defiance of sportsfishers and state authorities. Indian fishers in the Northwest had been arrested during similar "fishing wars" since the turn of the century, despite the 1854 Medicine Creek Treaty, which gave them the right to fish "…as long as the rivers run."[7] In 1974, U.S. Judge George Boldt ruled that Indians were entitled to catch as many as half the fish returning to off-reservation sites which had been the "usual and accustomed places" when the treaties were signed.[8] When Judge Boldt made his ruling in *U.S. v. Washington,* he realized that these rights were meaningless if there were no fish to catch. This issue was addressed by Judge William Orrick in Phase II of *U.S. v. Washington* in 1980. The judge ruled that "The most fundamental prerequisite to exercising the right to take fish is the existence of fish to be taken."[9] If the state of Washington were allowed to destroy the fishery habitat by licensing dams and logging operations, it would amount to an abrogation of the Indians' right to fish. The court ruled that treaty Indians have an implicit right to have the fishery habitat protected. Henceforth, state agencies, along with federal agencies and potential developers, such as timber companies, would have to "refrain from degrading the fish habitat to an extent that it would deprive the tribes of their moderate living needs."[10]

While the ruling did not give the Indians absolute power to veto development projects, it did give them legal standing to challenge actions or policies that might have a detrimental effect on their right to a fishery. The burden of proof was divided between the state and the tribes. The state would have to show that its action did not deprive the Indians of their right to fish; the tribes would have to show that the state action would degrade the fishery and reduce the fish available to the tribes.

Since Judge Orrick's decision, the Indians of the Skagit River—the Upper Skagit tribe, the Sauk-Suiattle tribe and the Swinomish tribal community—have used their treaty rights to protect the fish in the Skagit River on several occasions. In 1981, the tribes opposed a Seattle utility's proposal for a dam that would have inundated 11 miles of prime salmon spawning grounds in the Skagit River. The Skagit River tribes depend on the returning salmon for a major portion of their yearly income and they opposed the project through the environmental impact statement process. The Seattle City Council dropped its plans for the project, almost entirely in order to avoid a lengthy court battle over the Skagit River salmon.[11]

The Skagit River tribes have also battled Puget Sound Power and Light over licensing and construction of twin nuclear power plants just one mile from traditional salmon fishing grounds. In June 1978, the three Skagit River tribes intervened in federal licensing hearings because they feared the construction and operation of the plant would threaten salmon habitat. During normal operation, the plant would use river water for cooling and then discharge it back into the river several degrees warmer than when it was taken out. The tribes argued against this since salmon are very sensitive to changes in water temperature. Plant construction would also have wiped out salmon spawning grounds. "Without the treaty case law," said Russ Busch, attorney for the Upper Skagit and Sauk-Suiattle, "more than half of our arguments against nuclear plants would have no teeth."[12] The Skagit River tribes also took their case to the general public through a ballot initiative. With the help of non-Indians in Skagitonians Concerned About Nuclear Plants, the tribes placed a nuclear referendum before county voters. Over 70 percent voted against nukes in the Skagit Valley. Puget Power delayed its permit application indefinitely.

While the boundaries of the tribes' right to protect the environment are still being reviewed in the courts, the Indians have continued to develop their management capabilities to such an extent that state and federal agencies have been forced to acknowledge the region's tribes as co-managers of the fishery resource. After the 1974 Boldt decision, all of the Northwest tribes in the region covered by *U.S. v. Washington* developed management programs at either the tribal level or through some cooperative management program like the Skagit System Cooperative or the Point No Point Treaty Council. Through these programs, native people were actively involved in all phases of fisheries management, from habitat protection to fisheries enhancement and fisheries research.[13]

Another level of intertribal coordination is the Northwest Indian Fisheries Commission, which serves as a coordinating body for the entire region under the jurisdiction of *U.S. v. Washington*. In 1990, the 20 treaty Indian tribes of western Washington released nearly 43 million hatchery-reared fish, including a record 15.4 million fall chinook. "Everybody—Indians as well as non-Indians—benefits from the tribes' ongoing fishery enhancement efforts," said commission chair Bill Frank, Jr. "And the tribes are proud of the quality of the fish they release each year."[14] Some of the fish were released by the Indian tribes in conjunction with state and federal agencies, as well as Trout Unlimited and other sport angling organizations.

After more than two decades of resource conflict and anti-Indian backlash, the tribes have now established their treaty-guaranteed right to have a voice in the management of this critical resource. While it is premature to make any generalizations about co-management, fisheries experts have stated that the early results of state-tribal fisheries management indicate that it is working effectively.[15]

Regional Resource Co-Management in Wisconsin

Yet another possible model of resource co-management has developed out of the intense treaty rights conflict over Chippewa spearfishing in northern Wisconsin described in the last chapter. The prospect of a new resource colony (mining, oil, and gas) in northern Wisconsin—with multiple mines at the headwaters of the state's major rivers; oil wells on the shores of Lake Superior; and processing facilities, oil waste pits, and mountains of mine tailings throughout the region—is a nightmare scenario. Instead of the resource colony that the multinational mining and oil corporations, with active encouragement from the state of Wisconsin, is trying to impose on northern Wisconsin, *Anishinaabe Niijii* wants to declare an "environmental zone" to be jointly managed by the state and the Chippewa. "The ceded territory would be the first 'toxic free zone' in the state if not the country," says Walt Bresette. Rather than mines and toxic waste dumps, the zone would be a haven for vacationers and people seeking a healthy place to live. "Under this plan," writes Bresette and co-author James Yellowbank, "the 42 percent of northern Wisconsin, which is ceded land, would be phased into a co-management program that ultimately would prohibit pollution. It would simultaneously develop jobs and rural community reinvestment opportunities through a ten-year environmental cleanup program."[16]

One of the great ironies of the Chippewa spearfishing controversy is that the Chippewa and their white neighbors were fighting over the right to harvest contaminated fish. A recent Wisconsin Department of Natural Resources study shows that increased walleye consumption is leading to higher levels of mercury in Chippewa blood, posing a health risk, especially for pregnant women and young children.[17] The walleye is a large gamefish that is a staple in the Chippewa diet; it also has the most mercury-tainted flesh. The DNR's most recent "Health Guide for People Who Eat Sport Fish from Wisconsin Waters" lists 217 waterbodies with varying consumption limits for mercury-polluted fish.[18] As more lakes are tested, more lakes are added to the advisory list. Since 1982, the DNR has tested 700 of the state's 15,000 lakes; usually one out of three lakes makes it on to the advisory list.[19] Recently, Chippewa spearfishers actually refused to spear certain lakes because of DNR fish advisories. Walt Bresette angrily commented, "I refuse to eat the fish and I refuse to let my family eat the fish because of the toxins."

According to Carl Watras, a DNR scientist who has been studying mercury contamination in northern lakes, "Virtually all the mercury in these lakes comes from the sky."[20] The major sources of the mercury in rain and snow are latex paints and emissions from coal power plants. While mercury is being eliminated from latex paint, Wisconsin utilities are hoping to build six new coal power plants. And if new mines are constructed in northern Wisconsin, they will be a major new source of mercury contamination. Mercury is released during mineral processing and is leached into waterways from mine tailings. In the nearby upper peninsula of Michigan, the White Pine copper mine and smelter is being sued by the National Wildlife Federation and the Michigan United Conservation Clubs for emitting mercury, lead, and arsenic over the waters of nearby Lake Superior at five times the legal limit. The U.S. Environmental Protection Agency has listed Copper Range, the mine's owner, as Michigan's "most prolific polluter."[21] While the cumulative effects of multiple sources of mercury contamination are still unknown, the danger is real, nonetheless. "The bottom line here is that this is a real threat," according to Tom Sheffy, an environmental specialist with the DNR's Bureau of Water Resources. "Mercury exposure in infants is a potentially dangerous thing."[22]

The cumulative effects of an export-oriented extractive resource economy in northern Wisconsin will be neither long-term jobs nor a healthy environment. The Wisconsin DNR has estimated that the total direct and indirect employment that would be generated by the operation of four possible metal mines in northern Wisconsin would be 1,300 jobs, representing about 3.5 percent of the total employment spread out over four counties. "Based on the number of jobs that would be created from these four mines operating simultaneously, mining would provide a relatively minor regional economic stimulus."[23] Even then, the DNR assumes that these jobs will benefit local residents in these areas. However, the experience of mining boomtowns in the western United States suggests that the jobs would go primarily to outside workers temporarily living in the state.[24]

The DNR also assumes that mine pollution of the air and water will have no detrimental effect on the existing jobs in the region's primary industries—agriculture, forestry, and tourism. A study released by the Institute for Environmental Studies at the University of Wisconsin came to the opposite conclusion:

> Mining waste, because of acid drainage or the discovery of potentially carcinogenic material in the waste, may have long-term effects on the natural and cultural environment. Because these effects may occur only as an act of

God and long after the mining firm has left the area, repairs and compensation may become the responsibility of the public sector. In certain cases, the potential for damage may be so severe as to require perpetual monitoring and maintenance similar to that done by federal authorities with radioactive waste material."[25]

Notice the explicit assumption in this ecological disaster scenario that the public will bear the costs of these "acts of God" because the mining companies will be long gone and unaccountable. This scenario is simply another version of the "national sacrifice areas" that were proposed for those coal-rich lands, many on the Navajo and Hopi reservations in the arid southwestern United States, where reclamation was impossible.[26]

Racism clearly plays a critical role in these kinds of siting decisions. "Whether by conscious design or institutional neglect," argues sociologist Robert Bullard, "communities of color in urban ghettos, in rural 'poverty pockets,' or on economically impoverished Native-American reservations face some of the worst environmental devastation in the nation."[27] And it is precisely in these communities that have become "sacrifice zones" where the struggle for environmental justice is most intense.[28] Environmental racism is evident in the systematic effort to exclude people of color from participation in the decision-making process. Whether by narrowly defining the issues that can be raised in the environmental impact statement process or by ignoring the objections of those opposed to such projects, the voices of those most directly affected by these projects are silenced. This means that the question of "who *pays* and who *benefits* from current industrial and development policies" is not seriously addressed.[29] By proposing the general outlines of an alternative economic development plan for the ceded territory, Bresette and Yellowbank, along with their supporters in the Wisconsin Greens, want to reopen and broaden the public debate about the economic and environmental future of northern Wisconsin. At the same time, the serious consideration of such a plan poses a direct ideological challenge to the traditional export-based models of economic development.

If the goal is to provide jobs in an economically depressed rural economy, then investing in mining and oil and gas drilling is exactly the wrong way to accomplish this. Mining and oil and gas drilling are extremely capital-intensive. This means that for every dollar invested, relatively few jobs are produced. A recent study by the Worldwatch Institute concludes that "Polluting industries are at best a marginal—and now shrinking—source of jobs."[30] Investments in locally-owned small firms and in labor-intensive technologies such as tribal fish hatcheries, renewable energy, recycling, forest products, and organic farming would create far more jobs than mining, while also contributing to an environmentally sustainable economy. Menominee Tribal Enterprises, in Keshena, Wisconsin, has already received international recognition for its achievements in sustainable forestry. The Menominee system of intensive forest management, on its 220,000 acres of forested lands, "is now a recognized leader in shelterwood systems for uneven-aged management of white pine, hemlock, and hemlock-yellow birch ecosystems."[31]

Instead of encouraging electric utilities to build six new coal-fired power plants, the state of Wisconsin could encourage the utilities to buy locally-produced renewable energy. Northern States Power is already building a wind farm on Buffalo Ridge in Minnesota. The technologies are already available and cost effective. Moreover, as a Wisconsin Greens energy specialist has pointed out, "buying energy locally would benefit the regional cash flow, go far to stabilize the economy up North and on the farm, and would ease environmental stress, eg., the rates fish pick up mercury made available by acid rain."[32] Since the promise of job opportunities is the major, if not the only appeal of the mining, oil, and gas industries to depressed northern Wisconsin communities, the treaty-based alternative economic development plan for northern Wisconsin holds much promise as an ecologically-preferable way of creating sustainable jobs for both Indians and non-Indians.

Native Peoples and
Sustainable Development

In 1987, the United Nation's World Commission on Environment and Development, also known as the Brundtland Commission (after its chair, Prime Minister Gro Harlem Brundtland of Norway), published *Our Common Future*. The key concept of the report was "sustainable development," defined as "development that meets the needs of the present without compromising the ability of future generations to meet their own needs."[33] The report also acknowledged the crucial role of culture as an adaptive mechanism. In surveying the impact of externally-imposed development upon native cultures in the remote regions of the globe, the Brundtland report noted the "terrible irony" that "it tends to destroy the only cultures that have proved able to thrive in these environments." To counter this tendency, the report advocated "the recognition and protection of [native cultures'] traditional rights to land and the other resources that sustain their way of life—rights they may define in terms that do not fit into standard legal systems."[34]

The concept of sustainable development received a great deal of attention in the discussions leading up to the U.N. Conference on the Environment and Development, or the Earth Summit, held in Rio de Janeiro, Brazil in June 1992. Thomas N. Gladwin, a professor of management and international business at New York University, described the concept as "the cutting edge of social and economic reform."[35] But the cutting edge of this concept has been dulled as practically every major institution in the world economy—from multinational mining and logging companies to the World Bank—has embraced the concept. Even the International Atomic Energy Agency claimed that "the supply of energy for economic growth in a sustainable and environmentally acceptable manner is a central activity in the Agency's programme."[36] The real question that needs to be answered is: "sustainability of what and for whom?"[37]

The different interpretations of sustainable development have assumed a particular urgency in the context of recent international proposals for preserving the biological diversity in the world's rainforests. At least half of all known species are contained in the tropical rainforests.[38] One of the plans for preserving world biodiversity is the Tropical Forestry Action Plan, drawn up by the World Resources Institute in cooperation with the World Bank, the United Nations Development Program, and the Food and Agricultural Organization. The plan envisions an $8 billion action program to encourage production of fuel wood, commercial forestry, reforestation, and conservation of tropical forest ecosystems. Among the major shortcomings of the plan, according to a recent report by Marcus Colchester of the World Rainforest Movement, is that "it paid little attention to the needs and rights of forest dwellers and seemed unduly focused on funding commercial forestry and wood-based industries, while failing to identify the real causes of deforestation."[39] Among the real causes of deforestation, as we have seen, are large-scale agriculture, cattle breeding, road construction, logging, oil drilling, mining, and dams—all the activities financed by major financial institutions such as the World Bank. The implementation of the Tropical Forestry Action Plan at the national level "will promote a massive expansion of logging in primary forests. Despite the fact that rainforest logging is not being carried out in a sustainable fashion and is itself one of the principal causes of deforestation, under the Tropical Forestry Action Plan logging in primary forests will intensify."[40]

The Tropical Forestry Action Plan is just one example of the ethnocentric and neocolonial perspectives that ignore the role of native peoples in maintaining sustainable resource systems in the areas they still inhabit. Another example is the increasingly popular "debt for nature swaps" being promoted by banks and environmental groups. Here again, the knowledge and experience of native peoples is frequently overlooked as parts of the rainforest are set aside for conservation in return for the cancellation of foreign debt. "You must understand," says Santos Adam Afusa, a Peruvian Indian and member of the coordinating body for the Indigenous Peoples' Organization of the Amazon Basin, "that we try to maintain the forest as our ancestors have maintained, protected, and taken care of it. That is extremely important because the destruction of the forest would not only ruin our homelands but would have a worldwide effect. The issue is not just to protect the forest; the issue is also to [rely on] the people that are able and have for millennia been able to protect and maintain the forest."[41] Indeed, as Winona LaDuke has pointed out, there is a widespread assumption among those promoting these megaprojects that "Indigenous people do not have their own economic systems so someone should come and give them one. This development program is a war on subsistence."[42] The alternative to this "war on subsistence" is a type of sustainable development which recognizes "the right of each indigenous people to a land and resource base necessary to sustain an appropriate and sufficient economy and the right to exercise its authority and jurisdiction over the corresponding territory."[43]

We know from studies in ethnobotany that native peoples are often aware of differences in nature which are invisible to specialists from the outside. For example, in one Aymara community in the Bolivian Altiplano, peasant households named 38 "sweet" and nine "bitter" varieties of potato that they themselves cultivate.[44] "Their interest in maintaining crop diversity is based not on a belief in diversity for its own sake, but on the knowledge that diversity reduces their environmental vulnerability."[45] Darrell Posey, an ethnobiologist, has reached similar conclusions, based upon his research with the Kayapo in Brazil. According to Posey, the Kayapo use the heterogeneity of the Amazon to broaden their resource potential.[46] And after surveying native land-use practices in Central America, one study concludes that "there are no other land-use models for the tropical rainforest that preserve ecological stability or biological diversity as efficiently as those of the indigenous groups presently encountered there."[47]

We cannot expect to preserve fragile ecosystems while the native peoples who live in these areas are dispossessed and forcibly dislocated. This is the foundation of the emerging unity between native peoples and the international conservation movement. As ecologically-destructive megaprojects continue to penetrate the world's resource frontiers, the global problems of deforestation, desertification, depletion of fisheries, and soil erosion are major concerns of both groups.[48] In 1970, UNESCO provided a conceptual framework for integrating the goals of conservationists and native peoples with the creation of the "Man and the Biosphere" program. Among the major objectives of the program are the conservation of ecosystems which are ecologically self-sustaining, the promotion of research and monitoring on their appropriate use and management, and the involvement of native peoples in all phases of the project. Native rights advocate Bernard Nietschmann suggests that Man and the Biosphere reserves "are among the most attractive for expanding the role of traditional peoples in reserve design, management, and interactive research objectives."[49]

One of the more successful applications of the biosphere reserve concept is the Kuna Wildlands Project in Panama. The project area covers 60,000 hectares of protected wildlands on the Kuna Yala native reserve on the northeastern coast of Panama. Included in this reserve are coral reefs, islands, mangroves, coastal lagoons, gallery forest, and evergreen hardwood forest.[50] One of the first priorities of the park was the physical demarcation and protection of the entire reserve boundary of the Kuna people. Much of the success of the Kuna reserve can be attributed to their high degree of social organization and cohesion and a strong tradition of autonomy and self-reliance.[51] After surveying the experiences of native peoples with national parks in northern Canada, Alaska, and northern Australia, one study found that the most successful cases of native-conservationist relations occurred where there were organizational vehicles (native corporations, aboriginal land councils) to ensure native control over the land and input into planning.[52]

As native experience and knowledge is taken into account in managing biosphere reserves, there is an implicit challenge to the prevailing Western model of technology transfer from the "advanced" societies to the "less advanced" societies. The more we learn about native economies, the more appreciation we have for "small-scale economic development" models based on technologies that are low-cost, labor-intensive, and ecologically sound. In an explicit challenge to the entire "industrial model" of economic development, the World Council of Indigenous Peoples called upon the international community to recognize the important contributions of these native technologies to sustainable development. "The trend of industrial technology," according to the council statement, "has reduced the variety of technology that may be available for human development. The ability of human society to adapt to a variety of environmental and social changes has been correspondingly reduced. The contributions of diverse populations to the pool of technologies must be expanded rather than narrowed. Human diversity must be matched by technological diversity. The constant recognition of the value of technologies appropriate to political, human, and ecological circumstances is essential to achieving balanced development throughout the world."[53]

Clearly, the goal of sustainable development is inseparable from the goal of maintaining cultural diversity. In a recent Worldwatch paper, Alan Thein Durning argues that "the world's dominant cultures cannot sustain the earth's ecological health without the aid of the world's endangered cultures. Biological diversity—of paramount importance both to sustaining viable ecosystems and to improving human existence through scientific advances—is inextricably linked to cultural diversity."[54] The sooner that we stop labeling "native issues" as something separate and distinct from our own survival, the sooner we will appreciate the critical interconnections of the world's ecosystems and social systems. "At some point," says Thomas Meredith, a geographer at McGill University in Montreal, Canada, "it may be possible to recognize cultural adaptive diversity as having the same conservation value as genetic adaptive diversity...At the very least, however, the many culture groups whose knowledge and values lead them to favor environmental and economic circumstances that seem alien to modern Western culture must be recognized, as they have never been in practice, and given a share in determining the fate of their own habitat."[55] To facilitate this process, Meredith urges an appropriate process of environmental impact assessment, involving native peoples and including the study of "socio-ecosystems."

One of the most far-reaching recommendations of the World Conference of Indigenous Peoples on Territory, Environment, and Development, held at Kari-Oca Villages in Brazil in May 1992, was the call for a war crimes tribunal, modeled on the Nuremberg trials after World War II, to focus international public attention on those corporations and nation-states which impose megaprojects on native lands without obtaining consent or involving native peoples in the decision-making process. Such failures should be considered "crimes against indigenous peoples" and those responsible should be tried in a "world tribunal within the control of indigenous peoples set for such a purpose."[56] The September 1992 World Uranium Hearing in Salzburg, Austria was a step in that direction. Such a tribunal could serve as a focal point for bringing together regional, national, and international native-environmentalist alliances to provide an effective counterweight to the ability of multinational corporations and nation-states to wage future resource wars against native peoples.

Conclusion

In assessing the priorities for advocacy work on behalf of native peoples, Cultural Survival has observed that "The era of the resource wars is just beginning. At stake is not only the issue of ownership, but the value of resources and who has the right to manage and consume them."[57] Increasingly, native peoples are at the forefront of these battles because their lands are directly threatened by mining, lumber, hydroelectric, or military projects. Until quite recently, native peoples have had to defend themselves against multinational corporations and nation-states using their own very limited resources and with hardly any notice from the rest of the world. The situation has radically changed over the past decade. The integral connections between native survival and environmental protection have become apparent to even the most conservative environmental organizations. Now the assertion of native land rights takes place in the context of an environmental movement that is prepared to appreciate the knowledge native people have about their own environment and to accept native leadership in environmental battles.

A common thread running through the case studies of native and rural resistance to ecologically destructive projects in this book is the key role played by native assertion of treaty rights. Once the Chippewa of Wisconsin or the Cree and Inuit of Canada asserted their sovereignty and their rights to control the natural resources within their respective territories, the focus of the debate shifted from *how* this project will be developed, to *who* will be involved in the decision-making process.

This shift in the framework of the debate is most significant. Multinational corporations and pro-development governments rarely, if ever, make explicit provisions for real public participation in these resource decisions. For the most part, the extensive planning for these megaprojects is done in secret and presented to the public as a *fait accompli*. This helps to promote a "psychology of inevitability" about these projects and discourages any potential opposition from arising until it is too late to stop the project. This was certainly the case with the first phase of the James Bay project. However, once native groups are able to assert their right to participate in the decision-making process, the momentum of the corporate-state machine is slowed down, at least temporarily, as natives and their environmental allies share their concerns about the wide-ranging social, economic, and environmental impacts of these projects with a wider, larger audience. The most recent draft of the United Nations' Universal Declaration on the Rights of Indigenous Peoples makes explicit provisions for the right of native peoples to participate in this decision-making process. Article 17 states the importance of the "right to require that states consult with indigenous peoples and with both domestic and transnational corporations prior to the commencement of any large-scale projects, particularly natural resource projects or exploitation of mineral and other subsoil resources in order to enhance the projects' benefits and to mitigate any adverse economic, social, environmental, and cultural effect." It adds that "just and fair compensation shall be provided for any such activity or adverse consequence undertaken..."[58]

The success or failure of these efforts will depend greatly on the specific research, organizing, legal, lobbying, networking, media, and direct-action skills that the native rights and environmental movements can bring to bear in each situation. If these ecologically-destructive projects can be stopped, native peoples and their environmental allies can work on proposals for long-term sustainable economic development alternatives to the short-term wasteful projects of profit-maximizing corporations and growth-at-all-costs government policies.

Notes

Foreword

1. CIMI 1992.

Introduction

1. In 1978, while the international community was condemning the Chilean military junta for its widespread human rights violations, Exxon was investing $107 million in two Chilean copper mines. According to *Business Latin America*, Exxon's decision to invest heavily in Chile "constitutes a public relations breakthrough as much as an economic milestone for the country. Not only is it the largest single investment by a U.S. firm in many years, but it has been made by a large, image-conscious corporation, indicating that international business is giving its blessing to the Chilean military regime." See Gedicks 1979.
2. United Indian Planners Association 1977, p. 10.
3. American Indian Policy Review Commission 1977, p. 307.
4. Bartlett and Steele 1980.
5. Gedicks 1977.
6. Davis 1976, 1977. Roger Moody began editing the newspaper *Native Peoples News* in 1978.
7. See Miner 1976; Maxwell 1984.
8. See, for example, Chase 1991.
9. *Akwesasne Notes* 1978, p. 5.
10. Ibid. p. 6

Chapter 1

1. Ribeiro 1962, p. 101; cited in Davis 1977, p. 17.
2. Anthropology Resource Center 1981a, p. 6.
3. American Anthropological Association 1991; cited in Young 1992, p. 27.
4. Bodley 1982, p. 24.
5. Hernandez 1984, p. 38.
6. Linden 1991, p. 46.
7. Anthropology Resource Center 1981b, p. 2.
8. Curtis 1976.
9. See Chapter 5.

10. Turner and Nachowitz 1991, p. 473.
11. Webster 1992, p. 548.
12. McCutcheon 1991, p. 20.
13. Bourassa 1985, p. 4.
14. McCutcheon 1991; Webster 1992.
15. McCutcheon 1991, p. 4.
16. Pendleton 1990, p. 9.
17. Masty 1991, p. 14.
18. Ibid. p. 13.
19. Berkes 1988, p. 208.
20. Hazell 1991, p. 21.
21. Ibid.
22. Verhovek 1992a, p. 20.
23. Fadden 1991, p. 28; Shkilnyk 1985.
24. Kettl 1991, p. 61.
25. Rimmer 1991, p. 35.
26. Cited in Kapashesit 1991, p. x.
27. Dam the Dams Campaign and the Institute for Natural Progress 1988/89; Ross 1991.
28. Coon-Come 1991, p. 10.
29. McCutcheon 1991, p. 43.
30. Ibid., pp. 52-53.
31. Richardson 1991, p. 24.
32. Ibid., p. 25.
33. Ibid., p. 258.
34. Ibid., pp. 298-99.
35. Ibid., p. 299.
36. Feit 1982, pp. 291-292.
37. In October 1991, Hydro-Quebec signed an out-of-court settlement with the Cree in which they agreed that the Great Whale River Complex would be assessed and reviewed as a whole. See Grodinsky 1991, p. 51.
38. Ulbrich 1991.
39. Webster 1992, p. 548.
40. Ibid.
41. Farnsworth 1991, p. 5.
42. Goodman 1991, p. 44.
43. Cited in Thurston 1991, p. 52.
44. McCutcheon 1991, p. 185.
45. Turner 1991, p. 55.
46. Cited in McCutcheon 1991, p. 186.
47. Cited in Thurston 1991, p. 58.
48. McCutcheon 1991, p. 161.
49. Farnsworth 1991, p. 5.
50. Investor Responsibility Research Center (IRRC) 1992.
51. Verhovek 1992b, p. 1.
52. Verhovek 1992a, p. 21.

53. Verhovek 1992b, p. 1.
54. Brouse 1992.
55. Thiele 1992, p. 11.
56. Burger 1990, p. 18.
57. Burger 1987, p. 45.
58. Holt 1992, p. 11. Malaysia is a federation of states which is divided into a western half on the Malayan peninsula and an eastern half on the island of Borneo, consisting of two states, Sarawak and Sabah.
59. Chartier 1987, p. 65.
60. IWGIA 1990, p. 110.
61. Rainforest Action Network 1989, p. 29.
62. Sahabat Alam Malaysia 1988, p. 65.
63. Ibid., p. 69.
64. Hanbury-Tenison 1990, p. 29.
65. Ibid., pp. 67-68.
66. Chartier 1987, p. 65.
67. *Utusan Konsumer* 1987, p. 13.
68. Apin 1987, p. 11.
69. Rainforest Action Network 1988a, p. 5.
70. Ibid., p. 14.
71. Rainforest Action Network 1989, p. 30.
72. Rainforest Action Network 1988b, p. 7.
73. World Rainforest Movement 1989, p. 78.
74. *Utusan Konsumer* 1992, p. 42.
75. IWGIA 1990, p. 111.
76. Colchester 1992, p. 6.
77. MacDonald 1982, p. 28.
78. Cited in NACLA 1975, p. 29.
79. Ibid., p. 35.
80. Parlow 1991, p. 36.
81. Survival International 1987, p. 1.
82. IWGIA 1987, p. 36.
83. Hart 1973, p. 25.
84. NACLA 1975, p. 34.
85. IWGIA 1987, p. 37.
86. Rainforest Action Network 1991, p. 4.
87. Cooper 1992, p. 41.
88. Karten 1992, p. 4.
89. IWGIA 1990, p. 47.
90. Sheean 1992.
91. Burger 1990, p. 92.
92. Survival International 1987, p. 1.
93. Cooper 1991, p. 25.
94. Parlow 1991, p. 33.
95. Cited in Cooper 1991, p. 27.
96. Steller 1992.

97. Associated Press 1992.

98. Wald 1992, p. 7.
99. Burger 1990, p. 104.

Chapter 2

1. U.S. Council on Environmental Quality 1981, p. 382.
2. Young 1992, p. 5.
3. Burger 1990, p. 104.
4. Treece 1987, pp. 31-32.
5. Bosson 1977, pp. 31-32; Mikesell 1979, p. 24.
6. Nafziger 1979, p. 6.
7. Bello 1979, p. 34.
8. Lindsey 1988; Goldstick 1987.
9. Federal Trade Commission 1975, p. 9; Ambler 1990, p. 74.
10. According to a 1982 report of the Commission on Fiscal Accountability of the Nation's Energy Resources (CFANER), 240 of the nation's 300 federally recognized tribes have energy resources—most of which are still undeveloped. See Davis 1982, p. 16.
11. Cook 1981, p. 108.
12. *Business Week* 1979.
13. A strategic mineral is one for which the quantity required for essential civilian and military uses exceeds the reasonably secure domestic and foreign supplies, and for which acceptable substitutes are not available within a reasonable period of time. See U.S. Congress, Office of Technology Assessment 1985, p. 11. See also Fine 1981 and U.S. House of Representatives 1980a, p. 1. For an excellent critique of the national security rationale, see Zuckerman 1981.
14. The executive director of the National Strategy Information Center (NSIC) is Retired Admiral William C. Mott, U.S. Navy. *Mining Engineering* journal described him as a "good friend" to have in the nation's capital. See Kral 1989, p. 149. He is also chairman of the National Strategic Materials and Mineral Advisory Committee. NSIC's Council on Economics and National Security (CENS) assisted the American Geological Institute in organizing a press conference on the resource war just before the 1980 presidential election. CENS organized a number of resource war conferences in Dallas, St. Louis, Washington, D.C., and New York. Among NSIC board members are Charles F. Barber of Asarco Mining Co., and former Representative James D. Santini (D-Nevada), chairman of the Subcommittee on Mines and Mining in the U.S. Congress. See CENS 1980; 1981.
15. *Engineering and Mining Journal* 1982, p. 9.
16. Hopi Epicentre for International Outreach 1987, pp. 3-4.
17. The Center for Defense Information 1992, p. 6.
18. Trofimenko 1984, p. 39.
19. Churchill and LaDuke 1986, p. 69.
20. Snipp 1986, p. 459.

21. Jorgensen 1978, p. 51.
22. Pratt 1979, p. 45.
23. American Indian Policy Review Commision 1977, p. 339.
24. Americans for Indian Opportunity 1975, p. 2.
25. Snipp 1986, p. 458.
26. Mander 1991, p. 203.
27. Shuey 1982, p. 27.
28. International Indian Treaty Council 1977, p. 24.
29. The World Uranium Hearings 1992.
30. Gorz 1980, p. 25.
31. Lovins 1973, p. 23.
32. U.S. Environmental Protection Agency (EPA) 1985, pp. 2-10.
33. Barnet 1980, p. 118.
34. U.S. House of Representatives 1980b, p. 38.
35. Carter 1991, p. 21.
36. Michael Tanzer argues that the international oil corporations are the wave of the future in international capitalist mining. See Tanzer 1980, p. 177. Also, Atlantis 1983.
37. Satchell 1991, p. 46.
38. U.S. EPA 1985, pp. 2-4.
39. Landsberg 1976, p. 638.
40. *Engineering and Mining Journal* 1992, p. 16AA.
41. *The Northern Miner* 1992.
42. National Materials Advisory Board 1972, pp. 3-4; cited in Carpenter 1976, p. 667.
43. U.S. EPA, pp. 5-15; Macdonnell 1988, p. 327.
44. Gooding 1991b.
45. Zelms 1991, pp. 24-25.
46. *High Country News* 1992.
47. Murdoch 1943, p. 12.
48. Ibid., p. 13.
49. Schoolcraft 1821, p. 199; cited in Keller 1978, p. 16.
50. Keller 1978, p. 17.
51. Cited in Keller 1978, p. 17.
52. Walker 1973.
53. Keller 1978, p. 17.
54. Wrone 1989, p. 5.
55. Gates 1951; Walker 1973.
56. U.S. Bureau of Indian Affairs 1976, p. 1.
57. Button and Adams 1980, p. 33.
58. In 1982 the Center for Alternative Mining Development Policy published the results of its mineral leasing research in a pamphlet called *Land Grab: The Corporate Theft of Wisconsin's Mineral Resources.*
59. Rogers 1980.
60. Gedicks 1982. The effects of uranium mining on the Navajo and Pueblo Indians are described in Churchill and LaDuke 1986.
61. Gedicks 1984, p. 184.

Chapter 3

1. Gladwin 1987, p. 19.
2. U.S. House of Representatives 1980a; Brobst 1979; Landsberg 1976.
3. Piccone and Zaslavsky 1982, p. 18.
4. Neesham 1978, p. 55.
5. U.S. Government Accounting Office 1982.
6. Kirkland 1984, p, 31.
7. Davies 1982, p. 88.
8. Vennum 1988; Gough 1980.
9. Exxon 1983, p. 316.
10. Davis and Zannis 1973, p. 37.
11. Wisconsin Department of Natural Resources 1986.
12. Van Goethem 1982.
13. Beal 1978.
14. Wisconsin Department of Natural Resources 1986, p. 186.
15. May 1977, p. 44.
16. Dorgan 1977.
17. Nader 1982, p. 9.
18. Cook 1985, p. 72.
19. Schmidt 1982, p. 4.
20. Gedicks et al. 1982, p. 16.
21. McNamara 1976, p. 51.
22. Wisconsin Department of Natural Resources 1986, p. 167.
23. Davy McKee 1979.
24. Buettner 1985.
25. Gladwin 1987, p. 23.
26. Crown 1980, p. 1.
27. O'Brien 1983; LaDuke 1983; Kalka 1985.
28. Gladwin 1987, pp. 25-27.
29. Nelson 1977, p. 1.
30. Gladwin 1987, p. 27.
31. Hagerty 1980.
32. Wisconsin Department of Natural Resources 1986, p. 160.
33. *Mine Talk* 1982.
34. *The New York Times* 1982.
35. Investor Responsibility Research Center 1983, p. 15.
36. *Metals Week* 1981.
37. Shao 1982.
38. Gladwin 1987, p. 31.
39. Stowers 1986.
40. *Milwaukee Journal* 1986.
41. Maier and Bartelt 1986.
42. Investor Responsibility Research Center 1983, p. 15.
43. U. S. Department of the Interior 1986, p. 1.
44. *Milwaukee Journal* 1986. I immediately sent a copy of the *Milwaukee Journal*
    editorial to Mr. Lawrence Rawl, the chair and chief executive officer (CEO)

of Exxon, along with a little note, which said, "Exxon may be able to buy Governor Earl, Senator Kincaid, the Secretary of the DNR, the editor of the *Forest Republican* and a legion of lawyers but it can't buy public opinion. We think your company's Crandon Project days are numbered." Gedicks 1986.

45. Mayers and Seely 1990. Ex-governor Earl is now the chief lobbyist for Noranda, a large Canadian mining company seeking state approval for an open-pit zinc-copper mine near the Lac du Flambeau Chippewa reservation in Oneida County, Wisconsin.
46. Bruehl 1986.
47. Patton 1988, p. 4.
48. *Milwaukee Journal* 1988.
49. Stanley and Kalvelage 1992.
50. These figures are based on Exxon's own estimates of 7.9 billion pounds of zinc and 1.8 billion pounds of copper.
51. Seppa 1992b.
52. McCool 1981, p. 64.
53. See Chapters 4 and 5.
54. *Forest Republican* 1992.
55. *Milwaukee Sentinel* 1992c.

Chapter 4

1. Girvan 1972, p. 56.
2. Petras and Morley 1975.
3. Moran 1974, p. 136.
4. The earlier reference to a two million-ton deposit of 10.6 percent copper refers only to the enriched, upper 150-200 feet of the orebody. The lower-grade ores at greater depths will not be mined under the current proposal. This practice is known as "high-grading" a deposit.
5. Shilling 1976, p. 13.
6. May and Shilling 1977, p. 39.
7. Gooding 1991a.
8. These "new and improved mining and investment codes" provide a greater degree of protection for multinational mining companies against the threats of nationalization, expropriation, and restrictions on profit repatriation. See *Mining Journal* 1991a.
9. Flambeau Mining Corporation 1976, p. 119.
10. Rebufonni 1976.
11. Dorgan 1974a.
12. Ibid.
13. Dorgan 1974b.
14. Lyons 1979, pp. 1-2.
15. Bauman 1982.
16. Personal interview 1979.
17. Churchill 1980, p. 15.
18. Miller 1976a.

19. Personal interview 1979.
20. The EIS on the Kennecott mine contained 33 major environmental studies. The DNR had conducted three of the 33 studies. It had verified five of the studies. It accepted at face value the accuracy of the other 25 studies conducted by Kennecott. See Peshek and Dawson 1981, p. 12.
21. Miller 1976b.
22. Dorgan 1976.
23. Wisconsin DNR 1976, p. 119.
24. Cited in Peshek 1981a, p. 25.
25. Among the provisions of Rusk County's metallic mineral mining and prospecting ordinance is a county standard of nondegradation of groundwater. The ordinance states that "no activity which results in a degradation of the present quality or quantity of groundwater will be permitted." The ordinance also prohibits mining within 500 feet of a navigable river or stream, lake, pond, or flowage. Another provision in the ordinance calls for a mining firm to deposit in an interest-bearing trust account $1 million, or $5,000 for each well within two miles of the boundary line or property of the applicant, whichever is greater. The money would be used to pay for replacing any contaminated, damaged, or depleted wells and/or for providing water to any well owners whose well has been affected. Finally, a mining company is responsible for monitoring at its expense, all wells within two miles of mining company property for two years prior to the start of mining and for 30 years thereafter. See Rusk County Zoning Ordinance, 1984.
26. Bauman 1982.
27. The average concentration in most mining properties is 0.6 percent pure. See Geniesse, 1991.
28. Peshek 1981a, p. 26.
29. Ibid., p. 27.
30. Ibid.
31. Bachrach and Baratz have referred to this process as "non-decisionmaking." See Bachrach 1970, p. 44.
32. Brock 1981.
33. Barker 1981.
34. Hintz 1981. Only two tribes—the Menominee and the Forest County Potawatomi—endorsed the groundwater rules. The Sokaogon Chippewa, whose reservation would be most directly affected by Exxon's proposed underground zinc-copper mine, did not take a position on the rules. The Forest County Potawatomi tribe, just a few miles north of Exxon's proposed mine, was pressured into endorsing the groundwater rules with the threat that the tribes would be left out of the legislation making them eligible to receive up-front money from the newly created Mining Investment and Local Impact Fund Board (personal interview with James Thunder, former tribal chair of Forest County Potawatomi, 1981). The original draft of the legislation made local municipalities, but not tribal governments, eligible for grant money. The Lac Courte Oreilles Chippewa Tribe was outspoken in its opposition to the rules. In September 1981 the tribal council passed a

resolution "that notice is being given to the state of Wisconsin that in the event this or another rule becomes law the tribe shall seek all remedies under law to enjoin such enforcement as unconstitutional and a deprivation of a property right without due process of law, as well as being injurious to the personal health of tribal members." See Lac Courte Oreilles 1981.

35. Van Goethem 1981.
36. Amy 1985, p. 15.
37. The organizations included the Rusk County Citizens Action Group, Northern Thunder, Northwoods Alliance, Badger Safe Energy Alliance, the League Against Nuclear Dangers, and the Center for Alternative Mining Development Policy. The township mining impact committees included Grant, Doyle, and Reserve, Wisconsin.
38. Hoffman 1983.
39. Kennecott 1988a. Kennecott's position papers were obtained from the files of Wisconsin Secretary of Administration James Klauser through a Wisconsin open-records request.
40. Seely 1982.
41. Kennecott 1988a.
42. Helland 1987.
43. Churchill 1987.
44. Kennecott 1988b.
45. Ibid.
46. Seely 1991b.
47. Recent Supreme Court cases have ruled that putting conditions on development of land unrelated to the impact of the development amounted to an effort to confiscate the land, known as a "taking" without paying for it. See Peterson 1988. In August 1990, a Michigan court of claims ruled that the Michigan Department of Natural Resource's denial of an oil company's application to drill for oil in the Norhouse Dunes amounted to a "taking" or inverse condemnation, for which the state must either pay damages or grant permission to drill. John Forester, chief counsel for the Michigan Environmental Council, has emphasized that "If every state action which has the effect of restricting the development and/or use of land because of environmental concerns becomes a 'taking,' then the mandate of the Michigan Constitution to the legislature to 'provide for the protection of the air, water and other natural resources of the state from pollution, impairment and destruction' will become almost meaningless..." See Forester 1991. The most recent challenge to government's ability to regulate land use for environmental and other public values came in the June 1992 Supreme Court decision in *Lucas v. South Carolina Coastal Council.* By a 6-2 vote, the court said that even if a regulation addresses a serious harm, the government must compensate a property owner denied "all economically viable use of his land." See Barrett 1992.
48. Seely 1991b.
49. Ibid.
50. Wimmer 1988.
51. Mercando 1988.

52. Kennecott had originally planned to ship the ore to the White Pine smelter in Michigan. Those plans had to be canceled when the National Wildlife Federation and the Michigan United Conservation Clubs sued the smelter's owner for emitting mercury, lead, and arsenic over the waters of Lake Superior at five times the legal limit. Kennecott now plans to ship the crushed ore by rail to be processed by a Noranda affiliate company in Timmins, Ontario, and then smelted at the Rouyn-Noranda smelter in Quebec. This is a classic case of exporting pollution to the hinterlands.
53. Sevick 1987.
54. Wisconsin DNR 1990, p. 11.
55. Kennecott 1988c.
56. Ibid.
57. Ibid.
58. Kelley 1988.
59. Mayers 1991c.
60. Kennecott 1989.
61. Mayers 1991c.
62. Kennecott 1989.
63. Cited in Peshek 1981b.
64. Cited in Peshek 1979.
65. Mercando 1989, pp. 3-4.
66. Powers 1991b.
67. Kewley 1990a.
68. *Flambeau News* 1990.
69. Seely 1991b.
70. Associated Press 1991.
71. Kewley 1990b.
72. Cohen 1986, p. 137; Johnson 1988.
73. Bauerlein 1991.
74. Moody 1991, p. 166.
75. CRA is the largest company within the RTZ group, and, in 1989, it provided nearly a quarter of RTZ's profits. See Moody 1991, p. 15.
76. *Engineering and Mining Journal* 1990, p. 15.
77. Moody 1991, p. 168.
78. LCO News Release 1990.

Chapter 5

1. Moody 1991, p. 5.
2. Gedicks 1988.
3. Kelly 1991.
4. PARTIZANS 1989.
5. PARTIZANS 1990, p. 3.
6. Gooding 1990.
7. *Leader-Telegram* 1990.
8. Moody 1991, p. 167.

9. Gjording 1991.
10. *The Real Flambeau News* 1990.
11. Dean et al. 1989.
12. *The Flambeau News*, April 12, 1990. The National Wildlife Federation released a follow-up report entitled "Phantom Reductions," which said that Kennecott Utah Copper had reduced its reported toxic emissions from 158 million pounds in 1987 to only 12.5 million pounds in 1988 by redefining itself as a mining rather than manufacturing concern. Only the manufacturing sector is required to file toxic release inventory reports to the U.S. Environmental Protection Agency. Federation President Jay Hair said, "At best this is disingenuous." See Abrams 1990.
13. Mercando 1990a.
14. Schwarz 1990.
15. Olson 1990a.
16. Leventhal interpreted this partial concession as a "good faith" gesture by Kennecott/RTZ that would make it difficult for LCO to appeal the hearing examiner's decision on the grounds of an infringement of their due-process rights.
17. Kewley 1990c.
18. Just before the master hearing, Noranda Exploration of Toronto, Ontario, announced the discovery of several significant mineral deposits on 2,419 acres of Oneida County forest land that has been leased to Noranda. Noranda's proposed mine site is within the ceded territory of the Chippewa and near the Lac du Flambeau Chippewa reservation. See Chapter 4.
19. *Ladysmith News* 1990.
20. Powers 1990.
21. Thompson 1990.
22. Churchill 1990.
23. Skalitzky 1990.
24. Behm 1990.
25. Skalitzky 1990.
26. *Milwaukee Sentinel* 1991b.
27. Minewatch 1990.
28. Ness 1991.
29. Mercando 1990b.
30. *The Real Flambeau News*, 1990b.
31. Mercando 1990c.
32. Skille 1990.
33. Kennecott 1990.
34. The exemptions from specific locational, design, and operational require-ments which the DNR granted to Kennecott/RTZ include the following: (1) allowing mining within 140 feet of the Flambeau River, rather than requiring construction to remain at least 300 feet from a navigable river; (2) allowing construction within a flood plain; (3) allowing waste stockpiles and other mine components within 1,000 feet of a state highway; (4) allowing the company to forego groundwater testing for turbidity, radioactivity, and cer-

tain organic compounds such as pesticides; (5) allowing the company to disturb wetlands; and (6) allowing the company to locate project facilities within wetlands. See Wisconsin DNR 1990, p. 3.

35. Olson 1991a.
36. *Milwaukee Sentinel* 1991a.
37. Seely 1991a.
38. Mayers 1991a.
39. Powers 1991a.
40. Olson 1990b.
41. On March 5, 1991, attorney Harry Hertel, representing the class action plaintiffs, informed Kennecott attorney John Koeppl that he would be seeking a temporary restraining order against mine construction. The company had announced that mine construction would begin on April 26, 1991. On March 13, 1991, Hertel informed Koeppl that his motion for a restraining order had been withdrawn "with the understanding that in turn, Flambeau will not commence any actual physical work at the mine site..." See Hertel 1991b. In July 1991, the class action lawsuit was settled by a stipulation whereby Kennecott conceded "that the voicing of opposition to the Flambeau Mining project, hitherto or hereafter, by elected representatives of Rusk County, the city of Ladysmith, or the town of Grant constitutes neither a breach of section 31 of the Local Agreement nor an actionable default..." This was a substantial victory for opponents of the mine. Kennecott could no longer threaten court action against local officials who opposed the mine.
42. Mayers 1991b.
43. Mayers 1991d.
44. Mayers 1991e.
45. Ness 1991.
46. Town of Grant 1991.
47. *Milwaukee Sentinel* 1991c.
48. Olson 1991c.
49. *St. Paul Pioneer Press* 1991c.
50. Mercando 1991.
51. Flambeau Mining Company 1991.
52. Behm 1991a.
53. Olson 1991d.
54. Seely 1991d.
55. PARTIZANS 1991.
56. Imrie 1991.
57. Lavelette 1991.
58. *Capital Times* 1991; *Evening Telegram* 1991.
59. Behm 1991b.
60. Powers 1991d.
61. Olson 1991f.
62. Livick 1991.
63. Keahey 1991.

Chapter 6

1. Kewley 1991.
2. Worthington 1991.
3. Nicotera 1989.
4. Ibid.
5. Wisconsin DNR 1990, p. 36.
6. Ramharter 1991.
7. *St. Paul Pioneer Press* 1991b.
8. Olson 1991b.
9. *Milwaukee Sentinel* 1991b.
10. Bergquist 1991.
11. *St. Paul Pioneer Press* 1991a.
12. Gaiashkibos 1991.
13. *Wisconsin State Journal* 1991a.
14. Sheehan 1991.
15. *Wisconsin State Journal* 1991a.
16. Ibid.
17. Seely 1991e.
18. Stanley 1991a.
19. Eggleston 1991a.
20. Sierra Club 1991.
21. Mayers 1991f.
22. Kewley 1991.
23. Flambeau Summer 1991.
24. *Milwaukee Sentinel* 1991e.
25. Charges against the "Flambeau Five" were dropped when a Rusk County circuit judge ruled that the prosecuting attorney had failed to show that the property was properly posted to comply with a Rusk County trespassing ordinance. The signs on the construction site listed Flambeau Mining Company as the owner, but Judge Frederick Henderson ruled that the district attorney had failed to establish Flambeau Mining Co., rather than Kennecott Copper Corp., as the title holder to the 300-acre minesite. Jan Jacoby, a spokesperson for Flambeau Summer, and one of the defendants, said "They're gagging on their own shell game." See Olson 1991h.
26. Mayers 1991g.
27. Miller 1991.
28. Olson 1991g.
29. Stanley 1991b.
30. Stanley 1991c.
31. Wisconsin Administrative Code NR 132.03(25)(a) provides that plans proposed for surface mining are inherently unsuitable should they constitute a threat to the survival of a species. See *LCO/Sierra v. Wisconsin DNR,* 1991, p. 19.
32. Havlik 1991, p. 2.
33. Ibid., p. 4.
34. Busacker 1991, pp. 3-4.

35. Segall 1991a.
36. Ibid.
37. Northrup 1991a, p. 2.
38. Segall 1991b.
39. Eggleston 1991b.
40. Segall 1991b.
41. *Leader-Telegram* 1991.
42. Eggleston 1991b.
43. Judge Northrup responded to Mercando's concern about additional costs related to site stabilization in a letter to all the parties to the lawsuit. He said: "For reasons stated on the record, the Court believed that any substantial advancement of the project would be contrary to the Court's ruling on the injunctive relief. To the extent this may require Flambeau Mining Company to incur unforseen expenses, it must also be recognized that while the EIS which failed to discover the endangered and threatened species was issued by the DNR, that study essentially adopted the bulk of the studies done by Flambeau. *Had the studies done for Flambeau been more complete, it is likely that the additional expenses would have been avoided* (emphasis added)." See Northrup 1991b.
44. *Wisconsin State Journal* 1991b.
45. *Ladysmith News* 1991a.
46. Stanley 1991d.
47. *Flambeau News* 1991.
48. *Ladysmith News* 1991b.
49. Northrup 1991b.
50. Wisconsin DNR 1991a, p. 8.
51. Zichella 1991.
52. Ugoretz 1991.
53. Miller 1992.
54. Wisconsin DNR 1992a, p. 40.
55. Heath 1991.
56. Segall 1991c.
57. *Leader-Telegram* 1992.
58. Wisconsin DNR 1992a, p. 29.
59. Parejko 1992, p. 1.
60. Wisconsin DNR 1992a, p. i.
61. Seppa 1992a.
62. Gooding 1992.
63. Bresette 1992.
64. *Wisconsin State Journal* 1992.
65. With the help of the Milwaukee chapter of the American Civil Liberties Union, John La Forge filed a lawsuit against the City of Ladysmith for violating his constitutional rights by keeping him in jail for 20 hours without being charged. The City of Ladysmith later agreed to pay $3,500 to settle the lawsuit before it went to trial. "This should alert police across Wisconsin that there are consequences for violating the constitutional rights of demonstrators,"

said Chris Ahmuty of the ACLU. "Police should not let their views or the views of their superiors on public controversies blind them to their sworn duty to uphold the Constitution." *Saint Paul Pioneer Press* 1993.
66. *Saint Paul Pioneer Press* 1992.
67. Survival International 1992
68. *Institutional Investor,* 1992, pp. 23-24.

Chapter 7

1. Cited in Metz 1990a, p. 17.
2. Ibid.
3. Strickland 1990, p. 10. Rennard Strickland served as editor-in-chief of the 1982 revision of *The Handbook of Federal Indian Law* and is the author and editor of more than a dozen other books about Native Americans. He is now the Director of the American Indian Law and Policy Center at the University of Oklahoma. At the time the report was released, in April 1990, he was a professor specializing in American Indian law and policy in the University of Wisconsin School of Law. The report grew out of a meeting between Strickland and three senior members of the staff of the Senate Select Committee on Indian Affairs. After presenting his ideas to the staff in informal discussion, those staff members requested that he present these ideas in a form that could be read and reviewed. The result was the Strickland report. Co-authors included UW law professor Stephen J. Herzberg and law student Steven J. Owens.
4. Ibid., p. 24.
5. Busiahn 1991; U.S. Department of the Interior 1991.
6. Rÿser 1991, p. 3.
7. Cornell 1988, p. 54.
8. Rÿser 1991, p. 10.
9. Ibid., p. 4.
10. Thannum 1990, p. 15.
11. Wisconsin Department of Development 1987.
12. Wisconsin Department of Natural Resources 1979.
13. Strickland 1990, p. 20.
14. U.S. Environmental Protection Agency 1992, p. ix.
15. Midwest Treaty Network 1991, p. 1.
16. Gaiashkibos 1990.
17. Baker 1992, pp. 5-6.
18. Oberly 1989.
19. Winters 1991.
20. Klauser 1990.
21. *Mining Journal* 1988, p. 389.
22. *Mining Journal* 1991, p. 232.
23. Moody 1992, p. 520. Larry Mercando, vice-president of the Flambeau Mining Company in Ladysmith, Wisconsin, is currently chair of the consortium. See Chapter Three, p. 3.

24. Baldwin 1981.
25. *Milwaukee Sentinel* 1990. In October 1992, outspoken treaty rights advocate Tom Maulson defeated Mike Allen in the election for tribal chair of the Lac du Flambeau Chippewa tribe.
26. Anderson 1991.
27. Lang 1990.
28. Noranda employed 12 full-time lobbyists and spent more than $240,000 lobbying state officials on mining in 1991. See *Milwaukee Sentinel* 1992a. Besides ex-governor Tony Earl, Noranda hired former Wisconsin public intervenor Peter Peshek. As public intervenor, Peshek was responsible for inviting mining executives to help rewrite Wisconsin mining regulations. See Chapter Three.
29. Segall 1990.
30. GLIFWC 1992.
31. Kalvelage 1992.
32. Wisconsin DNR 1992c.
33. *Milwaukee Sentinel* 1992b.
34. Seppa 1992c.
35. Six months after Noranda announced it was getting rid of its mineral leases, the company still retains the leases. Noranda's announcement of a pullout from Wisconsin appears to have been a ploy designed to influence legislators to loosen environmental regulations. *Milwaukee Journal* 1993.
36. Youngstrum 1991.
37. Wagner 1986.
38. Behm 1985.
39. *Milwaukee Journal* 1984.
40. Kerr 1991.
41. Ibid.
42. Klump 1992.
43. Wisconsin DNR 1992d.
44. Israel 1976, pp. 617-618.
45. Burley 1982, p. 1645.
46. Rÿser 1991, p. 27.
47. Aukofer 1989.
48. Norman 1986.
49. Behm 1981, p. 19.
50. Nicks 1988, p. 2.
51. Rep. David Obey 1989.
52. Strickland 1990, p. 25.
53. Cited in Kerr 1990b, p. 20.
54. Schultze 1989.
55. Ibid.
56. Rinard 1989.
57. Jasperse 1989.
58. Strickland 1990, pp. 33-34.
59. Kerr 1990b, p. 23.

60. Rÿser 1991, p. 48.
61. Williams 1991.
62. Metz 1990b, p. 2.
63. Kerr 1990a.
64. Gaiashkibos 1990.
65. Kerr 1990a.
66. Smart 1990.
67. HONOR 1991.
68. Ibid.
69. Strickland 1990, p. 24.
70. Whaley 1991. See also Whaley and Bresette 1993.
71. *Milwaukee Journal* 1991.
72. GLIFWC 1991, p. 4.

Chapter 8

1. Josephy 1975.
2. Gray 1991; see also Taylor 1988.
3. Clay 1985, p. 2.
4. Greenberg 1985, p. 28.
5. Turnbull 1972; Calhoun 1991.
6. LaDuke 1989, p. xi.
7. Johansen 1979, p. 187.
8. Ibid., p. 188.
9. *U.S. v. Washington,* Phase II, 506 F. Supp. 187 (1980), p. 203; cited in Cohen 1986, p. 142.
10. Ibid., p. 208; cited in Cohen 1986, p. 143.
11. Cohen 1986, p. 144.
12. Garrity 1980, p. 10.
13. Cohen 1991, p. 159.
14. Northwest Indian Fisheries Commission 1991, p. 3.
15. Cohen 1991, p. 162.
16. Yellowbank and Bresette 1991, p. 2.
17. Seely 1992.
18. Wisconsin Department of Natural Resources (DNR) 1992b.
19. Fantle 1992, p. 1.
20. Ibid., p. 8.
21. *Milwaukee Journal* 1992.
22. Quoted in Seely 1992.
23. Wisconsin Department of Natural Resources 1991b, p. 6.
24. Little and Lovejoy 1979.
25. McNamara 1976, p. 51.
26. Box 1974, p. 85.
27. Bullard 1993, p. 17.
28. Chavis 1993, p. 4.
29. Bullard 1993, p. 21.

30. Renner 1991, pp. 11-12.
31. Bubser 1992, p. 29.
32. Hurrle 1992, p. 7.
33. WCED 1987, p. 43.
34. Ibid., p. 115.
35. Smith 1992, p. 68.
36. Court 1990, p. 124.
37. Meredith 1992, p. 126.
38. Gray 1991, p. 11.
39. Colchester and Lohmann, 1990, p. 2.
40. Ibid., p. 2.
41. Afusa 1991, p. 157.
42. LaDuke 1991a, pp. 17-19.
43. IWGIA 1988, p. 92.
44. Dandler and Sage 1985.
45. Redclift 1987, p. 153.
46. Posey 1985; cited in Gray 1991.
47. Houseal 1985, p. 10.
48. Clad 1988, p. 329.
49. Nietschmann 1984, p. 499.
50. Houseal 1985, p. 16.
51. Ibid.
52. Gardner 1988, p. 343.
53. World Council of Indigenous Peoples 1979.
54. Durning 1992, p. 7.
55. Meredith 1992, p. 126.
56. Kari-Oca Declaration 1992, p. 59.
57. Cultural Survival 1991, p. 31.
58. United Nations 1989.

Bibliography

Abrams, Jim
    1990   "Pollution-Cut Cheating Charged" *Wisconsin State Journal* (August 17)

Afusa, Santos Adam
    1991   "Indigenous People Can Save Rain Forests," in Matthew Polesetsky (ed.) *Global Resources: Opposing Viewpoints.* San Diego, California: Greenhaven Press.

Akwesasne Notes
    1978   "The Only Possible Future." Vol. 10, No. 2. Rooseveltown, New York (Late Spring).

Ambler, Marjane
    1990   *Breaking the Iron Bonds: Indian Control of Energy Development.* Lawrence, Kansas: University Press of Kansas.

American Indian Policy Review Commission
    1977   *Final Report.* Washington, D.C. U.S. Government Printing Office.

Americans for Indian Opportunity
    1975   "Real Choices in Indian Resource Development: Alternatives to Leasing." Report of a conference from Billings, Montana.

Amy, Douglas J.
    1985   "Potential Political Problems in Wisconsin's 'Consensus Process'" Unpublished paper.

Anderson, Terry
    1991   "Q. & A: Reclamation Important Part of Mining, Executives Say." *Green Bay Press Gazette.* (August 4).

Anthropology Resource Center (ARC)
    1981a   "The Yanomami Indian Park: A Call for Action." Cambridge, Massachusetts: ARC.
    1981b   "Transnational Corporations and Indigenous Peoples." *ARC Newsletter.* Vol. 5 No.3 (September).

Apin, Teresa
    1987   "Sarawak Blockade." *Utusan Konsumer* (June).

Associated Press
    1991   "Supervisor Paid for Mining Lease." *Wisconsin State Journal* (April 3)

1992   "Ecuador Indians Regain Title to Amazon Forest." *Milwaukee*
              Sentinel (June 20).

Atlantis, Inc.
1983   *Big Oil's Move into Mining.* Washington, D.C.: McGraw-Hill Pub-
              lications.

Aukofer, Frank
1980   "Sensenbrenner Blasted for Leaking Chippewa Bill." *Milwaukee*
              Journal (May).

Bachrach, Peter and Morton S. Baratz
1970   *Power and Poverty: Theory and Practice.* New York: Oxford Univ.

Baker, Al, Jr.
1992   Testimony at Wisconsin Department of Natural Resources Per-
              mit Modification Hearing in Ladysmith, Wisconsin (Sep-
              tember 16).

Baldwin, Janice
1981   "Memo to Legislative Council Mining Committee on Confidenti-
              ality of Core Samples." Madison, Wisconsin: Legislative
              Council (January 9).

Barker, Rocky
1981   "Two Tribes Endorse Proposed Rules to Regulate Mining" *Mil-*
              waukee Journal (September 16).

Barnet, Richard J.
1980   *The Lean Years: Politics in the Age of Scarcity.* New York: Simon
              and Schuster.

Barrett, Paul M.
1992   "States Must Compensate Landowners for Regulation." *Wall*
              Street Journal (June 30).

Bartlett, Donald and James Steele
1980   "Energy Anarchy." *The Philadelphia Inquirer* (December 7-13).

Bauerlein, Monika
1991a   "Bait and Switch" *Minneapolis City Pages,* Vol. 12 No. 542
              (April 24).

Bauman, Michael
1982   "Mining in Wisconsin: Treasure or Trouble?" *The Milwaukee*
              Journal, Insight Magazine (October 24).

Beal, David L.
1978   "$64 Question: Will New Mining Bring Pollution and Peril the
              Wolf River's Future." *Milwaukee Journal* (April 11).

Behm, Don
1981.   "Northern Environmental Stewards Oppose Consensus Trade-
              Offs." *Wisconsin Academy Review* vol. 28 no. 1 (December).
1985   "Tests Hint of Oil, Gas." *The Milwaukee Journal* (December 15).
1990   "Loftus Urges Moratorium on Metal-Ore Mining" *Milwaukee*
              Journal (July 24).

1991a   "Mine Rally Called a Threat." *Milwaukeee Journal* (July 2).

1991b   "Opponents of Mine Vow to Return to Site" *Milwaukee Journal* (July 11).

Bergquist, Lee

1991   "Miners Dig Up Dormant Issue." *Milwauke Sentinel* (July 23).

Bello, Walden, Peter Hayes and Lyuba Zarsky

1979   "Australian Uranium Connection." *Pacific Research.* Vol. 10 No. 1.

Berkes, Firket

1988   "The Intrinsic Difficulty of Predicting Impacts: Lessons from the James Bay Hydro Project." *Environmental Impact Assessment Review.* Vol. 8 , No. 3 (September).

Bodley, John H.

1982   *Victims of Progress.* Palo Alto, California: Mayfield. Second edition.

Bosson, Rex and Benison Varon

1977   *The Mining Industry and the Developing Countries.* London: Oxford University Press.

Bourassa, Robert

1985   *Power from the North.* Canada: Prentice Hall.

Box, Thadis et. al.

1974   *Rehabilitation Potential of Western Coal Lands.* National Academy of Sciences. Cambridge, Massachusetts: Ballinger Publishing.

Bresette, Walt

1992   "Chippewa Treaty Activist Joins Flambeau Summer." Press Release (May 12).

Brobst, Donald A.

1979   "Fundamental Concepts for the Analysis of Resource Availability" in V. Kerry Smith (ed.) *Scarcity and Growth Reconsidered.* Baltimore, Maryland: The Johns Hopkins University Press.

Brock, Thomas D.

1981   Testimony Before the Wisconsin Department of Natural Resources (September 17).

Brouse, Gary

1992   Letter to ICCR board members (March).

Bruehl, Becky

1986   "Menominees to Continue Fighting Mine Despite Delay." *Green Bay Press Gazette* (December 12).

Bubser, Dave

1992   "Menominee Sustainable Forestry." *Cultural Survival Quarterly* Vol. 16, No. 3 (Fall).

Buettner, Herbert
    1985   "Our Reasons for Concern that Environmental Damage and Con-
                tamination of Surface and Ground Waters Will Occur if
                Mining is Allowed to Develop and Operate Near Crandon,
                As Proposed by Exxon, in the Watershed of the Upper
                Wolf River" *Mimeo* (April 18).

Bullard, Robert
    1993   *Confronting Environmental Racism.* Boston: South End Press.

Burger, Julian
    1987   *Report from the Frontier: The State of the World's Indigenous Peo-
                ples.* London and Cambridge, Massachusetts: Zed Books
                and Cultural Survival.
    1990   *The Gaia Atlas of First Peoples.* New York: Anchor Books.

Burley, Carl L.
    1982   "Indian Lands—An Industry Dilemma." *Journal of the Rocky
                Mountain Mineral Law Institute* Vol. 28.

Busacker, Greg
    1991   Affidavit in LCO/Sierra v. Wisconsin DNR (August 19).

Busian, Thomas R.
    1991   *Chippewa Treaty Harvest of Natural Resources, Wisconsin 1983-
                1990.* Odanah, Wisconsin: Great Lakes Indian Fish and
                Wildlife Commission.

Business Week
    1979   "Now the Squeeze on Metals." No. 2592 (July 2).

Button, Andrew and Samuel S. Adams
    1980   *Geology and Recognition Criteria for Uranium Deposits of the
                Quartz-Pebble Conglomerate Type.* Washington, D.C.: U.S.
                Department of Energy (December).

Calhoun, John B.
    1991   "The Plight of the Ik," in Patrick C. West and Steven R. Brechin
                (eds.), *Resident Peoples and National Parks: Social Dilem-
                mas and Strategies in International Conservation.* Tuscon:
                University of Arizona.

CAMDP (Center for Alternative Mining Development Policy).
    1982   *Land Grab: The Corporate Theft of Wisconsin's Mineral Re-
                sources.* Madison, Wisconsin: CAMDP.

Capital Times
    1991   "Reporters aren't Cops." Editorial (July 5).

Carpenter, Richard A.
    1976   "Tensions Between Materials and Environmental Quality." *Sci-
                ence.* Vol. 191 No. 4228 (February).

Carter, Russell A.
    1991   "1991 Project Survey: Building on a Stable Base." *Engineering
                and Mining Journal* Vol. 192 No. 1.

CENS (Council on Economics and National Security).
    1980   "The Resource War and the U.S. Business Community: The
                Case for a Council on Economics and National Security—
                A White Paper." Washington, D.C.: CENS (June).
    1981   "Strategic Minerals: A Resource Crisis." Washington, D.C.:
                CENS).
Center for Defense Information
    1992   "Armed Force and Imported Resources." *The Defense Monitor.*
                Vol. 21 No. 2.
Chartier, Clem
    1987   "Malaysia: Logging greatest threat to indigenous peoples of
                Sarawak." Statement to the UN Working Group on Indige-
                nous Populations. *IWGIA Newsletter* No. 51/52 (Octo-
                ber/December).
Chase, Steve (ed.).
    1991   *Defending the Earth: A Dialogue Between Dave Foreman and
                Murray Bookchin.* Boston: South End Press.
Churchill, Ward and Winona LaDuke
    1986   "Native America: The Political Economy of Radioactive Colonial-
                ism." *The Insurgent Sociologist* Vol. 13 No. 3 (Spring).
Churchill, Roscoe
    1980   "The People are Mightier than the Corporation," *Clearwater
                Journal,* Vol. 1 No. 5 (Late Winter).
    1987   Letter to Peter Helland (October 19).
    1990   Public Testimony Before the State of Wisconsin, Division of
                Hearings and Appeals, Department of Administration (July
                17).
CIMI (Indian Missionary Council in South and Central America).
    1992   *Indian Information Center Newsletter* Vol. 6, No. 4. Berkeley, Cal-
                ifornia.
Clad, James C.
    1988   "Conservation and Indigenous Peoples: A Study of Convergent
                Interests," in John H. Bodley (ed.) *Tribal Peoples and Devel-
                opment Issues: A Global Overview.* Mountain View, Califor-
                nia: Mayfield Publishers.
Clay, Jason W.
    1985   "Parks and People." *Cultural Survival Quarterly* DVol. 9 No. 1
                (February).
Cohen, Fay G.
    1986   *Treaties on Trial: The Continuing Controversy over Northwest In-
                dian Fishing Rights.* Seattle: University of Washington
                Press.
    1991   "Implementing Indian Treaty Fishing Rights: Conflict and Coop-
                eration" in Ward Churchill (ed.), *Critical Issues in Native*

North America, Vol. II. Copenhagen, Denmark: International Work Group for Indigenous Affairs (IWGIA).

Colchester, Marcus
    1990   "The Tropical Forestry Action Plan: What Progress?" Cited in Andrew Gray, *Between the Spice of Life and the Melting Pot: Biodiversity Conservation and its Impact on Indigenous Peoples.* Copenhagen, Denmark: International Work Group for Indigenous Affairs (IWGIA). Document 70.
    1992   "Indigenous Unite." *Multinational Monitor* Vol. 13 No. 4 (April).

Cook, James
    1981   "New Hope on the Reservations." *Forbes* Vol. 128 No. 10 (November 9).
    1985   "Exxon Proves that Big Doesn't Mean Rigid." *Forbes* Vol. 135, No. 9 (April 29).

Coon-Come, Matthew
    1991   "Where Can You Buy a River?" *Northeast Indian Quarterly* Vol. 8 No. 4 (Winter).

Cooper, Marc
    1991   "Oil Slick." *Mother Jones* Vol. 16 No. 6 (Nov./Dec.).
    1992   "Rain Forest Crude." *Mother Jones* Vol. 17 No. 2 (March/April).

Cornell, Stephen
    1988   *The Return of the Native.* Chicago: Oxford University Press.

Court, Thijs de la
    1990   *Beyond Brundtland: Green Development in the 1990s.* Trans. by Ed Bayens and Nigel Harle. London: Zed Books.

Crown, Judith
    1980   "Exxon Steps Up Copper, Zinc Prospecting in Wisconsin." *American Metal Market* Vol. 88 No. 96 (May 16).

Cultural Survival
    1991   "'Sharing' the Wealth?" *Cultural Survival Quarterly* Vol. 15 No. 4 (Fall).

Curtis, Edward S.
    1976   *Visions of a Vanishing Race.* New York: Thomas Y. Crowell.

Dam the Dams Campaign and Institute for Natural Progress
    1988/89   "The Water Plot: Hydrological Rape in Northern Canada." in Ward Churchill (ed.) *Critical Issues in Native North America.* Copenhagen, Denmark: International Work Group for Indigenous Affairs (IWGIA).

Dandler, J. and Sage C.
    1985   "What is happening to Andean potatoes? A view from the grassroots." *Development Dialogue, 1* (Uppsala, Sweden). Cited in Michael Redclift, *Sustainable Development: Exploring the Contradictions.* London: Methuen. 1987.

Davies, Warnock
1982   "Managing Political Vulnerability." *Engineering and Mining Journal* Vol. 183 No. 2 (February).

Davis, Robert and Mark Zannis
1973   *The Genocide Machine in Canada.* Montreal, Quebec, Canada: Black Rose Books.

Davis, Shelton H. and Robert O. Mathews
1976   *The Geological Imperative: Anthropology and Development in the Amazon Basin of South America.* Cambridge, Massachusetts: Anthropology Resource Center.

Davis, Shelton H.
1977   *Victims of the Miracle: Development and the Indians of Brazil.* London: Cambridge University Press.
1982   *Native Resource Control and the Multinational Corporate Challenge: Aboriginal Rights in International Perspective: Background Documents.* Cambridge, Massachusetts: Anthropology Resource Center.

Davy Mc Kee Engineers
1979   "Crandon Project: Pyrite Processing Study" (November).

Dean, Norman L., Jerry Poje and Randall J. Burke
1989   "The Toxic 500: The 500 Largest Releases of Toxic Chemicals in the United States—1987." Washington, D.C.: National Wildlife Federation.

Dorgan, Michael
1974a   "Copper Bonanza Was Given Away As Kennecott Wrote Its Own Ticket." *Madison Capital Times* (July 29).
1974b   "Copper: Fool's Gold for Ladysmith?" *Madison Capital Times* (July 30).
1976   "Copper Mine Report Accepted but Doubted" *Madison Capital Times* (November 10).
1977   "Indians Claim They Own Land Bearing Exxon Ore." *The Capital Times.* Madison, Wisconsin (July 16).

Durning, Alan Thien
1992   *Guardians of the Land: Indigenous Peoples and the Health of the Earth.* Paper No. 112. Washington, D.C.: Worldwatch Institute.

Eggleston, Richard
1991a   "Chippewa, Sierra Club File Suit to Block Mine." *St. Paul Pioneer Press* (August 1).
1991b   "Judge Orders Suspension of Ladysmith Mine Work." *St. Paul Pioneer Press* (August 30).

Engineering and Mining Journal
1982   "U.S. must face minerals issues *now,* Asarco's Barber tells strategic resources conference." Vol. 183 No. 1 (January).

1990 "Bougainville Copper Withdraws Remaining Personnel," Vol. 191 No. 3 (March).

1992 "Public opinion on mining must be changed." Vol. 193 No. 7 (July).

Evening Telegram (Superior).
1991 "Tape Seizure Illegal, Immoral." (July 18).

Exxon
1983 *Forecast of Future Conditions: Socioeconomic Assessment, Crandon Project.* Prepared for Exxon Minerals by Research and Planning Consultants, Inc (October).

Fadden, Mary
1991 "The Hazards of Methylmercury." *Northeast Indian Quarterly* Vol. 8 No. 4 (Winter).

Fantle, Will
1992 "Fishing for Trouble." *Isthmus Newsweekly* (June 5-11).

Farnsworth, Clyde H.
1991 "Toughest Fight Yet for Hydro-Quebec" *The New York Times* (October 6).

Federal Trade Commission
1975 *Staff Report on Mineral Leasing on Indian Lands.* Washington, D.C.: U.S. Government Printing Office.

Feit, Harvey A.
1982 "Protecting Indigenous Hunters: The Social and Environmental Protection Regime in the James Bay and Northern Quebec Land Claims Agreement" in Charles C. Geisler et. al (eds.) *Indian SIA: The Social Impact Assessment of Rapid Resource Development on Native Peoples.* Ann Arbor: University of Michigan Natural Resources Sociology Research Lab. Monograph #3.

Fine, Daniel I.
1981 "Reshaping the Strategy Behind U.S. Mineral Policy." *Engineering and Mining Journal* Vol. 182 No. 4.

Flambeau Mining Corp.
1976 Mining Permit Application for Mining the Flambeau Copper Deposit, Rusk County, Wisconsin (September 14).

1991 "Setting the Record Straight...A Closer Look at the Facts" (June 27).

Flambeau News
1990 "Whose 'Real' News?" Vol. 1 No.6 (April 12).
1991 "Community Expresses Support for Flambeau Mining Project" Vol. 2 No. 21 (September 12).

Flambeau Summer Coalition
1991 "Environmental Emergency in Ladysmith." Press Release (August 2).

Forest Republican
    1992   "Tribal Leader Issues Statement on Exxon Plans." (September 3).

Forester, John
    1991   "Takings Ruling to Set Grave Precedent" CACC Clearinghouse Newsletter, Vol. 13 No. 5 (September/October).

Gaiashkibos
    1990   "Where are all the hellraisers?" Address given at Midwest Treaty Network forum in Madison, Wisconsin (May).
    1991   Letter to Carroll D. Besadny, Secretary, Wisconsin Department of Natural Resources (July 9).

Gardner, J.E. and J.G. Nelson
    1988   "National Parks and Native Peoples in Northern Canada, Alaska, and Northern Australia," in John II. Bodley (ed.) *Tribal Peoples and Development Issues: A Global Overview.* Mountain View, California: Mayfield Publishers.

Garrity, Michael
    1980   "The Pending Energy Wars: America's Final Act of Genocide," *Akwesasne Notes* (Spring).

Gates, William G., Jr.
    1951   *Michigan Copper and Boston Dollars.* New York: Russell and Russell.

Gedicks, Al *et al.*
    1982   *Land Grab: The Corporate Theft of Wisconsin's Mineral Resources.* Madison, Wisconsin: Center for Alternative Mining Development Policy.

Gedicks, Al
    1977   "Raw Materials: The Achilles Heel of American Imperialism?" *The Insurgent Sociologist* Vol. 7 No. 4 (Fall).
    1979   "Exxon and the Recolonization of Wisconsin and Chile." *CALA Newsletter* Vol. 7 No. 3 (February).
    1982   "Northern State Counties Fighting Uranium Miners." *Madison Capital Times* (September 27).
    1984   "Resource Wars in Chippewa Country," in Joseph G. Jorgensen (ed.) *Native Americans and Energy Development, II.* Boston: Anthropology Resource Center.
    1986   Letter to Lawrence Rawl, Chairman, Exxon Corporation (September 23).
    1988   "Exxon Minerals in Wisconsin: New Patterns of Rural Environmental Conflict," *The Wisconsin Sociologist,* Vol. 25 Nos. 2-3 (Spring/Summer).

Geniesse, Peter A.
    1991   "Mining's New Frontier." *Appleton Post-Crescent* (August 4).

Girvan, Norman
1972   *Copper in Chile: A Study in Conflict Between Corporate and National Economy.* Jamaica: University of the West Indies, Institute of Social and Economic Research.

Gjording, Chris N.
1991   *Conditions Not of Their Choosing: The Guaymi Indians and Mining Mulinationals in Panama.* Washington, D.C.: Smithsonian Institution Press.

Gladwin, Thomas N.
1987   "Patterns of Environmental Conflict over Industrial Facilities in the United States, 1970-1978" in Robert W. Lake (ed.), *Resolving Locational Conflict.* State University of New Jersey: Rutgers University.

GLIFWC (Great Lakes Indian Fish and Wildlife Commission).
1991   GLIFWC 1990 Annual Report. Odanah, Wisconsin: GLIFWC
1992   Comments on Noranda Minerals' Notice of Intent to Collect Data and Proposed Scope of Study, Lynne Project, Oneida County, Wisconsin (January).

Goldstick, Miles
1987   *Voices from Wollaston Lake: Resistance Against Uranium Mining and Genocide in Northern Saskatchewan.* Sweden: Earth Embassy and WISE.

Gooding, Kenneth
1990   "RTZ Annual Meeting." *London Financial Times* (May 10).
1991a   "Copper Mine with a Deep Green Finish." *London Financial Times* (March 13).
1991b   "Body Set up as a Voice for Safe Mining." *London Financial Times* (September 4).
1992   "U.S. Copper Project Defeats Ecological Mussel-Power." *London Financial Times* (April 28).

Goodman, Ian
1991   "Electricity Imports from Quebec: The Current and Historical Context." *Northeast Indian Quarterly* Vol. 8 No. 4 (Winter).

Gorz, André
1980   *Ecology as Politics.* Boston: South End Press.

Gough, Robert P.W.
1980   "A Cultural-Historical Assessment of the Wild Rice Resources of the Sokaogon Chippewa" in *An Analysis of the Socio-Economic and Environmental Impacts of Mining and Mineral Resource Development on the Sokaogon Chippewa Community.* Madison, Wisconsin: COACT Research. 2 volumes.

Gray, Andrew
1991   *Between the Spice of Life and the Melting Pot: Biodiversity Conservation and its Impact on Indigenous Peoples.* Copenhagen,

Denmark: International Work Group for Indigenous Affairs (IWGIA) (August).

Greenberg, Adolph M.
1985 "Game Conservation and Native Peoples in Northern Ontàrio." *Cultural Survival Quarterly* Vol. 9 No. 1 (February).

Grodinsky, William S.
1991 "The James Bay and Northern Quebec Agreement." *Northeast Indian Quarterly* Vol. 8 No. 4 (Winter).

Hagerty, Thomas J.
1980 "Exxon Cancels Plans for Crandon Test Mine." *Milwaukee Journal* (September 17).

Hanbury-Tenison, Robin
1990 "No Surrender in Sarawak." *New Scientist* (December 1).

Hart, Laurie
1973 "Pacifying the Last Frontiers: Story of the Wycliffe Translators." *NACLA's Latin America and Empire Report* Vol. 7 No. 10 (December).

Havlik, Marian
1991 Affidavit in *LCO/SIERRA v. Wisconsin DNR* (July 25).

Hazell, Stephen
1991 "Environmental Impacts of Hydro-Development in the James Bay Region." *Northeast Indian Quarterly* Vol. 8 No. 4 (Winter).

Heath, David
1991 "Comments on study design, mussels, Kennecott mine toxicity." Madison, Wisconsin: Department of Natural Resources (July 22).

Helland, Peter
1987 Report by the Governor's Ad Hoc Task Force on Mining

Hernandez, Deborah Pacini
1984 "Resource Development and Indigenous People: The El Cerrejón Coal Project in Guajira, Colombia." Cambridge, Massachusetts: Cultural Survival, Inc.

Hertel, Harry R.
1991a Letter to Attorney John Koeppl (March 5).
1991b Letter to Attorney John Koeppl (March 13).

High Country News
1992 Vol. 24 No. 24 (December 28).

Hintz, Gene
1981 "Truce on Mining Code Changes Forged by Alliance." *Milwaukee Journal* (September 16).

Hoffman, Arnie
1983 "Group Asks State to Suspend Exxon Mine Permit Debate." *Eau Claire Leader-Telegram* (March 24).

Holt, Lindsay II
    1992   "Multinational Logging Companies Destroying Penan Rainforest Home." *Forest Guardians,* #4 (Spring).
HONOR (Honor Our Neighbors Origins and Rights, Inc.).
    1991   "WCA Wants to Promote Mining on County Lands." *HONOR Digest* (February/March).
Hopi Epicentre for International Outreach
    1987   "Indian Economic Development: Fool's Gold." *Kahtsímkíwa* Vol. 1 No. 2 (Winter).
Houseal, Brian *et al.*
    1985   "Indigenous Cultures and Protected Areas in Central America." *Cultural Survival Quarterly* Vol. 9 No. 1 (February).
Hurrle, William
    1992   "Energy, Wisconsin Utilities and the Rest of Creation." Unpublished memo.
Imrie, Robert
    1991   "Mining Protestors Removed." *Wisconsin State Journal* (July 8).
Institutional Investor
    1992   "Managing Political risk." Vol. 26 No. 12 (November).
International Indian Treaty Council
    1977   "International NGO Conference on Discrimination Against Indigenous Populations in the Americas." *Treaty Council News* Vol. 1 No. 7 (October).
International Work Group for Indigenous Affairs (IWGIA).
    1987   "Ecuador: Transnational Oil Companies, Missionary Deaths and Huaorani Land Rights." *IWGIA Newsletter* No. 51/52 (October/December).
    1988   "Statement on Self-Determination by the Participants at the Indigenous Peoples Preparatory Meeting." *Yearbook 1987: Indigenous Peoples and Development.* Copenhagen, Denmark: IWGIA.
    1990   *Yearbook.* Copenhagen, Denmark: IWGIA.
    1991   *Arctic Environment: Indigenous Perspectives.* Document 69. Copenhagen, Denmark: IWGIA (August).
Investor Responsibility Research Center
    1983   Proxy Issues Report: Mining on Indian Lands (Exxon Corp.) *Analysis AA.* Washington, D.C.
    1992   "Shareholder Proposal Highlights Environmental Concerns over Controversial James Bay Hydroelectric Project." *News for Investors* (March).
Israel, Daniel H.
    1976   "The Reemergence of Tribal Nationalism and Its Impact on Reservation Resource Development." *University of Colorado Law Review* Vol. 47 No. 4 (Summer).

Jasperse, Patrick
    1989   "Spearfishing Critics Yield Little Ground." *The Milwaukee Journal* (April 20).

Johansen, Bruce and Roberto Maestas
    1979   *Wasi'chu: The Continuing Indian Wars.* New York: Monthly Review.

Johnson, Phillip
    1988   "Usual and Accustomed Grounds." *Whole Earth Review* (Spring).

Jorgensen, Joseph G.
    1978   "A Century of Political Economic Effects on American Indian Society, 1880-1980." *Journal of Ethnic Studies* Vol. 6 (Fall).

Josephy, Alvin M. Jr.
    1975   "Indian's Odd Foes." *The New York Times* (November 27).

Kalka, Chris
    1985   "Protecting Land and People" *North Country Anvil* No. 50 (Summer).

Kalvelage, James R.
    1992   "Holperin Reverses His Support of Proposed Mine." *The Milwaukee Sentinel* (June 2).

Kapashesit, Winona LaDuke
    1991   "Foreword" in Boyce Richardson, *Strangers Devour the Land.* Post Mills, Vermont: Chelsea Green.

Kari-Oca Declaration
    1992   "Indigenous People Earth Charter." International Work Group for Indigenous Affairs (IWGIA) Newsletter No. 4 (November-December).

Karten, Joe
    1992   "Conoco Out of Huaorani Territory but Battle for Forest Continues." *World Rainforest Report* Vol. 8 No. 1 (Jan./March).

Keahey, John
    1991   "Kennecott to Pay State for Water Pollution." *Salt Lake Tribune* (July 31).

Keller, Robert H.
    1978   "An Economic History of Indian Treaties in the Great Lakes Region." *American Indian Journal* Vol. 42 No. 2.

Kelley, Tim
    1988   "Errors Found in Copper Mine Plan." *Milwaukee Journal* (December 6).

Kelly, Sean
    1991   "RTZ Vows Clean Mine; Activist Challenges Agenda" *Wisconsin State Journal* (March 26).

Kennecott Copper Corporation
    1988a   Issue Paper #1: Local Agreement/Local Approvals (April 25).
    1988b   Issue Paper #2: Legalization of Local Agreement (April 25).

1988c   Issue Paper #5: Time for Procurement of DNR Permits (April 25).

1989   Issue Paper #8: Groundwater Modeling and EIS Scheduling (March 24).

1990   Status Report #3: Potential Litigation (November 30).

Kerr, Scott
1990a   "Conference on Treaties Sparks Anger." *The Milwaukee Journal* (January 14).

1990b   "The New Indian Wars." *The Progressive* DVol. 54 No. 4 (April).

1991   "Stakes High over Proposed Test Oil Well." *Saint Paul Pioneer Press* (July 7).

Kettl, Paul A.
1991   "Suicide and Homicide: The Other Costs of Development." *Northeast Indian Quarterly* Vol. 8 No. 4 (Winter).

Kewley, Mary Jo
1990a   "Mine Divides Neighbors." *Wausau Daily Herald* (July 16).

1990b   "Band Opposes Mine on Spiritual Grounds." *Wausau Daily Herald* (July 16).

1990c   "Environmentalists Plan Filibuster." *Wausau Daily Herald* (July 16).

1991   "Clam May Stall Mine's Digging." *Wausau Daily Herald* (June 4).

Kirkland, Richard I. Jr.
1984   "Exxon Rededicates Itself to Oil." *Fortune* Vol. 110 No. 2 (July 23).

Klauser, James R.
1990   Letter from Wisconsin Secretary of Administration Klauser to Michael Donnelly, Noranda's Lynne project manager (November 27).

Klump, Dianne
1992   "LCO Attempts to Halt Exploratory Drilling by Terra, Demands EIS." *News from Indian Country* Vol. 6 No. 6 (March).

Kral, Steve
1989   "President's education must include the problems of mining." *Mining Engineering* Vol. 41 No. 3 (March).

LaDuke, Winona
1983   "The Mortality of Wealth: Native America and the Frontier Mentality." *Radical America* Vol. 17 Nos. 2-3.

1989   "Prelude: Succeeding into Native North America" in Ward Churchill (ed.), *Critical Issues in Native North America.* Document 62. Copenhagen, Denmark: International Work Group for Indigenous Affairs (IWGIA).

1991a   "Environmental Work: An Indigenous Perspective," *Northeast Indian Quarterly* Vol. 8 No. 4 (Winter).

1991b   Foreword in Boyce Richardson, *Strangers Devour the Land.*
         Port Mills, Vermont: Chelsea Green.
Lac Court Oreilles Chippewa Tribe
    1981   Resolution 81-79 In Opposition to DNR Administrative Rule NR
            182 (September 14).
    1990   Press Release—Gaiashkibos in London (May 7).
    1991   *LCO Band of Lake Superior Chippewa Indians and Sierra Club,*
            John Muir Chapter v. Wisconsin Department of Natural Re-
            sources (July 31).

Ladysmith News
    1990   "Muskies, Inc. Wildlife Federation Oppose Flambeau Mining
            Project." (July 19).
    1991a   "Judge Halts Work at Mine Site; Company to Appeal Injunc-
            tion." (September 5).
    1991b   "We Are Concerned" Advertisement (September 26).
    1992   "Opposing Views Voiced at Mine Hearings." (September 24).

Landsberg, Hans H.
    1976   "Materials: Some Recent Trends and Issues." *Science* Vol. 191
            No. 4228 (February).

Lang, Dale R.
    1990   Letter from North Central District Headquarters of the Wiscon-
            sin Department of Natural Resources (DNR) to Steve
            Ostermann, Oneida County Zoning Administrator (Octo-
            ber 10).

Lavelette, Bill
    1991   "Tape Seized from TV Cameraman May Be Evidence in Mine
            Protest." *St. Paul Pioneer Press* (July 12).

Leader-Telegram
    1990   "Tribal Leader Rips Mining Firm After Meeting." (May 11).
    1991   "Judge Halts Mine Work." (August 30).
    1992   "Dragonfly Found at Mine may be Endangered." (January 15).

Linden, Eugene
    1991   "Lost Tribes, Lost Knowledge." *Time* (September 23).

Lindsey, Anne
    1988   "A Tribal Gathering in the World's Uranium Capital." *Earth Is-*
            land Journal (Fall).

Little, Ronald L. and Stephen B. Lovejoy
    1979   "Energy Development and Local Employment." *The Social Sci-*
            ence Journal Vol. 16 No. 2 (April).

Livick, William
    1991   "Six Madison Residents Arrested in Mine Protest" *Madison Cap-*
            ital Times (July 13-14).

Local Agreement
    1988   Local Agreement Between Rusk County, the Town of Grant, the City of Ladysmith and Kennecott Explorations (Australia) Ltd. for Development of the Kennecott Flambeau Mine.

Lovins, Amory
    1973   *Openpit Mining.* London: Earth Island.

Lyons, Kevin
    1979   "A First Environmental Case." Unpublished Paper.

Macdonald, Theodore
    1982   "Ecuador," in Sally Swenson (ed.) *Native Resource Control and the Multinational Corporate Challenge: Aboriginal Rights in International Perspective.* Cambridge, Massachusetts: Anthropology Resource Center.

Macdonnell, Lawrence J.
    1988   "Regulation of Wastes from the Metals Mining Industry: The Shape of Things to Come." *Mineral Processing and Extractive Metallurgy Review* Vol. 3 Nos. 1-4.

Maier, Harry and James Bartelt
    1986   "Price Boost Might Revive Exxon Mine." *Green Bay Press Gazette* (December 11).

Mander, Jerry
    1991   *In the Absence of the Sacred: The Failure of Technology and the Survival of the Indian Nations.* San Francisco: Sierra Club.

Masty, David, Sr.
    1991   "Traditional Use of Fish and Other Resources of the Great Whale River Region." *Northeast Indian Quarterly* Vol. 8 No. 4 (Winter).

Maxwell, Jean A.
    1984   "Colvilles on the Verge of Development," in Joseph G. Jorgensen (ed.) *Native Americans and Energy Development II.* Cambridge, Massachusetts: Anthropology Resource Center.

May, Edwarde R. and Robert W. Shilling
    1977   "Case Study of Environmemtal Impact—Flambeau Project," *Mining Congess Journal* (January).

Mayers, Jeff and Ron Seely
    1990   "Conflict Tugs on State Resources." *Wisconsin State Journal* (March 4).

Mayers, Jeff
    1991a   "DNR Rejects Mine Review." *Wisconsin State Journal* (February 21).
    1991b   "Mine Official Criticizes Pollution Accusations." *Wisconsin State Journal* (February 27).

1991c   "Sophisticated Lobbying Neutralizes Mining Foes." *Wisconsin State Journal* (March 24).
1991d   "La Follette: Kennecott is 'Scared.' " *Wisconsin State Journal* (March 16).
1991e   "Mining Firms Dig for Support." *Wisconsin State Journal* (August 1).
1991f   "Sierra Club Suit Opposes Mine." *Wisconsin State Journal* (August 1).
1991g   "DNR Wants New Study for Mine." *Wisconsin State Journal* (August 3).

McCool, Daniel
1981   "Federal Indian Policy and the Sacred Mountains of the Papago Indians." *Journal of Ethnic Studies* Vol. 9 No. 3 (Fall).

McCutcheon, Sean
1991   *Electric Rivers: The Story of the James Bay Project.* Montreal: Black Rose.

McNamara, Michael D.
1976   *Metallic Mining in the Lake Superior Region: Perspectives and Projections.* University of Wisconsin, Institute for Environmental Studies, Report 64.

Mercando, Lawrence E.
1988   Letter to James Wimmer (August 25).
1989   Testimony before the State of Wisconsin, Division of Hearings and Appeals, Department of Administration (December 20).
1990a   Letter to Ray Kramer et. al (April 25).
1990b   "No Justification for Moratorium on Mining," *Flambeau News,* Vol. 1 No. 23 (September 27).
1990c   "An Open Letter from Larry Mercando," *Flambeau News,* Vol. 1 No. 27 (November 8).
1991   Letter to Rusk County Neighbors (June 7).

Meredith, Thomas C.
1992   "Environmental Impact Assessment, Cultural Diversity, and Sustainable Rural Development." *Environmental Impact Assessment Review* Vol. 12 Nos. 1/2 (March/June).

Metals Week
1981   "Exxon Minerals May Shelve Many of its 'Expensive' Minerals Projects" (December 28).

Metz, Sharon
1990a   "A Legacy of Broken Promises." *Sojourners* (June).
1990b   "Background Paper on WCA Coalition Organizing Effort." Unpublished Memo.

Midwest Treaty Network
1991   *Wisconsin Treaties: What's the Problem?* Madison, Wisconsin.

Mikesell, Raymond F.
    1979   *New Patterns of World Mineral Development.* London: British-
            North American Committee.

Miller, Mike
    1976a   "Citizens Group Appeals Copper Mine Statement." *Madison
            Capital Times* (August 4).
    1976b   "Mine Statement is Called Industry Rubber Stamp." *Madison
            Capital Times* (November 8).
    1991   "Request to Halt Mine Site Preparation Denied." *Madison Capi-
            tal Times* (August 5).

Miller, Glenn
    1992   Testimony in *LCO/Sierra v. Wisconsin DNR* (June 2).

Milwaukee Journal
    1984   "Legislator Predicts Wisconsin Oil Rush." (August 1).
    1986   "Case for Exxon Mine Still Doubtful." (September 21).
    1988   "Langlade County, Exxon Protest Proposed Protection for Wolf
            River." (June 1).
    1990   "Indians Criticize State Officials." (February 25).
    1991   "Spearing Opponents Settle Suit." (November 8).
    1992   "Environmental Groups Sue over Air Emissions." (August 18).
    1993   "Mining Company Retaining its Leases." (February 9).

Milwaukee Sentinel
    1990   "Tribal Leader Opposes Mining Plan" (June 23).
    1991a   "Lac Courte Oreilles Band Blasts Mine Decision." (January 23).
    1991b   "Legislator Cites Confidence in His Mining Bill." (January 28).
    1991c   "Mine Opponents Could Face Arrest at Rally." (June 25).
    1991d   "Lawmakers Say Site Needed Survey." (July 1).
    1991e   "Mining Protestors Take Case to Company Office." (August 3).
    1992a   "Firm Spent $240,000 to Lobby." (February 5).
    1992b   "Firm May Alter Mining Plans." (July 25).
    1992c   "Mining Deal Falls Through." (December 15).

Mine Talk
    1982   "Exxon Shocks the Synfuels World; Colony Pullout Leaves
            Workers, Western Colorado Towns in Haze." Albuquer-
            que, New Mexico: Southwest Research and Information
            Center (Summer/Fall).

Miner, H. Craig
    1976   *The Corporation and the Indian: Tribal Sovereignty and Industial
            Civilization in Indian Territory, 1865-1907.* Norman, Okla-
            homa: University of Oklahoma.

Minewatch
    1990   "What and Who is Minewatch?" London, England.

Mining Journal
    1988   (November 11). London.
    1991a   "The Right Climate" London, England (March 22).

1991b   "Noranda Consolidates." (March 22).

Moody, Roger
1991   *Plunder!* London, England: PARTIZANS/CAFCA.
1992   *The Gulliver File: Mines, People and Land: A Global Battlefield.* London: Minewatch.

Moran, Theodore
1974   *Multinational Corporations and the Politics of Dependence: Copper in Chile.* New Jersey: Princeton University Press.

Murdoch, Angus
1943   *Boom Copper, the Story of the First U.S. Mining Boom.* New York: Macmillan.

NACLA (North American Congress on Latin America).
1975   "Ecuador: Oil Up for Grabs." *NACLA's Latin America and Empire Report* Vol. 9 No. 8 (November).

Nader, Ralph
1982   "Approaching Strategy for Confronting the Corporate Threat." *Akwesasne Notes* Vol. 14 No. 6 (Winter). Rooseveltown, New York.

Nafziger, Richard
1979   "The Energy Corporations and Indian Development." Albuquerque, New Mexico: University of New Mexico, Native American Studies Center, Development Series, Occasional Paper.

National Materials Advisory Board
1972   *Elements of a National Materials Policy.* Washington, D.C.: National Academy of Sciences.

Neesham, Robin
1978   "Exxon Emerging as a Major Mining Firm." *Engineering and Mining Journal* Vol. 179 No. 7 (July 1978).

Nelson, Mervin C. & Assocs.
1977   "Cost and Time Analysis of the Mining and Environmental Requirements in the Pre-mining Stage for Copper Mining in the Northern Highland, Wisconsin." *Research Proposal to the U.S. Department of the Interior, Bureau of Mines.* Milwaukee, Wisconsin.

Ness, Eric
1991   "Mining: A Showdown Looms in Ladysmith" *Isthmus Newsweekly* Vol. 16 No. 27 (July 5).

New York Times
1982   "Exxon Pullout Halts a Rockie's Boom." (October 10).

Nicks, Stephen
1988   Draft Settlement Agreement Between the Mole Lake Band and the State of Wisconsin. Madison, Wisconsin: Wisconsin Department of Justice.

Nicotera, Ronald F.
  1989   Memo to Ed Jepsen, Environmental Analysis Division of the
          Wisconsin Department of Natural Resources (July 5).

Nietschmann, B.
  1984   "Biosphere Reserves and Traditional Societies," in *Conservation,
          Science and Society: Contributions to the First International
          Biosphere Reserve Congress, Minsk, Byelorussia/USSR.*
          Paris: United Nations Educational, Scientific and Cultural
          Organization (UNESCO).

Norman, Jack
  1986   "Will Klauser Aid Business?" *Milwaukee Journal* (November 20).

Northern Miner
  1992   "Pollution Laws More Stringent." Toronto, Canada Vol. 78 No.
          25 (August 24).

Northrup, George
  1991a   Order in *LCO/Sierra vs. Wisconsin DNR and Flambeau Mining
          Company*
  1991b   Letter to Counsel in *LCO/Sierra vs. Wisconsin DNR and Flam-
          beau Mining Company* (September 26).

Northwest Indian Fisheries Commission
  1991   "Tribes Release Millions of Fish." *NIFC News,* Vol. 17 No. 1

Oberly, James W.
  1989   "Communalism, Individualism and Corporate Capitalism: The
          Lac Courte Oreilles Indians, Northern State Power Com-
          pany and the 1921 Chippewa Flowage Dam." Unpublished
          paper, Department of History, University of Wisconsin,
          Eau Claire.

Obey, David R. (Rep.)
  1989   Correspondence to Tribal Chairmen, Lake Superior Chippewas
          (April 18).

O'Brien, Jim
  1983   "Environmentalism as a Mass Movement: Historical Notes. *Rad-
          ical America* Vol. 17 Nos. 2 and 3.

Olson, Kathy
  1990a   "Tribe Requests Delay in Copper Mine Case." *St. Paul Pioneer
          Press* (April 25).
  1990b   "Suit Filed to Block Copper Mining Project." *St. Paul Pioneer
          Press* (December 21).
  1991a   "State Official Approves Copper Mining Permits." *St. Paul Pio-
          neer Press* (January 16).
  1991b   "DNR Biologist Forbidden from Discussing River Clams." *St.
          Paul Pioneer Press* (July 2).
  1991c   "Dragonfly Larvae Spur Rally in Mining Town." *St. Paul Pio-
          neer Press* (June 26).

1991d   "Anti-Mine Rally Draws 400; Some Camp Near Ladysmith." *St. Paul Pioneer Press* (July 7).

1991e   "Ecologist to Undertake Flambeau River Testing." *St. Paul Pioneer Press* (July 10).

1991f   "Seven More Protestors Arrested at Ladysmith." *St. Paul Pioneer Press* (July 13).

1991g   "Anti-Mine Group Begins Own Study of Nearby River." *St. Paul Pioneer Press* (August 17).

1991h   "Mistrial is Declared in Mine Protest Case." *St. Paul Pioneer Press* (October 17).

Parejko, Ken
1991   Macroinvertebrate Biotic Index Monitoring of the Flambeau River. Department of Biology, Saginaw Valley State University, Michigan.

1992   Comments on Flambeau Mine Supplementary EIS (April 23).

Parlow, Anita
1991   "Worlds in Collision." *The Amicus Journal* Vol. 13 (Spring).

PARTIZANS
1989   *Parting Company* (Autumn). London, England.

1990   Special Report on the 1990 RTZ Annual General Meeting, Parting Company (Autumn) London, England.

1991   "Fly-In Fly-Out System Hits RTZ London" Press Release (July 6, 1991).

Patton, James D.
1988   Letter to Carroll D. Besadny, Secretary, Wisconsin Department of Natural Resources (May 20).

Pendleton, Scott
1990   "Hydro-Quebec Pushes New Dams." *The Christian Science Monitor* (August 29).

Peshek, Peter
1979   "The Adoption of Adminitrative Rules to Regulate Metallic Mining Wastes" Testimony before the state of Wisconsin, Department of Natural Resources, Metallic Mining Council (May 29).

1981a   "New Metal Mining in Wisconsin: A Classic Environmental, Economic, and Political Dilemma," *Wisconsin Academy Review* Vol. 28 No.1 (December).

1981b   "Wisconsin's Strategy for Preparing for a Mew Mining Industry -Consensus or Conflict" Paper presented at the Center for Public Resources, Task Force on Environmental Disputes (May).

Peshek, Peter and Thomas Dawson
1981   "The Role of an Attorney in a Wetlands Destruction Case" Unpublished paper (January).

Peterson, Iver
    1988   "Builders Battle 'Takings' of Property." *The New York Times*
            (February 28).
Petras, James and Morris Morley
    1975   *The United States and Chile: Imperialism and the Overthrow of
            the Allende Government.* New York: Monthly Review Press.
Piccone, Paul and Victor Zaslavsky
    1981-82 "The Socio-Economic Roots of Re-Armament." *Telos.* No, 50.
Posey, Darrell
    1985   "Nature and Indigenous Guidelines for New Amazonian Devel-
            opment Strategies: Understanding Biological Diversity
            through Ethnoecology," in J. Hemming (ed.) *Change in the
            Amazon Basin* Vol. 1: *Man's Impact on Forests and Rivers.*
            Manchester University Press.
Powers, Pam
    1990   "Mine Opponents Scuffle with Police." *Eau Claire Leader-Tel-
            gram* (July 17).
    1991a   "Tribal Chairman Says Environment Will Be 'the Loser'." *Eau
            Claire Leader-Telegram* (March 26).
    1991b   "Mine Manager Tells of Involvement in Conservation." *Eau
            Claire Leader-Telegram* (July 7).
    1991c   "Protestors Hunker Down." *Eau Claire Leader-Telegram* (July
            7).
    1991d   "Mining Official Says Project Won't Cave in to Protestors." *Eau
            Claire Leader-Telegram* (July 11).
Pratt, Raymond B.
    1979   "Tribal Sovereignty and Resource Exploitation." *Southwest Econ-
            omy and Society* Vol. 4 No. 3.
Rainforest Action Network
    1988a   "Crackdown in Malaysia." *Earth Island Journal* Vol. 3 No. 1
            (Winter).
    1988b   "Rainforest People Resume Blockade of Logging." *Earth Island
            Journal* Vol. 3 No. 4 (Fall).
    1989   "With the Penan at the Last Blockade." *Earth Island Journal* Vol.
            4 No. 2 (Spring).
    1991   "Ecuador: ARCO, UNOCAL Drilling in Amazon." *World Rainfor-
            est Report* (Jan./March).
Ramharter Robert
    1991   Memo to Linda Bochert, Executive Assistant to Carroll D.
            Besadny, DNR Secretary (June 17).
The Real Flambeau News
    1990a   "Kennecott Makes 'Top Ten' Polluters List." Vol. 1 No. 7
            Ladysmith: Rusk County Citizens Action Group.
    1990b   "Freedom March." (November).

Rebufonni Dean
1976   "Town Finds More to Copper Industry Than Coin." *Minneapolis Tribune* (November 28).

Redclift, Michael
1987   *Sustainable Development: Exploring the Contradictions.* London and New York: Methuen.

Renner, Michael
1991   *Jobs in a Sustainable Economy.* Worldwatch Paper 104. Washington, D.C.: Worldwatch Institute (September).

Ribeiro, Darcy
1962   *A Politica Indigenista Brasileira.* Rio de Janeiro: Ministrio da Agricultura, Serviçio de Informao Agricola.

Richardson, Boyce
1991   *Strangers Devour the Land.* Post Mills, Vermont: Chelsea Green.

Rimmer, Chris
1991   "The Significance of James Bay to Migratory Birds." *Northeast Indian Quarterly* Vol. 8 No. 4 (Winter).

Rinard, Amy
1989   "Mining foe sees 'hidden agenda' for treaty talks." *The Milwaukee Sentinel* (July 25).

Rogers, Deborah
1980   "Mineral Rights Under Forest County Potawtomi Tribal Lands: An Agreement Between Kerr-McGee and Chicago Northwestern Railroad." Madison, Wisconsin: Center for Alternative Mining Development Policy. Technical Paper (May).

Ross, Alan
1991   "The Manitoba Hydro-Electric Projects." *Northeast Indian Quarterly* Vol. 8 No. 4 (Winter).

Rusk County
1984   Rusk County Zoning Ordinance, Section 6.25 Metallic Mineral Mining and Prospecting Section.

Rÿser, Rudolph C.
1991   "Anti-Indian Movement on the Tribal Frontier." Occasional Paper # 16. Kenmore, Washington: Center for World Indigenous Studies.

Sahabat Alam Malaysia (SAM).
1988   "Malaysia: Appeal by the Orang Ulu to Protect their Lands, Forests and Resources." *IWGIA Newsletter.* No. 53/54 (May/August). Copenhagen, Denmark: IWGIA.

Saint Paul Pioneer Press
1991a   "Chequamegon Mining Project Loses Financing" (June 5).
1991b   "Second Rare Clam Found at Mine Site" (June 20).
1991c   "Town of Grant Will Permit Anti-Mining Demonstration" (June 29).

    1992   "Judge Dismisses Lawsuit to Block Open-Pit Mine." (June 13).

Satchell, Michael
    1991   "The New Gold Rush." *U.S. News & World Report* Vol. 111 No.
             18 (October 28).

Schmidt, Jack
    1982   "Problems with Tailings Ponds: Incomplete Regulation, Inconsis-
             tent Review, Threats to Water." *Down to Earth*. Helena,
             Montana.

Schoolcraft, Henry R.
    1821   *Narrative Journal of Travels through the Northwestern Regions of
             the United States*. Albany: E. & E. Hosford.

Schultze, Steve
    1989   "Chippewas Felt Treaty Deal Put their Heritage at Stake." *The
             Milwaukee Journal* (October 29).

Schwarz, David
    1990   Memo to Kurt Schacht, Deputy Secretary, Wisconsin Depart-
             ment of Administration.

Seely, Ron
    1982   "Mining Has Strong Poential in Wisconsin." *Wisconsin State
             Journal* (January 31).
    1991a   "Chippewa Band Asks DNR to Reverse Copper Mine OK." *Wis-
             consin State Journal* (February 6).
    1991b   "Northern Officials Give State Poor Grades." *Wisconsin State
             Journal* (March 24).
    1991c   "Mining Company Donations: Generosity or Bribe?" *Wisconsin
             State Journal* (March 28).
    1991d   "Protest Taken to Mining Site." *Wisconsin State Journal* (July
             7).
    1991e   "Protestors Urge Survey at Mine Site." *Wisconsin State Journal*
             (July 16).
    1992   "Toxic Fish Taint Spearer's Victory." *Wisconsin State Journal*
             (May 17).

Segall, Cary
    1990   "Willow Battle Heats Up." *Wisconsin State Journal* (December
             15).
    1991a   "Judge Delays Decision on Mine Construction." *Wisconsin
             State Journal* (August 24).
    1991b   "Judge Halts Mine Project." *Wisconsin State Journal* (August
             30).
    1991c   "Sierra Club Official Rips DNR." *Wisconsin State Journal* (No-
             vember 11).

Seppa, Nathan
    1992a   "Mine Protestors Plan Action." *Wisconsin State Journal* (April
             30).

1992b   "Exxon, Phelps Dodge re-examine zinc-copper mine near Crandon." *Wisconsin State Journal* (August 26).

1992c   "Zinc Mine Plans Fade." *Wisconsin State Journal* (October 20).

Sevick, Jerry
1987   Letter to Gordon Reinke, Wisconsin Department of Natural Resources (October 7).

Shao, Maria
1982   "Metal Fatigue." *Wall Street Journal* (August 31).

Sheean, Olga
1992   "Fool's Gold in Ecuador." *World Wildlife Fund News* (January/February).

Sheehan, Tim
1991   "Two Arrested at Mining Headquarters." *Eau Claire Leader-Telegram* (August 3).

Shilling, Robert W.
1976   "Flambeau: A Case Study in Developing a Copper Mine in Wisconsin," Seminar on Mininig in Wisconsin (November 18).

Shkilnyk, Anastasia M.
1985   *A Poison Stronger than Love: The Destruction of an Ojibwa Community.* New Haven: Yale University.

Shuey, Chris
1982   "Church Rock Revisited." *Mine Talk* Vol. 2 Nos. 1-2.

Sierra Club
1991   "Sierra Club Sues State of Wisconsin to Protect Endangered Species, Stop Copper Mine." Press Release.

Skalitzky Lori
1990   "Loftus Calls for Moratroim on State Mining Pending Study." *Milwaukee Sentinel* (July 23).

Skille, Donna
1990   "Five Hundred People Opposed to Mining March on Ladysmith, Wisconsin." *News from Indian Country* (Mid-November).

Smart, Christopher
1990   "Indian Groups Disrupt Treaty Meeting." *The Milwaukee Sentinel* (January 19).

Smith, Emily T.
1992   "Growth vs. Environment." *Business Week* No. 3265 (May 11).

Snipp, Matthew C.
1986   "American Indians and Natural Resource Development: Indigenous Peoples' Land, Now Sought After, Has Produced New Indian-White Problems." *American Journal of Economics and Sociology* Vol. 45 No. 4 (October).

Stanley, George and James Kalvelage
1992   "Exxon to proceed with Crandon mine." *The Milwaukee Sentinel* (August 26).

Stanley, George
    1991a   "Group Will Ask Judge to Halt Mine for Review on Species."
               Milwaukee Sentinel (July 26).
    1991b   "Environmental Suit Called Too Late." *Milwaukee Sentinel* (August 17).
    1991c   "Clam Census was Only DNR Survey." *Milwaukee Sentinel* (August 24).
    1991d   "Rain Wipes Out Mining Firm's Erosion Control." *Milwaukee Sentinel* (September 14).

Steller, Tim
    1992   "Ecuador's Rain Forest Natives Struggle for Lands." *The Circle* Vol. 13 No.5 (April).

Stowers, Bonnie
    1986   "Prospect Holds Appeal: Indians Like Idea of Tax-Free Mine." *Milwaukee Journal* (November 23).

Strauss, Simon D.
    1981   "Oil and Copper Don't Mix." *The New York Times* (April 12).

Strickland, Rennard *et al.*
    1990   *Keeping Our Word: Indian Treaty Rights and Public Responsibilities.* Madison, Wisconsin.

Survival International
    1987   "Ecuador: Indians Kill Bishop as Oil Companies Invade." *Urgent Action Bulletin* (August).
    1990   Yanomami Survival Campaign.
    1992   Survival International's Top Ten List. London (September).

Tanzer, Michael
    1980   *The Race for Resources: Continuing Struggles over Minerals and Fuels.* New York: Monthly Review Press.

Taylor, Lynda et. al.
    1988   "The Importance of Cross-Cultural Communication between Environmentalists and Land-Based People." *The Workbook,* Vol. 13 No. 3 (July/September) Albuquerque, New Mexico: Southwest Research and Information Center.

Thannum, Jim
    1990   *Chippewa Spearing Season—Conflict and Cooperation: The Two States of Wisconsin.* Odanah, Wisconsin: Great Lakes Indian Fish and Wildlife Commission.

Thiele, Scott
    1992   "James Bay Victory." *Earth First!* Vol. 12 No. 5 (May).

Thompson, Chris
    1990   "Mining Officials Hope to Avoid Controversy" *Duluth News Tribune* (July 22).

Thurston, Harry
    1991   "Power in a Land of Remembrance" *Audubon Magazine* (NovemberDecember).

Town of Grant
    1991   Ordinance to Regulate Use of Town Property (June 11).

Treece, Dave
    1987   *Bound in Misery and Iron: The Impact of the Grande Carajás Programme on the Indians of Brazil.* London: Survival International.

Trofimenko, Genrikh
    1984   "Challenges to Global Stability in the 1980s: A Soviet View." in Adam M. Garfinkle (ed.), *Global Perspectives on Arms Control.* New York: Praeger.

Turnbull, Colin
    1972   *The Mountain People.* New York: Simon and Schuster.

Turner, Steve and Todd Nachowitz
    1991   "Damming of Native Lands." *The Nation.* Vol. 253 No. 13 (October 21).

Turner, Terry
    1991   "The World Struggle to Save James Bay." *Northeast Indian Quarterly* Vol. 8 No. 4 (Winter).

U.S. Bureau of Indian Affairs
    1976   *Status of Mineral Resource Information for the Bad River, Lac Courte Oreilles, Lac du Flambeau, Mole Lake Community, Potawatomi, Red Cliff, Public Domain and St. Croix, and Stockbridge-Munsee Indian Reservations of Wisconsin.* Administrative Report BIA-20. Washington, D.C.

U.S. Congress
    1985   *Strategic Minerals: Technologies to Reduce U.S. Import Vulnerability.* Washington, D.C.: Office of Technology Assessment.

U.S. Council on Environmental Quality
    1981   *The Global 2000 Report to the President.* Washington, D.C.: U.S. Government Printing Office.

U.S. Department of the Interior
    1986   Comments on Exxon Minerals Company Zinc-Copper Mine, Draft EIS. Washington, D.C (July 31).
    1991   *Casting Light Upon the Waters: A Joint Fishery Assessment of the Wisconsin Ceded Territory.* Minneapolis, MN: Bureau of Indian Affairs.

U.S. Environmental Protection Agency
    1985   *Report to Congress: Wastes from the Extraction and Beneficiation of Metallic Ores, Phosphate Rock, Asbestos, Overburden from Uranium Mining, and Oil Shale* (December).

1992   *Tribes at Risk: The Wisconsin Tribes Comparative Risk Project.*
        Washington, D.C. (October).

U.S. Government Accounting Office
    1982   *Changing Ownership Within the U.S. Minerals Industry: Possible
            Causes and Steps Needed to Determine the Effects.* Washington, D.C.

U.S. House of Representatives
    1980a   "Nonfuel Minerals Policy Review." Washington, D.C.: Subcommittee on Mines and Mining, Committee on Interior and Insular Affairs. 96th Congress; 2nd Session (September).
    1980b   "U.S. Minerals Vulnerability: National Policy Implications."
            Washington, D.C.: Subcommittee on Mines and Mining,
            Committee on Interior and Insular Affairs (November).

Ugoretz, Steven
    1991   Letter to Carl Zichella and Caryl Terrell, Sierra Club Midwest Office (October 25).

Ulbrich, Jeffrey
    1991   "Cree Win Major Victory: Court Orders Environmental Review
            of Great Whale Hydro Project" *News from Indian Country*
            (Late September).

United Indian Planners Association
    1977   "Minerals: The Way it was at Lac du Flambeau." (January).

United Nations
    1989   "Universal Declaration on the Rights of Indigenous Peoples"
            Draft. Geneva, Switzerland: Working Group on Indigenous
            Populations.

Utusan Konsumer
    1992   "Sarawak: The Plight of Natives Worsens." *IWGIA Newsletter*
            No. 1 (Jan./March).

Van Goethem, Larry
    1981   "Split Develops on Mining Rules." *Milwaukee Journal* (August 26).
    1982   "Exxon Mine Will Feature Elaborate Waste Water Plan." *Milwaukee Journal* (March 28).

Vennum, Thomas Jr.
    1988   *Wild Rice and the Ojibway People.* St. Paul, Minnesota: Minnesota Historical Society Press.

Verhovek, Sam Howe
    1992a   "Power Struggle." *The New York Times Magazine* (January 12).
    1992b   "Cuomo, Citing Economic Issues, Cancels Quebec Power Contract." *The New York Times* (March 28).

Wagner, Herbert
    1986   "Area Oil Rush Temporarily at Rest." *Superior Evening Telegram* (October 14).

Wald, Matthew
     1992   "The Shrinking of the American Oil Industry." *The New York Times* (July 19).
Walker, David Allan
     1973   "Discovery and Exploitation of Iron Ore Resources in Northeastern Minnesota: The Formative Years, 1865-1901." Unpublished Ph.D. dissertation, University of Wisconsin, Madison.
WCED (World Commission on Environment and Development).
     1987   *Our Common Future.* Oxford: Oxford University Press.
Webster, Paul
     1992   "Quebec Inc. Unplugged." *The Nation* Vol. 254 No. 16 (April 27).
Whaley, Rick
     1991   "Witness for Nonviolence: Green Politics in Action." *Green Letter* San Francisco, California (Fall).
Whaley, Rick and Walter Bresette
     1993   *Walleye Warriors: An Effective Strategy Against Racism and for the Earth.* Philadelphia: New Society Publishers.
Williams, Florence
     1991   "People for the West Fronts for the Mining Industry." *High Country News* (July 1).
Wimmer, James
     1988   Memo to James Klauser (March 1).
Winters, Ron
     1991   Speech to Protect the Earth Survival Gathering and Pow-Wow, Lac Courte Oreilles Reservation, Hayward, Wisconsin (September).
Wisconsin Department of Development
     1987   "The Wisconsin Tourism Industry Study—Second Home Ownership, 1981 Data." Madison, Wisconsin.
Wisconsin Department of Natural Resources (DNR)
     1976   Final Environmental Impact Statement—Flambeau Mining Corporation Copper Mine, Rusk County, Wisconsin (February).
     1979   *Long Range Management Plan: Muskellunge Management Plan at 7-1 to 7-7; Walleye management Plan at 9-1 to 9-7.*
     1986   Draft Environmental Impact Statement. Exxon Minerals Company, Zinc-Copper Mine, Crandon, Wisconsin. Madison, Wisconsin: DNR.
     1990   Final Environmental Impact Statement—Flambeau Mining Co.—Copper Mine, Ladysmith, Wisconsin (March).
     1991a   Status Report and Staff Recommendations on Issues Related to Endangered Resources in the Flambeau River (August 2).
     1991b   "Information Sheet on Potential Mining Development in Northern Wisconsin" (October).

1992a   *An Evaluation of Endangered Resources in the Flambeau River and A Supplement to the Environmental Impact Statement for the Flambeau Mine Project.* Madison, Wisconsin (April 15).

1992b   "Health Guide for People Who Eat Sport Fish from Wisconsin Waters" (April).

1992c   Letter from William Tans, DNR mine project coordinator, to James Cahoon, Noranda's Lynne project manager (July 7).

1992d   Personal conversation with Archie Wilson, Chief, DNR North Central District (August 19).

Wisconsin State Journal

1991a   "Mining Opponents Distrust Company's Promise on Wildlife." (July 5).

1991b   "Mining Halt Faces Appeal." (August 31).

1992   "Mine Foes, Backers State Cases at DNR Hearings." (June 5).

World Council of Indigenous Peoples (WCIP).

1979   Submission Concerning the United Nations Third Development Decade, United Nations Economic and Social Council. Cited in "Transnational Corporations and Indigenous Peoples." Anthropology Resource Center Position Paper. Cambridge, Massachusetts: Anthropology Resource Center. 1981.

World Rainforest Movement

1989   "Declaration of the World Rainforest Movement." *IWGIA Newsletter* No. 59 (December). Copenhagen, Denmark: IWGIA.

World Uranium Hearings

1992   "Why on Earth, a World Uranium Hearing?" Salzburg, Austria.

Worthington, Rogers

1991   "Tiny Clam Provides Big Surprise for Wisconsin Mine, State Agency." *Chicago Tribune* (July 11).

Wrone, David R.

1989   "Economic Impact of the 1837 and 1842 Chippewa Treaties." Unpublished paper. Department of History, University of Wisconsin, Stevens Point (July 20).

Yellowbank, James and Walt Bresette

1991   "Regional Resource Co-Management: Saving the Land for the Next Seven Generations." *Indian Treaty Rights Newsletter* Vol. 2 No. 1 (Winter).

Young, John E.

1992   *Mining the Earth.* Washington, D.C.: Worldwatch Institute. Paper No. 109.

Youngstrum, Daryl

1991   "Mining, Environmental Considerations at Willow Reservoir Discussed at Outstanding Waterway Designation Meeting." *The Daily News.* Rhinelander, Wisconsin (December 22).

Zelms, Jeffrey L.
  1991   "Let George Do It?" *Engineering and Mining Journal* Vol. 192
            No. 11 (November).
Zichella, Carl A.
  1991   Letter to Carroll D. Besadny, DNR Secretary (September 20).
Zuckerman, Sam
  1981   "The Interior Department Goes to War." *Environmental Action*
            Vol. 13 No. 1.

INDEX

A

Aboriginal Mining Information Centre, 44

Achttien, Donald, 76, 178

Acid mine waste: at Crandon, WI, 62,65-66; at Ladysmith, WI, 88, 100; at Lynne, WI, 170; at Mole Lake, WI, 61; in western United States, 46

Ackley, Arlyn, 75

ACLU, 132, 185

adat, 28

Afusa, Santos Adam, 199

Agassiz, 51

Akwesasne Notes, 8

Allen, Michael, 171

Allende, Salvador (Pres.), 1, 83

Amazon Basin, 13

Amazon Crude, 36

American Freedom Coalition, 180

American Indian Movement, 3, 184

American Indian Policy Review Commission, 3, 42

American Metal Market, 67

American Mining Congress, 41

Americans for Indian Opportunity, 3, 67

Anishinaabe Niijii: benefit concert for, 160; and Bresette, Walt, 157; coalition success, 161; and decla-

ration of an "environmental zone," 194; and Flambeau Summer, 126; formation of, 109; and Maulson, Tom, 174; and newspaper ad, 113; as a political force, 190; and publication of *Real Flambeau News,* 111; and Protect the Earth Survival Gathering, 119; and witnesses for nonviolence, 184

Anthropology Resource Center, 5, 14

Anti-Indian movment: anti-Indian sentiment and mineral interests, 164-165; and Citizens Equal Rights Alliance, 180; Crist, Dean, 180; Equal Rights for Everyone, 177; Interstate Congress for Equal Rights and Responsibilities, 165; National Coalition on Federal Indian Policy, 181; Peterson, Larry, 177; Protect Americans' Rights and Resources, 164-165, 178; Sensenbrenner, James (Rep.), 179; Stop Treaty Abuse, 164-165; 184; Wisconsin Alliance for Rights and Resources, 177

Anti-Slavery Society, 38

Antigo Journal, 71

Arts, Waltraud, 68

About South End Press

South End Press is a nonprofit, collectively-run book publisher with over 175 titles in print. Since our founding in 1977, we have tried to meet the needs of readers who are exploring, or are already committed to, the politics of radical social change.

Our goal is to publish books that encourage critical thinking and constructive action on the key political, cultural, social, economic, and ecological issues shaping life in the United States and in the world. In this way, we hope to give expression to a wide diversity of democratic social movements and to provide an alternative to the products of corporate publishing.

If you would like a free catalog of South End Press books or information about our membership program—which offers two free books and a 40% discount on all titles—please write to us at South End Press, 116 Saint Botolph Street, Boston, MA 02115.

Other SEP Titles of Interest

Confronting Environmental Racism
Voices from the Grassroots
Edited by Robert D. Bullard

The State of Native America
Genocide, Colonization, and Resistance
Edited by M. Annette Jaimes

How Capitalism Underdeveloped Black America
Manning Marable

Defending the Earth
A Dialogue Between Murray Bookchin and Dave Foreman
Edited with an introduction by Steve Chase